BY LUCY MOORE

The Thieves' Opera (1997)
Amphibious Thing: The Life of Lord Hervey (2000)

Con Men and Cutpurses

Scenes from the Hogarthian Underworld

Edited by LUCY MOORE

ALLEN LANE
THE PENGUIN PRESS

ALLEN LANE
THE PENGUIN PRESS

Published by the Penguin Group
Penguin Books Ltd, 27 Wrights Lane, London w8 5TZ, England
Penguin Putnam Inc., 375 Hudson Street, New York, New York 10014, USA
Penguin Books Australia Ltd, Ringwood, Victoria, Australia
Penguin Books Canada Ltd, 10 Alcorn Avenue, Toronto, Ontario, Canada M4V 3B2
Penguin Books (NZ) Ltd, Private Bag 102902, NSMC, Auckland, New Zealand

Penguin Books Ltd, Registered Offices: Harmondsworth, Middlesex, England

First published 2000
1 3 5 7 9 10 8 6 4 2

Set in 11/13.5 pt Monotype Van Dijck
Typeset by Rowland Phototypesetting Ltd, Bury St Edmunds, Suffolk
Printed in Great Britain by The Bath Press, Bath

A CIP catalogue record for this book is available from the British library

ISBN 0-713-99392-8

Contents

Introduction

Imagine a damp winter morning in the middle of the eighteenth century at Tyburn, now Marble Arch. In those days, Tyburn was at the edge of London: the newly-built West End houses of the nobility reached up to it from the south-east, and the villages of Hampstead in the north and Kensington, with Chelsea past it to the south-west, were just visible in daylight. But this early it is still dark, and misty, and the people jostling around you – climbing up the temporary wooden stands known as Mother Procter's Pews to ensure the best view later, quarrelling over the price of an apple or a ballad-sheet – are like shadows.

Fresh straw is strewn on the ground, and there is the clean smell of cold mud, but mostly the smells are unpleasant, aggravated by the close anonymity of the crowd: the stale sweat that comes after a night of drinking, rotten stumps of teeth that have never been cleaned, ragged clothes taken off not for sleeping nor sex nor disease. The rich will come later, slumming, and pay for their places high up in the stands (although they could not claim to be much cleaner); these are poor people, here to celebrate the life and death of one of their own.

The route from Newgate Prison, next to the Old Bailey, runs by the church of St Sepulchre, where as the condemned men pass the bells toll for their souls, through the meat-market at Smithfield and past the taverns and whorehouses of Holborn and Covent Garden and Soho up to Oxford Road (now Oxford Street) and on to the makeshift stadium at Tyburn. The victim – our hero – sits in a jolting, open cart, his cold hands unbound, between two chaplains repeating like a dirge the need for salvation to a man who has seen few instances of mercy or hope in his short life. Ahead of him is the carriage carrying the Ordinary, or head chaplain of Newgate; half-a-dozen pike-bearing Javelin Men wearing the livery of the City of London bring up the rear on horseback. He is enclosed by the representatives of what the cynical might call hypocritical piety – one eighteenth-century Ordinary not only published accounts of his charges' last days, which most of them did, but also ran a profitable funeral business for them – on one side, and those of an inefficient, parochial system of justice on the other. It is no surprise that the men on the tumbrel pride themselves on dying unbowed and unrepentant before their peers.

Finally, after the prayers have been said by the chaplain, a coin pressed into the palm of the executioner and his last words cried out by the dying man, the cart lurches off out from under his feet and, as the saying went, 'with a stiff neck and a wet pair of breeches', he swings out into the hereafter. This moment on the gallows is the final breath of the condemned man but it is the starting point, and central focus, of the following pieces of writing that document and describe criminal life in eighteenth-century London.

The criminal's heroic identity and the tradition of criminal literature

Although some criminals hanged at Tyburn were not working class, the majority were young and poor, and determined to assert with a flourish their freedom from the restrictions of the life that had driven them to crime. As the pirate Captain Bartholomew Roberts asserted in Captain Johnson's 1724 *A General History of the Robberies and Murders of the Most Notorious Pyrates*: 'In an honest service, there is commonly low wages and hard labour; in this [a life of crime], plenty, satiety, pleasure and ease, liberty and power; and who would not balance creditor on this side, when all the hazard that is run for it at worst, is only a sour look or two at choking? No – a merry life and a short one, shall be my motto.' Roberts was one of the lucky ones. He escaped the gallows but died in a sea battle, having ordered his men to throw his body overboard if he was wounded and might be captured.

Poor women bore a double burden of discrimination as well as poverty; and so if they dared, the advantages of turning to crime were commensurably greater. Although Moll Flanders is fictional, her story illustrates the ways in which a woman might try to escape the curse of being no more than a chattel by viewing herself as a commodity that she – rather than a father or husband or master – might exploit. The women who dressed as men, like the pirates Mary Read and Anne Bonny, had courage and ambition which only living as a man in a man's world could satisfy; both, apparently, were highly attractive to men, both freely used their femininity and neither seems to have disguised herself for any sexual reason – in fact, both dropped their disguises with alacrity at the prospect of romance. The thief Sarah Stanley, on the other hand, who was described as being of masculine mien, may well have dressed as a man and joined the army because she did not want to be a woman at all.

For a man or woman born into the lower orders, the alternatives to a life of crime were miserable: back-breaking work for pitiful wages, the constant threat of disease, cramped and unsanitary living conditions. It is no wonder that so many turned to gin; one slang name for it in Newgate was 'Kill-Grief'. Crime had about it an air (however illusory) of glamour, and brought with it the hope (however short-term) of liberty. A downtrodden scullery maid watching her idol, maybe a footman-turned-highwayman like Claude Du Vall, pass by in his wagon on the way to Tyburn might feel that someone, at least, had escaped the hardship of the life-style they once shared. As Mrs Peachum, in John Gay's 1727 musical comedy, *The Beggar's Opera*, sang: 'The youth in his cart hath the air of a lord, and we cry, there dies an Adonis.'

It was important both for the condemned man to display his lack of concern for death, and for the onlookers publicly to express their sympathy with him. Girls wore white dresses and held nosegays up for handsome young rebels. The crowd heckled and occasionally rose if they did not think the executioner was doing his job as painlessly as possible. Efforts were made to save the bodies of criminals, relics of which were thought to possess supernatural powers that would heal illness and bring good luck, from the 'anatomists', or Royal College of Surgeons, who were allowed to use the corpses of murderers in their lectures. One of the reasons audiences at hangings were increasingly restricted over the eighteenth century and eventually abolished altogether in 1868 was that public hanging days were used by the dying as platforms for their defiance. The punishment seemed only to encourage other criminals. 'The notions which the vulgar have of courage, as well as honour and shame, are full of dangerous errors,' wrote Bernard de Mandeville in *An Enquiry into the Causes of the Frequent Executions at Tyburn* (1725).

It was as easy then as it is today to glamorize the life of crime, as Daniel Defoe noted with disapproval in the early part of the eighteenth century, and as Charles Dickens, in his preface to *Oliver Twist* in 1837, explained: 'In every book I know, where such characters [criminals] are treated of, allurements and fascinations are thrown around them. Even in *The Beggar's Opera*, the thieves are represented as leading a life which is rather to be envied than otherwise.' Handsome Captain Macheath, with his air of authority, his success as a ladies-man and the love of a beautiful, virtuous girl, is as much to be admired and emulated as a gallant soldier, whose title Macheath even appropriates. As Dickens says:

[Dr] Johnson's question, whether any man will turn thief because Macheath is reprieved, seems to me beside the matter. I ask myself, whether any man will be deterred from turning thief because of Macheath's being sentenced to death, and because of the existence of Peachum and Lockit; and remembering the captain's roaring life, great appearance, vast success and strong advantages, I feel assured that nobody having a bent that way will take any warning from him, or will see anything in the play but a flowery and pleasant road, conducting an honourable ambition – in course of time – to Tyburn Tree.

Dickens's avowed intention, with *Oliver Twist*, was to show London's criminal underworld in its true light, a reaction against his peers' Gothic, salacious romanticism. To encourage Oliver to theft, Fagin shows him a *Newgate Calendar*, its pages 'soiled and thumbed with use'. Oliver, the innocent, is horrified and appalled by what he reads: 'The terrible descriptions were so real and vivid, that the sallow pages seemed to turn red with gore; and the words upon them, to be sounded in his ears, as if they were whispered, in hollow murmurs, by the spirits of the dead.' This, Dickens is saying, is how every civilized person should respond to these criminal narratives: they are not heroic epics to be emulated, as the Artful Dodger, manipulated by the evil Fagin, believes, but sad indictments on a society which has ignored the plight of its poorest members. 'I had read of thieves by the scores,' Dickens writes in the Preface,

seductive fellows (amiable for the most part), faultless in dress, plump in pocket, choice in horse-flesh, bold in bearing, fortunate in gallantry, great at a song, a bottle, pack of cards or dice-box, and fit companions for the bravest. But I had never met (except in Hogarth) with the miserable reality. It appeared to me that to draw a knot of such associates in crime as really did exist; to paint them in all their deformity, in all their wretchedness, in all the squalid misery of their lives; to show them as they really are, for ever skulking uneasily through the dirtiest paths of life, with the great black ghastly gallows closing up their prospect, turn them where they might; it appeared to me that to do this, would be to attempt a something which was needed, and which would be a service to society.

The tradition of crime-writing which Dickens hoped to debunk dated back to the late part of the seventeenth century. For the first time, printing was cheap enough to reach the masses and in parallel, literacy rates were increasing. Chapbook writers, ballad-sellers and cheap biographers flourished. London was still a small enough city to be intimate: of a population of perhaps 75,000 in central London (about 650,000 in greater London), a thousand people visited the house-breaker and escapologist Jack Sheppard in Newgate the first week after his last spectacular escape and recapture; many more would have read of his adventures in newspaper reports and pamphlets. Defoe, who, like Dickens, thought that sensationalist literature about criminals like Sheppard only incited others to crime, overcame his scruples to ghostwrite Sheppard's autobiography. His concession to his principles was the insertion of moralistic exhortations supposedly uttered by Sheppard (but incompatible with any other opinion Sheppard is known to have held) as he prepared for death.

It was not until the advent of Henry Fielding, novelist and JP of Bow Street Magistrate's Court in Covent Garden, that the first seeds of doubt over the efficacy of the death penalty, as well as policing and the criminal justice system (see below), were sown. Captain Smith, author in 1714 of *A General History of the Lives of the . . . Highwaymen*, believed that the executions of the criminals of whom he wrote ought not inspire pity in his readers: 'As their unparalleled insolence insulted over the laws of God and man, by taking an unaccountable pride and ambition in breaking both [the laws of God and man], we ought not to be sorry at the hangman's meritorious act of sending such case-hardened villains out of the land of the living.' His treatment of his subjects belied this statement, though: they seized opportunities and defied justice with a gusto and swagger that cannot have failed to inspire his readers if not with the desire to kick over the traces themselves at least with a certain rueful admiration.

In 1751 Fielding for the first time questioned the society that bred the criminals hanged at Tyburn, rather than automatically condemning the criminals themselves. 'Upon the whole, something should be, nay must be done, or much worse consequences than have hitherto happened, are very soon to be apprehended,' he concluded his *An Enquiry into the Causes of the Late Increase in Robbers*.

Nay, as the matter now stands, not only care for the public safety, but common humanity, exacts our concern on this occasion; for that many cart-loads of our fellow-creatures are once in six weeks carried to slaughter, is a dreadful consideration; and that this is heightened by reflecting, that, with proper care and proper regulations, much the greater part of these wretches might have been made not only happy in themselves, but very useful members of the society, which they now so greatly dishonour in the sight of all Christendom.

Fielding's view, however, was not a commonly held one in the eighteenth century. People of all classes enjoyed the spectacle of the Hanging Match, as the six-weekly hanging days at Tyburn were known. For every courageous man like Dick Turpin (actually hanged at York), who was respected for stamping his legs vigorously to quell their involuntary twitching before hurling himself off the scaffold to meet eternity, there was another like Blueskin Blake, Jack Sheppard's accomplice, who had not the courage to face his end sober, or Dr Dodd, whose emotional confession and repentance at Tyburn had his audience of tens of thousands sobbing into their handkerchiefs. It was criminals like these that the government hoped would serve as an example to their peers; unfortunately, those who managed to retain their dignity and bravado served as an inspiration instead.

It was because they were so inspirational – besides living such flamboyant lives – that these figures were such rich material for contemporary and subsequent commentators and novelists. The nineteenth-century 'Newgate Novel' depicted this underworld with relish. Its heroes were noble savages like Jack Sheppard, or villains like Jonathan Wild, who was the model for countless anti-heroes from Gay's Peachum to Dickens's Fagin. Gradually, the dominant figure became not the criminal, but the man pursuing him. By the twentieth century Moriarty (also modelled in part on Wild) has been side-lined by Sherlock Holmes; today films and television find as much material in policemen and detectives as in the criminals who are their quarry. This collection, which tells the stories of the eighteenth-century originals, often in their own words, illuminates both the literary tradition they inspired and the historical basis for that tradition.

The police and the justice system; or, the story of a criminal

As this anthology shows, crime flourished in eighteenth-century London. Conditions could not have been better: a chaotic, sprawling, higgledy-piggledy city full of hide-outs and safe houses; a commercial boom, creating unprecedented wealth – and the desire to consume its fruits conspicuously – in both the upper and middle classes, and a corresponding gulf between the rich and the poor; an ineffectual justice system; and most importantly, no police force we would recognize today.

This story is a familiar one, told time and again – best by William Hogarth in the *Industry & Idleness* series – a stereotypical case. A young apprentice is frustrated by his cruel master (but equally it could be a girl turned out of a parish workhouse on to the streets, or a boy newly arrived in London to seek his fortune). He is restricted, chastised, beaten; having nowhere to turn – no parents, no system of social assistance – he determines to run away, and make his own way in life. So he leaves the home in which he has lived for a period of up to seven years, with no money because he has never been paid, only given the barest minimum of room and board.

And he sets out to look for work and a home; no luck except for a pile of straw in the dank corner of a brandy shop. After a few days, lonely and hungry, he is almost ready to swallow his pride and go back to his sadistic master but someone approaches him and offers him a way to survive. It may be a thief-taker like Jonathan Wild, who loved to trawl the backstreets of London in search of the desperate and down-and-out. The more miserable a person was when Wild found him, the better, Wild reasoned: he would be willing to do anything for a chance; and if Wild did help him get set up as a highwayman or footpad, he would owe Wild his life and serve him loyally. Or it might be a sympathetic whore, encouraging the boy to become her twang, or bully, to scare her client at the moment of climax and enable her to pick his exposed pocket.

The first few times, it's easy: he climbs into the open window of a darkened house and takes a roll of fabric or a couple of silver spoons. On one occasion there is even a purse with six gold crowns (5 shillings each) in it lying on a table; that lasts him weeks. A man walks past him on the street with his silk handkerchief carelessly exposed; a quick tug and it's his. These kinds of goods are easy to dispose of – there is even a market near St Paul's dealing exclusively in stolen handkerchiefs. Gradually he becomes not just an opportunist, but a real criminal. Finding fences for the goods he's stolen leads him into flash houses and taverns frequented by the professionals, who encourage him to take bigger risks for greater rewards. He develops a taste for drink, and fine clothes, and women; perhaps he acquires a mistress who pesters him to steal trinkets and furbelows for her. He begins to subscribe to the thieves' mantra outlined by the highwayman Macleane's accomplice Plunkett: 'A brave man cannot want; he has a right to live, and need not want the conveniences of life, while the dull, plodding, busy knaves carry cash in their pockets. We must draw upon them to supply our wants; there needs only impudence, and getting the better of a few idle scruples; there is scarce courage necessary; all we have to deal with are such mere poltroons.'

The first time he's arrested – a citizen's arrest, a swift hand on his arm in a crowd after the cry for 'A pickpocket!' goes up – he's let off for lack of evidence. His accomplice – to whom he'd handed the snatched watch – had got away, and there wasn't enough proof to convict him. The thief-taker who has watched his career with interest makes sure there are witnesses in court who'll swear to his good character. These perjuring witnesses were known as straw-men, who promenaded up and down outside the Old Bailey with straw tucked into their shoes, advertising their willingness to accept a bribe in return for giving false evidence.

This first brush with justice does not put him off crime. The baying crowd who'd hauled him before the magistrate were frightening, but because there was neither a witness nor the watch, his innocence was assumed and held up by the blasé JP. It was easy to stand up and explain that he'd merely been in the wrong place at the wrong time;

his victim did not even try to bring the case to court. In many ways, in a situation like this, it was far more difficult for the prosecutor, who had to bear all the costs of bringing a case until he had proved the defendant guilty, and, like the defendant, received no free legal advice. If an offence had been committed, nothing could be done without money. Women, particularly, who could not own property in their own name, were dependent on the financial support of a husband or father to bring a case to court.

After a night in the Roundhouse, the prison in St Giles used as a temporary receptacle for minor criminals waiting for their hearings, he's sent home. At first he thinks he's got off scot-free. Maybe for a few hours he determines to put his life of crime behind him and open a little apothecary's shop, the trade he was originally trained to: settle down. But all too soon the thief-taker pays him a visit in his attic room in Covent Garden. Empty bottles, crumpled ballad-sheets and dice lie on the uneven wooden floor beside the straw pallet on which he is sprawled beside his sleeping mistress. The thief-taker is succinct. He got our hero out of trouble, and now he expects a return. Everything the boy steals from now on must be fenced through the thief-taker's office; and the more valuable the booty, the more secure his future in the informal corporation of thieves the thief-taker runs.

So he is thrust, almost despite himself, into the criminal under-world. He might survive for several years, working his way up the hierarchy of thieves which is an inverse of the social scale in 'normal' society, his fate inextricably linked to his master's; or he might refuse the thief-taker's double-edged protection, and carry on alone. This will reduce his chances of a long life. As soon as it becomes clear that he has chosen independence, the thief-taker will be out for blood. No one can be allowed to defy the thief-taker, refuse him and still thrive. It would be bad for business.

And so one day, sitting in a smoke-filled tavern, an acquaintance tells him of a sure thing – a house near Soho Square that is known to be full of silver, where his lover works as a servant-girl. Our hero's help is enlisted, the date set. On a moonless night the three youths creep in through a window left open by the girl, and start piling silver chocolate-pots and plates into a burlap sack. They leave the house by the same window, but this time, silver clinking, they attract the notice of a passer-by, led by a link-boy with a lantern, returning home to bed from a long night at the faro-tables in White's Chocolate House. The man confronts the robbers; the link-boy runs away; a rickety pistol is drawn and in the scuffle the man is shot. Dropping their bag of silver, the three flee the scene, but the damage has been done.

There is no police force to call, no central means of justice to set in motion to find the unknown killer and his band of thugs. When the aged parish watchman passes by at dawn and finds the cold figure lying on the cobblestones, he ambles off to tell the local JP what he's found. Parish watches were an archaic, parochial neighbourhood watch system, a year-long unpaid duty that theoretically would be divided among the parish's fit, male inhabitants, but in fact was usually farmed out (by the chosen member of the parish, not the parish itself) to a deputy constable, usually the cheapest individual available. These deputies, in all but the richest of parishes, were notorious for their lack of enthusiasm and susceptibility to bribery as well as their varying states of decrepitude. They were further hindered by the parish system itself, which decreed that each parish (there were 676 in the City of London alone) had to deal with its own crimes. A thief being pursued by a deputy in his own parish – should the deputy muster up enough energy to pursue him at all – could often simply cross the street into another parish to elude arrest. The local JPs, or magistrates, were often equally hopeless and generally as immoral. In Kent in 1714, only three-quarters of the newly appointed JPs even bothered to take the optional oath to play an active role in office.

The reason that there was no police force, as there was, by this time, in other European countries, was the long-standing fear of infringement of the traditional liberties of the freeborn Englishman. John Bull stood upright on his own, supported by the laws of Parliament; he had no need of interference. A police force was seen as little more than, at best, a network of government spies, and at worst, a standing army that the king might use to enforce his own will against that of the people. It was not until Henry and John Fieldings' consecutive tenures as magistrates at Bow Street from 1749 that an effective anti-crime force was formed, founded on the belief that true liberty consisted of each citizen being free to enjoy his or her life in security. This, the Bow Street Runners, was largely based on Jonathan Wild's methods of thief-taking, the underworld machinery it was instituted to control. Not until 1819 did Robert Peel introduce the concept of a policeman that survives to this day, the 'Bobby' on the beat.

And so, in the absence of any other institution to turn to, the thief-taker is called upon to find the killer, and a reward of up to 200 guineas is set for his capture either by the government or the murdered man's family. Did our hero do it? No matter, for the thief-taker soon finds one of the three – maybe the murderer himself – who is scared enough to inform on his accomplices. In return for the promise of a pardon, he squeals for his life. He tells the thief-taker that it was the apothecary's apprentice; and the search begins.

The hunted boy hides out in a variety of places. He goes to his mistress's mother's brandy shop – where she had first sauntered up to him, only a few months earlier – but it is too obvious, and after a trembling hour in a huge vat, hidden by a layer of salt cod, as the thief-taker's men ransacked the house, he decides to leave. For a few days he lives in a disused outbuilding just past Vauxhall, sneaking out to forage for food at night, but he gets bored, and lonely. One night he takes a boat across the river to see his mistress; and when she asks, he can't help letting slip where his hideout is. Within hours of his return he hears the ominous sounds of hooves pounding up to his isolated barn: it is the thief-taker and his goons. Alone, there is little point in resisting, and so, meekly, he holds out his wrists for the shackles.

This arrest is a very different affair from the first. As an accused murderer, with witnesses willing to swear to his guilt, he is thrown straight into the condemned hold at Newgate to await his trial. If he thought he had been cold, or hungry, or lice-infested before, he had been wrong. Conditions in Newgate were akin to the wildest excesses of a Gothic imagination of a dungeon: damp, dark, with no fresh air; rats so bold they'd attack sleeping babies; no food, nor water, nor blankets; so many lice on the ground that their shells crackled underfoot. A room in the Press Yard cost the same as the rent of a fully equipped and staffed house in St James's – although there were privileges that went along with it, such as the right to bring your wife and children to live with you, and to have your meals brought in from outside; the keeper was careful to allow rich prisoners their luxuries if they were willing to pay. But for the poor, life inside Newgate was harder even than life on the streets.

At court, too, everything was against him. The thief-taker was there again, but this time he sat in the spectators' gallery, surrounded by his henchmen, a smile of vengeful satisfaction playing around his lips. The witnesses against him, their stories planned and co-ordinated, told of how they were inveigled into the robbery, and how our hero unhesitatingly reached for his pistol and shot the man dead when he approached them. It was no good for the boy to protest that he had not known his accomplices before the robbery – now, of course, he realized that they had been planted by the thief-taker to entrap him – had never seen the gun before that night, would never have fired it. The sentence was pronounced against him: guilty of murder, and the sentence of death read out to him. 'The law is, that thou shall return from hence, to the place whence thou camest, and from thence to the place of execution, where thou shalt hang by the neck till the body be dead! dead! dead! and the Lord have mercy upon thy soul.'

At this point, for a crime less serious than murder, the condemned man might hope for a pardon, or a mitigation of his punishment from death to transportation (instituted in 1719 as an alternative to capital punishment). The death penalty was the legal punishment for over two hundred crimes – from murder to rape to the theft of anything worth over a shilling – because the government believed that being able to dispense mercy was an essential part of gaining the populace's respect. The result of this policy was that men like Colonel Charteris were pardoned their crimes, because of who they knew, and men with no connections suffered. Jack Sheppard, for instance, whose crime, non-violent burglary, would be seen today as far less serious than Charteris's rape (his second), died on the gallows as an example to others of the lower classes who threatened the property of the rich – to protect which was seen as the role of the law; while Charteris received a royal pardon and was set free.

For our hero, there is little hope of any such mercy. He returns to Newgate to contemplate his short life and untimely death, and to prepare himself to put on a brave face when he will ride, palely, through the screaming crowds to Tyburn and the gallows; thinking, as Fagin did when he sat in the condemned cell, of 'one dark cluster of objects in the centre of all – the black stage, the cross-beam, the rope, and all the hideous apparatus'.

This story is an amalgam of several different lives, but it contains within it the most typical elements of crime, justice and punishment in the eighteenth century: the lack of legitimate opportunity that led bright, healthy young men and women into crime; the difficulty of extricating oneself from the criminal milieu once initially drawn into it; the anachronistic parochialism of the police and judicial systems, whose objective was to protect the property of the rich over and above the welfare of the poor; and the grim hopelessness of the eighteenth-century penal system.

The selections which follow do not contain all – or sometimes even any – of these elements; they are atypical, which is why they are interesting; but this introduction, I hope, will provide a context in which to set the stories and lives that follow. For more specific and more academic analysis of eighteenth-century criminal history, consult the reading list which follows.

Organization and the material

I have divided the chapters according to the type of criminal. This I believe to be the most straightforward approach, with one exception: women. I considered including a separate chapter on women, but eventually decided against it because it seemed anachronistic to try to separate the sexes. Female criminals were predominantly (but by no means exclusively) either thieves or prostitutes; but they do feature in the majority of the chapters. It is important to remember that most criminals were men; the selections included here are not necessarily disproportionate – the division is about two-thirds men to one-third women – but they were chosen not necessarily because they are typical but because they are interesting. Women like Jenny Diver (Mary Young) were notorious in their day precisely because it was so unusual for a woman to be successful in what was generally a male domain. The stories of the cross-dressers Anne Bonny, Mary Read and Sarah Stanley show to what extent women needed to take on masculine characteristics to succeed at crime, as well as to attain a sense of individual freedom and control over their own lives. They chose to live by men's rules, but often still using feminine wiles, and this is what makes them so interesting to the contemporary reader.

Jews in eighteenth-century London are another group deserving of mention. They were a minority, persecuted and alienated from the rest of English society. Principally involved in either the cloth trade or money lending, they inhabited London's East End. Negative cultural stereotypes of the Jew as miser and scavenger were firmly in place at this time, as evidenced by Dickens's description of Fagin as a Jew.

The majority of the pieces are taken from one of the *Newgate Calendars* – the first anonymously edited edition published in 1779 and the last by the attorneys Andrew Knapp and William Baldwin in 1826 – and the *Select Trials at the Old Bailey*, published periodically throughout the eighteenth century, although I generally used the latest version published in 1764. All of these books are noted below.

I also tried to include examples of all the different genres of criminal writing and observation: newspaper reports, ballads, pulp biographies, travel-writing, pamphlets, poems, chapbooks and satires. The only type of writing I avoided was fiction (but I have added a list of relevant novels to the reading list). Some pieces are published in full, others are excerpts; but again, I tried to provide as comprehensive a picture as possible of criminals' lives, and the changes undergone in this period, using the various materials. I included two entries on individuals who were not actual criminals (i.e. were not arrested and tried): the courtesan Harriette Wilson, and Edward Trelawny, who wrote about piracy on the South China Seas. Both excerpts, taken from autobiographies written by literate and amusing characters, add spice as well as breadth to their respective chapters. For those who are interested, I have appended the 1723 Black Act as an example of the law-making and legal style of the times.

The period this collection spans is a broad (and vague) one, ranging from Captain Hind, who was executed in 1652, to Harriette Wilson, writing in 1825. Roughly I tried to stay within the eighteenth century, but I did not restrict myself if there was a fascinating or influential character outside this boundary. Hind was important because he was the first highwayman to incorporate the elements of gallantry, altruism and fame that we associate with the stereotype of highwaymen today; Wilson uniquely described a dissolute world that was at its zenith during her lifetime. My principal concern was that the people I used lived in a pre-industrial and pre-Victorian age. In the book's subtitle, the Hogarthian Underworld, is a reference to the pictorial world created by the painter and engraver William Hogarth (1697–1764), which chronicled the lives and deaths of characters like those whose words are collected here.

A Note on the Texts

The sources range from contemporary publications to modern (and modernized) reprintings. Where earlier publications have been used, the many capitals used for nouns, etc. are lower cased, the long 's' is modernized and the ampersand and '*&c.*' are expanded, but the eighteenth-century spelling and punctuation have been retained, so readers get the flavour of the period. There is some house styling: double quotation marks are made into singles and the punctuation in relation to them standardized; the comma before 'and' in a series is omitted; dashes are modernized; and clear typographical errors are corrected.

Sources

(All published in London)

Anonymous, *The Malefactor's Register; or, the Newgate and Tyburn Calendar*, 5 vols. (1779)

Jackson, W., *The New and Complete Newgate Calendar; or, villainy displayed in all its branches*, 6 vols. (1795)

Johnson, Captain C., *A General History of the Robberies and Murders of the Most Notorious Pyrates* . . . (1724)

—, *A General History of the Lives and Adventures of the Most Famous Highwaymen, Murderers, Street-Robbers, &c.* (1714; 1734)

Knapp, A., and W. Baldwin, *Criminal Chronology; or, the New Newgate*

Calendar, 4 vols. (1809); subsequent editions entitled *Newgate Calendar* (1824, 1826)

Select Trials at the Old Bailey (1734, 1742 and 1764)

Smith, Captain A., *A Compleat History of the Lives and Robberies of the Most Notorious Highwaymen, Footpads, Shop-lifts, and Cheats, of Both Sexes* . . . (1719; new edition, 1926)

—, *The General History of the Lives of the Most Notorious Highwaymen* . . . (1714)

Thompson, G., *Newgate Calendar, containing the lives of the most notorious characters who have violated the laws of their country* (1840)

Further Reading

Eighteenth- and nineteenth-century fiction

Ainsworth, W. H., *Jack Sheppard* (London, 1839)
—, *Rookwood* (London, 1837)
Defoe, D., *Moll Flanders* (London, 1722)
Dickens, C., *Oliver Twist* (London, 1837)
Fielding, H., *Amelia* (London, 1751)
—, *Jonathan Wild the Great* (London, 1743)
Gay, J., *The Beggar's Opera* (London, 1727)
Godwin, W., *Caleb Williams* (London, 1794)

Non-fiction

Beattie, J. M., *Crime and the Courts in England* (Oxford, 1986)
Bender, J., *Imagining the Penitentiary: Fiction and the Architecture of Mind in the Eighteenth Century* (Chicago, 1987)
Burford, E. J., *Wits, Wenchers and Wantons* (London, 1986)
Clery, E. C., *The Rise of Supernatural Fiction* (Cambridge, 1995)
Cockburn, J. S. (ed.), *Crime in England* (London, 1977)
Earle, P., *A City Full of People* (London, 1994)
Foucault, M., *Discipline and Punish*, trans. A. Sheridan (London, 1977)
Gatrell, V. A. C., *The Hanging Tree: Execution and the English People, 1770–1868* (Oxford, 1994)

George, M. D., *London Life in the Eighteenth Century* (London, 1925)

Hay, D., Linebaugh, P., and E. P. Thompson (eds.), *Albion's Fatal Tree* (London, 1975)

Hibbert, C., *The Road to Tyburn* (London, 1957)

Holmes, R., *Dr Johnson and Mr Savage* (London, 1993)

Howson, G., *Thief-Taker General* (London, 1970)

Glendinning, V., *Swift* (London, 1998)

Ignatieff, M., *A Just Measure of Pain* (London, 1978)

Judges, A. V., *The Elizabethan Underworld* (London, 1930)

Linebaugh, P., *The London Hanged* (London, 1991)

McLynn, F., *Crime and Punishment in Eighteenth Century England* (London, 1989)

Marshall, T., *Murdering to Dissect* (Manchester, 1995)

Moore, L., *The Thieves Opera* (London, 1997)

Paulson, R., *Hogarth: High Art and Low 1732–1750* (Cambridge, 1992)

—, *Hogarth: The Modern Moral Subject 1697–1732* (Cambridge, 1992)

Plumb, J. H., *England in the Eighteenth Century* (Harmondsworth, 1950)

Porter, R., *English Society in the Eighteenth Century* (London, 1982)

—, *London: A Social History* (London, 1994)

Richardson, R., *Death, Dissection and the Destitute* (London, 1987)

Rogers, P., *Hacks and Dunces* (London, 1980)

Sharpe, J. A., *Crime in Early Modern England* (London, 1984)

Stater, V., *Duke Hamilton is Dead!* (New York, 1999)

Thompson, E. P., *Whigs and Hunters* (London, 1975)

Trumbach, R., *Sex and the Gender Revolution. Homosexuality and the Third Gender in Enlightenment London* (London, 1998)

I

The Hogarthian Underworld

NED WARD
From *Secret History of London Clubs* (1709)

This little book included chapters like 'The Beggars' Club' and 'The Mollies' Club' (about homosexuals) – populist satires on the different groups that peopled London's underworld. Ned Ward (1667–1731) was a journalist, an observer of contemporary London life, whose career like Defoe's and Swift's was built upon the newly literate lower and middle classes. Even if a labourer in London could not read, he could go to a coffee house and hear the news read out there; servants often had access to their masters' libraries; politics and society gossip were discussed at all levels of society. In this intimate, informed world, the actions of miscreants like Jonathan Wild or Jenny Diver (Mary Young) – propagated by men like Ward – were of interest to men and women from every background. Ward's easy, slangy style made him a popular chronicler of the rowdy, unprincipled London in which he lived.

THE THIEVES' CLUB

This Tyburn-looked Society of Desperado's, who commonly have the fortune to wear their destiny in their faces, formerly kept their club at a certain tavern not far from Flat Ditch, but now remov'd to a more obscure place on the north west side of *London*: where a remarkable thief-taker can help anybody to their stolen goods, provided the gratitude the loser offer'd amounted to about half the value of what the raparees[1] had depriv'd him of; which is commonly as the rogues with safety are able to make of their booty, because the receivers, who either buy or lend money upon such cargoes, always guess by their chapmen how honestly they are come by, and therefore will not deal without reasonable advantage. This thief-takers house take their sanctuary at, and both day and night at his tipling tenement,[2]

[1] thieves.   [2] tavern.

3

where the Society of the Devil's operators project their hellish roguries, and what they got over the Devil's back, they spend under his belly.

Thus all sorts of villanies are daily harbour'd under this unhallow'd roof, by him who knows their practices, till they foolishly waste what they have villainously gotten; and if any of 'em grow lazy, and don't exercise their tallent, their master the thief-taker will take him up and hang him out of their way as a worthless scoundrel who was only a dabler in a misery that he knew not how to live by.

> Just so reforming, stables protect,
> The harlot that can bribe as they expect
> But if she once grows poor through want of trade
> In triumph then they flog the needy jade.

Then amidst their jollity, when the power of *Bacchus* had forc'd open hell's cabbins, one to make a jest of his villiany, wou'd merrily discover that he once robb'd an old lady of three hundred pound by the confederacy of one of his misses, who was got in to be chamber maid, and would mimick how heartily the old granny begg'd, at fourscore that she might not be ravish'd. Another to show his gallantry, would boast how three of them stopp'd five gentlemen upon the road, robb'd four of them, and the other being an old parson, they drag'd him into a wood, and told him if he would preach a sermon to them, he should go unrifled. I thank you reply'd the parson; but 'tis a little too short a warning for a good sermon, however, I will do the best I can, which said one of the rogues was to this effect,

Gentlemen, you are the most like the old apostles of any men in the world, for they were wanderers upon the earth, and so are you, they had neither lands nor tenements they could call their own, neither as I presume, have you. They were despis'd of all but their own profession, and so I believe are you: they were often hurr'd into gaols and prisons, were persecuted by the people, and endured great hardships, all which circumstances, I presume, have been undergone by you; their Profession brought them all to untimely death, and so will yours bring you, if you continue in your courses.

4

But beloved (with permission) in this point, you will mightily differ from the apostles, for they from the tree ascended into heaven and thither I fear you will hardly ever come; and as their deaths were recompensed with eternal glory, yours will be rewarded with eternal shame and misery, unless you mend your manners. Upon which harrangue the man of God was dismist, with thanks for his favourable comparisons. And thus they made a jest of those wicked villanies, that they ought to blush every time they speak of 'em much more boast and glory in.

> For he that will no human laws obey,
> Will ne'er be aw'd by what the priest can say,
> But harden'd in his ills, will still rebel,
> And hazard life and Heaven instead of Hell.
> Let it, O youth, be then thy early care
>
> To truly know what thy companions are.
> That from the bad thou may'st select the good,
> And shun the poys'nous converse of the lude,[1]
> For he that rowls[2] in nettles man be stung,
> Nor can the fool be clean that wades in dung.
>
> Therefore the only way to be secure
> And keep an honest reputation pure
> Is to show wisely, it is your care to be
> Distinguished by your virtuous company.

BERNARD DE MANDEVILLE
From *An Enquiry into the Causes of the Frequent Executions at Tyburn* (1725)

The Dutch political commentator, Mandeville (1670–1733), took a Hobbesian view on social order: he believed it was the duty of the landed classes to rule; that the poor would always be insubordinate if

---

[1] crowd.   [2] rolls.

allowed to be; and that only firm punishments would act as an effective deterrent against crime. This long essay was first published serially in the British Journal *(a weekly newspaper) at the same time that Jonathan Wild was being tried (although it had been written before his arrest), making Mandeville's observations particularly apposite. Mandeville's most famous work was* The Fable of the Bees, *which was much admired throughout the eighteenth century; Dr Johnson was just one of his fans.*

CHAPTER I

Of THEFTBOTE;[1] *or, the Crime of Compounding of Felony*

The multitude of unhappy wretches, that every year are put to death for trifles in our great metropolis, has long been afflicting to men of pity and humanity; and continues to give great uneasiness to every person, who has a value for his kind. Many good projects have been thought of to cure this evil, by sapping the foundation of it: a society has been set up to reform our manners; and neither workhouses, nor discipline on small crimes, have been wanting: an act has been made against prophane cursing and swearing; and many charity schools have been erected. But the event has not answer'd hitherto the good design of those endeavours. This city abounds as much with loose, lazy and dishonest poor; there is as much mischief done by ordinary felons; and executions for theft and burglary are as frequent, at least, as ever: nay, it is believed, that *London* is more pester'd with low villany than any other place whatever, the proportion of bigness between them not left unconsider'd. As there is no effect without a cause, so something must be the reason of this calamity. I have long and carefully examined into this matter, and am forced to ascribe the mischief complained of to two palpable evils, distinct from those we have in common with other large overgrown cities. One regards prosecutions; the other the treatment that is given to malefactors after they are taken. I shall begin with the first: I mean the neglect

[1] thieftaking.

of them, occasion'd by our shameful negotiations with thieves, or their agents, for the recovery of stolen goods, by which, in reality, we become aiders and abetters to them.

The law of *England* is so tender of men's lives, that whoever justly prosecutes, and convicts a person of a capital crime, has nothing to answer for to his conscience, but, on the contrary, has done a service to his country, without offence to God, or the least breach of charity to his neighbour. But as every body has not strength of mind and resolution enough to perform duties that are repugnant to his nature, so, making allowances for human frailties, I could excuse the backwardness of a meek home-bred person, who should complain, that to appear in open court, and speak before a judge, are terrible things to him. But I think it unpardonable, that a man should knowingly act against the law, and by so doing powerfully contribute to the increase, as well as safety and maintenance, of pilferers and robbers, from no other principle, than a criminal selfishness, accompany'd with an utter disregard to the publick: yet nothing is more common among us. As soon as any thing is missing, suspected to be stolen, the first course we steer is directly to the office of Mr *Jonathan Wild*. If what we want is a trinket, either enamel'd, or otherwise curiously wrought; if there is painting about it; if it be a particular ring, the gift of a friend; or any thing which we esteem above the real value, and offer more for it than Mr *Thief* can make of it, we are look'd upon as good chaps, and welcome to redeem it. But if it be plain gold or silver, we shall hardly see it again, unless we pay the worth of it. Some years ago, it is true, a man might, for half a piece, have fetch'd back a snuff-box that weigh'd twenty or thirty shillings: but this was in the infancy of the establishment. Now they are grown wiser, and calculate exactly what such a thing will melt down for: to offer less is thought unreasonable; and unless Mr *Thief-catcher* stands your friend indeed, if you have it, you will seldom save any thing but the fashion. If in this place you can hear no tidings of your goods, it is counted a sign, that they are in the hands of irregular practitioners, that steal without permission of the board. In this case we immediately put in an advertisement in some news-paper or other, with a promise, that

such a reward will be given, and no questions asked. I own, that in
the printing of these short epistles there is no manner of harm, if we
abstract the act itself from the concern the publick has in it. The
tenor of them is rather benevolent than injurious: and a panegyrist
on the present times might justly say of them, that in no performances
the true spirit of Christianity was so conspicuous as in these: that
they were not only free from calumny and ill language, but likewise
so void of reproach, that speaking to a thief, we never call'd him so
in those charitable addresses: that in them the very catalogues of
injuries receiv'd, were penn'd with as little heat, or resentment, as
ever tradesman shew'd in a bill of parcels directed to his best customer:
that here we are so far from hating our enemy, that we proffer him
a recompence for his trouble, if he will condescend to let us have our
own again; and leaving all revenge to God, to shew that we are willing
to forgive and forget, we consult, in the most effectual manner, the
safety of a person that deserves hanging for the wrong he has done
us. Yet, notwithstanding the kind of constructions that may be put
on these civil offers, they all tend to the *compounding of felony*, and are
the occasion of a double mischief: they invite the indigent and lazy
to pick pockets, and render the negligent more careless than probably
they would be, was this practice abolish'd. A pocket-book, or memor-
andum, may be stole from a man that is of vast concern to him, and
yet of no use but to the owner: if this be taken by a regular thief, a
listed pilferer, it is easily recover'd for a small reward. I don't suppose
any one so silly, that therefore he would go to places, and into
companies, on purpose to have his pocket pick'd; but I can't help
thinking, that if those things were never to be heard of again, and
the loss irretrievable, many young rakes, and other loose reprobates,
would be under greater apprehensions, and more upon their guard,
at least when they had such a charge about them, than the generality
of them now are. And again, if nothing could be made of letters,
papers and things of that nature, such as have no known worth, and
are not readily turned into money, the numbers of whores and rogues,
young and old, that are employ'd in the diving trade,[1] would decrease

---

[1] pickpocketing; thievery.

considerably; many of them, from a principle of prudence, refusing to meddle with any thing else. For as on most of the things now spoke of, no real value can be set, the punishment would be inconsiderable, if any, should the things be found upon them, or themselves be taken in the fact. Most men will agree to all this, whilst unconcern'd; but when private interest is touch'd, it soon stifles these considerations. I should be a fool, says one, when a thing of value is stolen from me, not to get it back, if I can, for a trifle. If I lose a sword, or a watch, I must have another; and to save the fashion in these things is considerable: it is better to lose the half than the Whole. I have nothing to do with the thief, says another, if I have my own again, it is all I want: what good would it do to me to have a poor fellow hang'd? A third, more compassionate, will tell us, that if he knew the thief, he would not meddle with him; and that he would lose ten times the value of what has been taken from him, rather than be the occasion of a man's death. To these I reply, that the legislators seem to have known how the generality of men would argue, and what excuses they would make; they had an eye on the frailty of our nature; consider'd, that all prosecutions are troublesome, and often very expensive; that most men preferred their own interest, their ease and pleasure, to any regard of the publick; and therefore they provided against our passions with so much severity. *Compounding of felony* is not prohibited under a small penalty, or attoned for by a little fine; it is next to felony; and the most creditable citizen, that is convicted of it, ceases to be an honest man.

The offence in our law is call'd THEFTBOTE; of which my Lord Chief Justice *Coke* says, 'That it is an offence beyond misprision of felony; for that is only a bare concealment of his bare knowledge: but that it is THEFTBOTE when the owner not only knows of the felony, but takes of the thief his goods again, or amends for the same to favour or maintain him, that is, not to prosecute him, to the intent he may escape. The punishment of THEFTBOTE is ransom and Imprisonment.' Sir *Matthew Hale*,[1] in his *Pleas of the Crown*, says, 'That

---

[1] Sir Edward Coke (1552–1634) and Hale (1609–76) were Lord Chief Justices and lawmakers.

THEFTBOTE is more than a bare misprision of felony, and is, where the owner doth not only know the felony, but takes his goods again, or other amends, not to prosecute.'

This rigour of the legislature is a full demonstration, that they thought it a crime of the most pernicious consequence to the society; yet it is become familiar to us; and our remissness in several matters, relating to felons, is not to be parallell'd in any other civiliz'd nation. That rogues should be industriously dispers'd throughout the city and suburbs; that different hours and stations should be observ'd among them, and regular books kept of stollen goods; that the superintendent in this hopeful oeconomy should almost every sessions, for a reward, betray, prosecute, and hang one or more of this his acquaintance, and at the same time keep on his correspondence amongst the survivors, whom, one after another, he sends all to their triangular home;[1] that magistrates should not only know and see this, but likewise continue to make use of such a person for an evidence, and in a manner own that they are beholden to him in the administration of justice; that, I say, all these things should be facts, is something very extraordinary, in the principal city, and the home management of a kingdom, so formidable abroad, and of such moment in the balance of *Europe*, as that of *Great Britain*.

The mischief that one man can do as a thief, is a very trifle to what he may be the occasion of, as an agent or concealer of felons. The longer this practice continues, the more the number of rogues must hourly encrease; and therefore it is high time that regular book-keeping of stolen goods should cease, and that all gangs and knots of thieves should be broke and destroy'd as much as is possible, at least, none of them suffer'd to form themselves into societies that are under discipline, and act by order of a superior. It is highly criminal in any man, for lucre, to connive at a piece of felony which he could have hinder'd: but a profess'd thief-catcher, above all, ought to be severely punish'd, if it can be proved that he has suffer'd a known rogue to go on in his villany, tho' but one day, after it was

---

[1] the gallows.

10

in his power to apprehend and convict him, more especially if it appears that he was a sharer in the profit.

. . .

CHAPTER III

Of Execution Day, the Journey to Tyburn,
and a Word in behalf of Anatomical Dissections

When the day of execution is come, among extraordinary sinners, and persons condemned for their crimes, who have but that morning to live, one would expect a deep sense of sorrow, with all the signs of a thorough contrition, and the utmost concern; that either silence, or a sober sadness, should prevail; and that all, who had any business there, should be grave and serious, and behave themselves, at least, with common decency, and a deportment suitable to the occasion. But the very reverse is true. The horrid aspects of turnkeys and gaolers, in discontent and hurry; the sharp and dreadful looks of rogues, that beg in irons, but would rob you with greater satisfaction, if they could; the bellowings of half a dozen names at a time, that are perpetually made in the enquiries after one another; the variety of strong voices, that are heard, of howling in one place, scolding and quarrelling in another, and loud laughter in a third; the substantial breakfasts that are made in the midst of all this; the seas of beer that are swill'd; the never-ceasing outcries for more; and the bawling answers of the tapsters as continual; the quantity and varieties of more entoxicating liquors, that are swallow'd in every part of *Newgate*; the impudence, and unseasonable jests of those, who administer them; their black hands, and nastiness all over; all these, joined together, are astonishing and terrible, without mentioning the oaths and imprecations, that from every corner are echo'd about, for trifles; or the little, light and general squallor of the gaol itself, accompany'd with the melancholy noise of fetters, differently sounding, according to their weight: but what is most shocking to a thinking man, is, the behaviour of the condemn'd, whom (for the greatest part) you'll find, either drinking madly, or uttering the vilest ribaldry, and jeering others, that are less impenitent; whilst the Ordinary bustles among them, and shifting from one to another, distributes scraps of good counsel to unattentive hearers; and near him, the hangman, impatient to be gone, swears at their delays; and, as fast as he can, does his part, in preparing them for their journey.

CESAR DE SAUSSURE
From *A Foreign View of England in the Reigns of George I and George II* (1725–9)

Cesar de Saussure (b. 1705) was a Swiss man who travelled through England in the late 1720s writing home to his family descriptions of where he went, who he met and what he saw on his travels. His letters, though not published until the early twentieth century, were much admired during his lifetime when they were read in manuscript by the likes of Voltaire. The advantage of his account for modern readers is the (typically Swiss) detail into which he goes, the result of trying to bring to life for his family hundreds of miles away the customs, laws and rituals of early eighteenth-century England.

Some time after my arrival in London I witnessed a spectacle which certainly was not as magnificent or as brilliant as the Lord Mayor's show; it is true it was quite a different kind of entertainment. I saw thirteen criminals all hanged at the same time. It will interest you, no doubt, to know something about justice in England, how it is practised, how criminals are punished, in what manner they are executed, as here it is done in quite a different way to what it is in other countries.

In London there are a great number of minor magistrates. When a crime or a robbery has been committed, the relations of the murdered person or of those who have been robbed, or in their stead the attorney for the Crown, declare the fact to the magistrate and accuse the persons whom they suspect. They must give bail or appear in court whenever the case comes on. The magistrate then gives out a warrant or order to take the accused person prisoner. The constable or officers of police do this latter work. As soon as the guilty man is discovered they exhibit their warrant and their staff or mark of office, on which are painted the arms of the King. If the accused threatens them and refuses to allow himself to be made prisoner, all those persons who by chance are present are obliged, if the constables desire it, to come to their aid. When the criminal is secured he is conveyed to Newgate, one of the big gates of London, near which the prison is situated. Sometimes a rather peculiar plan is adopted in order to discover and arrest those who have committed a crime, if it is thought that they have several accomplices. An announcement is published in the gazettes and other public papers that those among the suspected who will deliver themselves up to justice, constitute themselves prisoners, denounce their accomplices and give evidence against them, will be pardoned. Sometimes they are even rewarded by receiving sums varying from twenty to a hundred guineas, according to the seriousness of the case. By this means many criminals who would otherwise escape the gibbets are caught.

The criminals remain in prison till the day of the assizes, which come on every six weeks in London, and every three months in the provinces. In the former place they are held at Old Bailey, close to the prison of Newgate. This tribunal is composed of one of the twelve chief justices of the kingdom, of the sheriff of the province, the attorney for the Crown, the King's recorder, a secretary, and twelve jurymen, who must be of the same social order as the accused. Should a peer of the realm be judged, the jury would consist of twelve peers; if a gentleman, he must be judged by twelve gentlemen; and if a man of the lower classes, the jury must be plebeian likewise, but educated – that is to say, able to read and write, and each having the reputation of being an honest man. Six-and-thirty persons are chosen as jurymen. The accused is allowed to refuse twelve of the number without giving any reason, and twelve others, but giving his reasons, and the twelve remaining men will constitute the jury. You must not think, however, that the jury is changed for every criminal, for as these habitually come from the scum of the people, honest artisans are usually chosen for the whole assizes, which lasts from three to four days, according to the number of prisoners to be judged. In this country torture is not resorted to to make a man confess a crime; it is thought that many an innocent person might be sacrificed were this barbarous custom adopted. Englishmen say that it is better that twelve culprits should escape human justice rather than that one innocent man should perish. Still there is a sort of question called the 'Press', which is made use of when an accused person refuses to plead or contest the authority of the tribunal over him. In these cases he is stretched on the ground, his feet and hands are tied to stakes, and on his stomach is placed a plank with weights, more weights being added every four hours. The accused remains without food in this position until he consents to plead his cause and to recognise the validity of the tribunal. Cases have been known of criminals preferring to die in this fashion, after two or three days of atrocious suffering, rather than by the hands of the executioner, and this in order not to leave a mark of infamy on their families, and to save their possessions from going to the Crown according to the law. It is, however, very rarely that the King makes use of this privilege, and almost always gives up these possessions in favour of the families of the criminals.

Let us now consider the judgment. When the tribunal is formed and the prisoner stands at the bar, the twelve jurymen take the oath on the Gospel that they will, according to their consciences, endeavour to judge rightly. The magistrate's report is then read, giving the reasons why the accused has been arrested and at whose instigation. After hearing this report the Lord Chief Justice asks the prisoner whether he is guilty of the crime of which he is accused, to which he must answer 'No', otherwise, were he to own himself guilty, his case would be ended, and he would be judged according to the law. But this rarely occurs, for every criminal prefers trying to escape by pleading 'Not Guilty'. The person who has been the cause of his arrest appears and takes the oath, swearing he will speak nothing but the truth. He proceeds to give a detailed account of the circumstances which have led to the prisoner's arrest. Should there be any more witnesses, they also take the oath before speaking, and should any person be able to declare on his oath that the accused is a person of bad antecedents, and suspected of such and such a bad action, he will be listened to with attention. When every person willing to speak against the prisoner has been heard, he is asked whether he has anything to say in self-defence, and he may speak as long as he likes. Should he have witnesses to put forward in his own favour, they take the oath and speak. I wish you to understand that a prisoner's good reputation is of great value. If several persons take the oath and say that he has always been an honest man, his case will be considered in quite a different light to what it would have been had he been suspected on other occasions of villainy. When everything has been heard and said for either side, the Lord Chief Justice addresses the jury and makes a summing-up of the whole case. He weighs in general more upon the good than upon the bad. The jury then retire into a room where they have no light and no food, and here they must remain until they are unanimous as to whether the accused is guilty or innocent. I am told that there have been cases of eleven out of the twelve jurymen being convinced of the guilt of the accused and condemning him, whilst the one wishing to save him has insisted on declaring him innocent, and after remaining an entire day and even two without food, forcing the others to come round to his opinion; but such a case is extremely rare.

The jury being unanimous, return to the court of justice and announce their decision. If they find the prisoner innocent he is immediately set free; but if they find him guilty the Lord Chief Justice, donning his red[1] cap, pronounces him guilty according to the law and without the benefit of the clergy. I must tell you the meaning of this latter phrase. It was formerly a privilege accorded to churchmen, but which to-day also belongs to laymen convicted of certain crimes, particularly for cases of involuntary murder. In virtue of this privilege a New Testament, printed in Latin with Gothic letters, is presented to the accused, out of which he must read two

[1] Probably a mistake for black.

verses. A person is chosen to listen, and if he pronounces these words 'Legit ut Clericus',[1] which is always said, even were the accused to read abominably, his only punishment will consist of being branded on the palms of the hands with a red-hot iron; but by paying thirteen and a half pence he has a right to have the iron dipped in cold water before being touched with it. I think that this institution must have been invented in former times to encourage the ignorant clergy to learn to read. The judge having pronounced the sentence, the criminal is conducted back to prison covered with chains, and shut up in a dungeon. When the assizes are over and all the prisoners have been judged, the King is presented with a list of the condemned to death, for in England no criminal can be executed without the consent and approbation of the King, who occasionally pardons one or two of the least guilty ones, or changes their condemnation to transportation to the English plantations of America, where malefactors are condemned to slavery for periods of five, ten, fifteen or twenty years, and sometimes for life. Should a transported prisoner escape and return to England before his time is up, he will, if caught, be hanged without mercy.

Criminals are not executed immediately after their trial, as they are abroad, but are given several days to prepare for death. During that time they may ask for anything that they require either for the soul or for the body. The chaplain of the prison[2] (for there is one) does not leave them, and offers every consolation in his power. The day before the execution those who desire it may receive the sacrament, provided the chaplain thinks that they have sincerely repented and are worthy of it. On the day of execution the condemned prisoners, wearing a sort of white linen shirt over their clothes and a cap on their heads, are tied two together and placed on carts with their backs to the horses' tails. These carts are guarded and surrounded by constables and other police officers on horseback, each armed with

[1] He reads, therefore he is a cleric. This practice was known as pleading 'the benefit of the clergy'.
[2] Known as the Ordinary.

16

a sort of pike. In this way part of the town is crossed, and Tyburn, which is a good half-mile from the last suburb, is reached, and here stands the gibbet. One often sees criminals going to their death perfectly unconcerned, others so impenitent that they fill themselves full of liquor and mock at those who are repentant. When all the prisoners arrive at their destination they are made to mount on a very wide cart made expressly for the purpose, a cord is passed round their necks and the end fastened to the gibbet, which is not very high. The chaplain who accompanies the condemned men is also on the cart; he makes them pray and sing a few verses of the Psalms. The relatives are permitted to mount the cart and take farewell. When the time is up – that is to say about a quarter of an hour – the chaplain and relations get off the cart, the executioner covers the eyes and faces of the prisoners with their caps, lashes the horses that draw the cart, which slips from under the condemned men's feet, and in this way they remain all hanging together. You often see friends and relations tugging at the hanging men's feet so that they should die quicker and not suffer. The bodies and clothes of the dead belong to the executioner; relatives must, if they wish for them, buy them from him, and unclaimed bodies are sold to surgeons to be dissected. You see most amusing scenes between the people who do not like the bodies to be cut up and the messengers the surgeons have sent for the bodies; blows are given and returned before they can be got away, and sometimes in the turmoil the bodies are quickly removed and buried. Again, the populace often come to blows as to who will carry the bought corpses to the parents who are waiting in coaches and cabs to receive them, for the carriers are well paid for their trouble. All these scenes are most diverting, the noise and confusion is unbelievable, and can be witnessed from a sort of amphitheatre erected for spectators near the gibbet. There is no other form of execution but hanging; it is thought that the taking of life is sufficient punishment for any crime without worse torture. After hanging murderers are, however, punished in a particular fashion. They are first hung on the common gibbet, their bodies are then covered with tallow and fat substances, over this is placed a tarred shirt fastened down with iron bands, and the bodies are hung with chains to the gibbet, which is erected on the spot, or as near as possible to the place, where the crime was committed, and there it hangs till it falls to dust. This is what is called in this country to 'hang in chains'. The lower classes do not consider it a great disgrace to be simply hanged, but have a great horror of the hanging in chains, and the shame of it is terrible for the relatives of the condemned. Peers of the realm are executed by beheading; their heads are placed on the block and severed with a hatchet. Women who have murdered their husbands are put to death in what I consider to be an unjust way: they are condemned to be burned alive. Men who murder their wives are only hanged, but the English say that any person guilty of treason, that is to say of murdering those to whom they owe faith and allegiance, must be punished in an exemplary and terrible fashion. Such would be the case of a woman murdering her husband, a slave or servant his master, a clerk his bishop and, in short, any person who is guilty of the death of his lord and superior.

Executions are frequent in London; they take place every six weeks, and five, ten or fifteen criminals are hanged on these occasions. Notwithstanding this, there are in this country a surprising quantity of robbers. They may be classed in three divisions – highwaymen, footpads and pickpockets, all very audacious and bold. Highwaymen are generally well mounted; one of them will stop a coach containing six or seven travellers. With one hand he will present a pistol, with the other his hat, asking the unfortunate passengers most politely for their purses or their lives. No one caring to run the risk of being killed or maimed, a share of every traveller's money is thrown into the hat, for were one to make the slightest attempt at self-defence the ruffian would turn bridle and fly, but not before attempting to revenge himself by killing you. If, on the contrary, he receives a reasonable contribution, he retires without doing you any injury. When there are several highwaymen together, they will search you thoroughly and leave nothing. Again, others take only a part of what they find; but all these robbers ill-treat only those who try to defend themselves. I have been told that some highwaymen are quite polite and generous, begging to be excused for being forced to rob, and leaving passengers the wherewithal to continue their journey. All highwaymen that are caught are hanged without mercy.

There is a queer law to encourage counties to get rid of thieves. If a person is robbed of a considerable sum in the daytime and on the high road, and if he declares the theft to the sheriff of the county before the sun sets, and can prove that the sum has been taken from him in such and such a place, the county in which he has been robbed is obliged to refund him the sum. This happened to a friend of mine, who was robbed of two hundred guineas. Being able to declare the theft, and to prove it before the sun went down, he had no difficulty in recovering the amount from the sheriff of the county of Hertfordshire.

Footpads are met with in towns, especially in and around London. Should they meet any well-dressed person at night in some unfrequented spot, they will collar him, put the muzzle of a pistol to his throat and threaten to kill him if he makes the slightest movement or calls for help. During that time another rascal will rob the victim of any valuables he may possess. These thieves, when caught, are also hanged. Pickpockets are legion. With extraordinary dexterity they will steal handkerchiefs, snuff-boxes, watches – in short, anything they can find in your pockets. Their profession is practised in the streets, in churches, at the play and especially in crowds. Quite lately a valuable snuff-box was stolen from me. I had placed it in the pocket of my carefully-buttoned waistcoat; my coat was buttoned likewise, and I was holding both my hands over the pockets of my coat. It is true the theft occurred in a very narrow, crowded street, or more properly called passage, leading into a park. These rascals are so impudent, they steal even under the gibbet. There never is any execution without handkerchiefs and other articles being stolen. When any of these pickpockets are caught in the act and are given over to the populace, they are dragged to the nearest fountain or well and dipped in the water till nearly drowned. When a pickpocket appears before a magistrate for the first time, he is sent to a house of correction called Bridewell; but if he is an old hand at the trade and has already been punished, he is sent to the prison of Newgate, where he remains till the assizes; he is then judged, and generally condemned to transportation to America, where he becomes a slave.

All horse stealers or thieves who break into a house at night through doors and windows are hanged without mercy. You will without doubt think all these details exceedingly lengthy, but I think they are very curious and will interest you, who are so accustomed to Swiss honesty. I am convinced that in the thirteen cantons and their allies fewer robbers are caught in a year than there are judged in a single London assizes. Before leaving the subject allow me to say a few more words concerning a famous robber captain, Jonathan Wild, who was one of the thirteen I saw executed. During the ten or twelve years of his successful career in London, this man had had almost all the thieves of the town under his control. He used to give them so much money for all stolen goods brought to him. Were you robbed, you had only to address yourself to him and you were sure of recovering your property, by paying half its value or perhaps a trifle over, for he consented to be satisfied with a small profit. By this arrangement thieves were certain of not being caught with the stolen goods on them, and were paid besides; those persons who had been robbed were delighted to recover for half their value the things they had lost, and everyone was satisfied. Perhaps you will be surprised at this business going on so long, but I must tell you there was then no law against receivers of stolen goods. Jonathan Wild was never personally guilty of robbery, and was quite friendly with justice, for he would occasionally give up to the hangman one or two of the least skilful of his underlings, or one of those he was displeased with, by giving evidence against them. However, things went too far, and an act of Parliament being passed against receivers of stolen goods, and Jonathan Wild continuing his profession notwithstanding this new law, was taken, condemned and hanged. Many persons consider that more harm was done than good by the execution of this famous thief, for there is now no one to go to who will help you to recover your stolen property; the government has certainly got rid of a robber, but he was only one, whereas by his help several were hanged every year.

HENRY FIELDING
From *An Enquiry into the Causes of the Late Increase of Robbers*
(1751)

Henry Fielding (1707–54) took a more moderate view than Mandeville, one more humane. As Magistrate at Bow Street (succeeded by his brother Sir John) from 1748 to 1754, Fielding founded the Bow Street Runners, a thief-taking force based on the system used so successfully by Jonathan Wild – but under his aegis, a force for order rather than crime and chaos. Fielding's work as JP was an integral part of the foundation of the modern British police force, just as his novels were of the foundation of modern British fiction. In this piece, he argued that Britain's new-found wealth, derived from trade, gave the poor a new proximity and access to luxuries, drink and gambling, which incited them to crime; this was the start of the modern attitude to crime which seeks to resolve the causes of crime rather than merely punishing the perpetrators. Poor laws, argued Fielding, were archaic and inadequate which aggravated their hardships and further stimulated crime. Further, it was easy to get rid of stolen property and to elude arrest; once arrested, difficult to convict a suspect; and once convicted, there was always hope of a pardon. Finally, ultimately, public executions did nothing to deter criminals: 'The day appointed by law for the thief's shame is the day of glory in his own opinion.'

But nothing hath wrought such an alteration in this order of people, as the introduction of trade. This hath indeed given a new face to the whole nation, hath in a great measure subverted the former state of affairs, and hath almost totally changed the manners, customs and habits of the people, more especially of the lower sort. The narrowness of their fortune is changed into wealth; the simplicity of their manners into craft; their frugality into luxury; their humility into pride, and their subjection into equality . . .

[The] politician finds many emoluments to compensate all the moral evils introduced by trade, by which the grandeur and power of the nation is carried to a pitch that it could never otherwise have reached; arts and sciences are improved, and human life is imbellished with every ornament, and furnished with every comfort which it is capable of tasting.

In all these assertions he is right: but surely he forgets himself a little, when he joins the philosopher in lamenting the introduction of luxury as a casual evil; for as riches are the *certain* consequence of trade, so is luxury the no less *certain* consequence of riches: nay, trade and luxury do indeed support each other; and this latter, in its turn, becomes as useful to trade, as trade had been before to the support of luxury.

To prevent this consequence therefore of a flourishing commerce is totally to change the nature of things, and to separate the effect from the cause. A matter as impossible in the political body as in the natural. Vices and diseases, with like physical necessity, arise from certain habits in both; and to restrain and palliate the evil consequences, is all that lies within the reach of art. How far it is the business of the politician to interfere in the case of luxury, we have attempted to shew in the following treatise.

Now, to conceive that so great a change as this in the people should produce no change in the constitution, is to discover, I think, as great ignorance as would appear in the physician who should assert, that the whole state of the blood may be entirely altered from poor to rich, from cool to inflamed, without producing any alteration in the constitution of the man.

To put this in the clearest light: there appear to me to be four sorts of political power; that of bodily strength, that of the mind, the power of the purse and the power of the sword. Under the second of these divisions may be ranged all the art of the legislator and politician, all the power of laws and government. These do constitute the civil power; and a state may then be said to be in good order, when all the other powers are subservient to this; when they own its superior excellence and energy, pay it a ready obedience, and all unite in support of its rule.

But so far are these powers from paying such voluntary submission, that they are all extremely apt to rebel, and to assert their own superiority; but none is more rebellious in its nature, or more difficult to be governed than that of the purse or money. Self-opinion, arrogance, insolence and impatience of rule, are its almost inseparable companions.

Now if these assertions are true, what an immense accession of this power hath accrued to the commonalty by the increase of trade? for tho' the other orders have acquired an addition by the same means, this is not in the same proportion, as every reader, who will revolve the proposition but a moment in his own mind, must be satisfied.

And what may we hence conclude? Is that civil power, which was adapted to the government of this order of people in that state in which they were at the conquest, capable of ruling them in their present situation? Hath this civil power kept equal pace with them in the increase of its force, or hath it not rather, by the remissness of the Magistrate, lost much of its antient energy? Where is now that power of the Sheriff, which could formerly awaken and arm a whole county in an instant? Where is that *Posse Comitatus*,[1] which attended at his beck? What is become of the constitutions of *Alfred*,[2] which the reader will find set forth at large in the following treatise? What of the antient conservators of the peace? Have the Justices, on whom this whole power devolves, an authority sufficient for the purpose? In some counties, perhaps, you may find an overgrown tyrant, who lords it over his neighbours and tenants with despotic sway, and who is as regardless of the law as he is ignorant of it, but as to the Magistrate of a less fortune, and more knowledge, every riotous independent butcher or baker, with two or three thousand pounds in his pocket, laughs at his power, and every pettyfogger makes him tremble.

It is a common and popular complaint, that the Justices of Peace

---

[1] 'Power of the people', legal term for the men of the community whom the sheriff called together to catch a criminal and bring him to justice.
[2] King Alfred (849–99), earliest English king to legislate extensively.

have already too much power. Indeed a very little is too much, if it be abused; but, in truth, this complaint proceeds from a mistake of business for power: The business of the Justice is indeed multiplied by a great number of statutes; but I know not of any (the Riot Act[1] perhaps excepted) which hath at all enlarged his power. And what the force of that act is, and how able the Magistrate is, by means of the civil power alone, to execute it in any popular commotion, I have myself experienced. But when a mob of chairmen[2] or servants, or a gang of thieves and sharpers, are almost too big for the civil authority to suppress, what must be the case in a seditious tumult, or general riot of the people?

From what hath been said, I may, I think, conclude, that the constitution of this country is alerted from its antient state.

2dly, That the power of the commonalty hath received an immense addition; and that the civil power having not increased, but decreased, in the same proportion, is not able to govern them.

What may and must be the consequence of this, as well as what remedy can be applied to it, I leave to the consideration of others: I have proceeded far enough already on the subject, to draw sufficient ill-will on myself, from unmeaning or ill-meaning people, who either do not foresee the mischievous tendency of a total relaxation of government, or who have some private wicked purpose to effect from publick confusion.

In plain truth, the principal design of this whole work, is to rouse the CIVIL power from its present lethargic state. A design which alike opposes those wild notions of liberty that are inconsistent with all government, and those pernicious schemes of government, which are destructive of true liberty. However contrary indeed these principles may seem to each other, they have both the same common interest; or rather, the former are the wretched tools of the latter: for anarchy is almost sure to end in some kind of tyranny.

. . .

[1] Law allowing Justices of the Peace to put down riots.
[2] sedan-chair porters, thought of as unruly.

SECTION V

Of the Punishment of RECEIVERS OF STOLEN GOODS

Now one great encouragement to theft of all kinds is the ease and safety with which stolen goods may be disposed of. It is a very old and vulgar, but a very true saying, 'that if there were no receivers, there would be no thieves'. Indeed could not the thief find a market for his goods, there would be an absolute end of several kinds of theft; such as shop-lifting, burglary, *etc.* the objects of which are generally goods and not money. Nay robberies on the highway would so seldom answer the purpose of the adventurer, that very few would think it worth their while to risque so much with such small expectations.

But at present, instead of meeting with any such discouragement, the thief disposes of his goods with almost as much safety as the honestest tradesman: for first, if he hath made a booty of any value, he is almost sure of seeing it advertised within a day or two, directing him *to bring the goods to a certain place where he is to receive a reward* (sometimes the full value of the booty) *and no questions asked.* This method of recovering stolen goods by the owner, a very learned Judge formerly declared to have been, in his opinion, a composition of felony. And surely if this be proved to be carried into execution, I think it must amount to a full conviction of that crime. But, indeed, such advertisements are in themselves so very scandalous, and of such pernicious consequence, that if men are not ashamed to own they prefer an old watch or a diamond ring to the good of the society, it is pity some effectual law was not contrived to prevent their giving this public countenance to robbery for the future.

But if the person robbed should prove either too honest, or too obstinate, to take this method of recovering his goods, the thief is under no difficulty in turning them into money. Among the great number of brokers and pawnbrokers several are to be found, who are always ready to receive a gold watch at an easy rate, and where no questions are asked, or, at least, where no answer is expected but such as the thief can very readily make.

Besides, the clandestine dealers this way who satisfy their

consciences with telling a ragged fellow, or wench, that *they hope* they came honestly by silver, and gold, and diamonds; there are others who scorn such pitiful subterfuges, who engage openly with the thieves, and who have warehouses filled with stolen goods only. Among the *Jews* who live in a certain place in the city, there have been, and still are, some notable dealers this way, who in an almost public manner have carried on a trade for many years with *Rotterdam*,[1] where they have their warehouses and factors,[2] and whither they export their goods with prodigious profit, and as prodigious impunity. And all this appeared very plainly last winter in the examination of one *Cadosa* a *Jew*,[3] in the presence of the late excellent Duke of *Richmond*, and many other noblemen and Magistrates.

What then shall we say? Is not this mischief worthy of some remedy, or is it not capable of it? The noble Duke (one of the worthiest of Magistrates as well as of the best of men) thought otherwise, as would have appeared, had his valuable life, for the good of mankind, been prolonged.

Certain it is, that the law as it now stands is ineffectual to cure the evil. Let us see therefore, if possible, where the defect lies.

At the common law, any one might lawfully (says Lord *Hale*) have received his own goods from the felon who stole them. But if he had received them upon agreement not to prosecute, or to prosecute faintly, this would have been theftbote punishable by imprisonment and ransom.

But in neither of the foregoing cases would the receiver of the goods have become an accessary to the felon. So if one man had bought another's goods of the thief, though he had known them to be stolen, if he had given the just value for them, he would not have become an accessary. But if he had bought them at an undervalue, this, Sir *Richard Hyde* held, would have made him an accessary. My Lord *Hale* differs from his opinion, and his reason to some readers

---

[1] Known smugglers' port.   [2] agent or manager.
[3] A Jewish fence convicted in a famous trial in 1749 for smuggling stolen goods to Holland and reselling them.

may seem a pleasant one; *for if there be any odds* (says he) *he that gives more, benefits the felon more than he that gives less than value.* However this, his lordship thinks, may be a misdemeanor punishable by fine and imprisonment; but that the bare receiving of goods knowing them to be stolen makes not an accessary.

So says the great Lord *Hale*, and so indeed was the Law; though the Judges seem not to have been unanimous in their opinion. In the book of *Assizes*, *Scrope* is said to have held otherwise; and though *Shard* there quashed an appeal of felony for receiving stolen goods only, yet I cannot help observing, that the reporter of the case hath left a note of astonishment at the judgment of the court. This, says he, was wonderful! and wonderful surely it is, if he who receives, relieves, comforts or assists a felon, shall be an accessary, that he shall not be so, who knowingly buys the goods of the felon; which is generally, I believe, the strongest relief, comfort and assistance which can be given him, and without the hope and expectation of which, he would never have committed the theft or robbery.

It is unnecessary, however, to enter further into this controversy; since it is now expressly declared by statute, 'That the receivers of stolen goods, knowing them to be stolen, shall be deemed accessaries after the fact.'

But this statute, though it removed the former absurdity of the law, was not sufficient to remedy the evil; there yet remaining many difficulties in bringing these pernicious miscreants to justice, consistent with legal rules. For,

1. As the offence of the accessary is dependant on that of the principal, he could not be tried or out-lawed, till after the conviction or attainder of the principal; so that however strong evidence there might be against the receiver, he was still safe, unless the thief could be apprehended.

2. If the thief on his trial should be acquitted, as often happens through some defect of evidence in the most notorious cases, the receiver, being only an accessary, tho' he hath confessed his crime, or tho' the most undeniable evidence could be brought against him, must be acquitted likewise.

3. In petit larceny there can be no such accessary: for tho' the statute says, that a receiver of stolen goods, knowing, *etc.* shall be an accessary after the fact, that is, legally understood to mean only in cases where such accessary may be by law; and that is confined to such felonies as are to receive judgment of death, or to have the benefit of clergy. Now, for petit larceny, which is the stealing goods of less value than a shilling, the punishment at common law is whipping; and this was properly enough considered as too trifling an offence to extend the guilt to criminals in a second degree. But since juries have taken upon them to consider the value of goods as immaterial, and to find upon their oaths, that what is proved to be worth several shillings, and sometimes several pounds, is of the value of tenpence, this is become a matter of more consequence. For instance: if a pickpocket steal several handkerchiefs, or other things, to the value of twenty shillings, and the receiver of these, knowing them to be stolen, is discovered, and both are indicted, the one as principal, the other as accessary, as they must be; if the jury convict the principal, and find the goods to be of as high value as a shilling, he must receive judgment of death; whereas, by finding the goods (which they do upon their oaths) to be of the value of tenpence, the thief is ordinarily sentenced to be whipt, and returns immediately to his trade of picking pockets, and the accessary is of course discharged, and of course returns to his trade of receiving the booty. Thus the jury are perjured, the public highly injured, and two excellent Acts of Parliament defeated, that two miscreants may laugh at their prosecutors, and at the law.

The two former of these defects are indeed remedied by a later statute, which enacts, 'That the buyers and receivers of stolen goods, knowing them to be stolen, may be prosecuted for a misdemeanour, and punished by fine and imprisonment, though the principal felon be not before convicted of felony.'

This last statute is again repeated in the 5th of Queen *Anne*; and there the power of the court to punish in the case of the misdemeanour, is farther encreased to any other corporal punishment, which the court shall think fit to inflict, instead of fine and imprisonment; and, in the case of the felony, the accessary is to receive judgment of death; but the benefit of clergy is not taken away. Lastly, By the statute of *George* II the receivers of stolen goods, knowing, *etc.* are to be transported for 14 years. And by the same statute, every person taking money or reward, directly or indirectly, under pretence or upon account of helping any to stolen goods, unless such person apprehend and bring to his trial the felon, and give evidence against him, is made guilty of felony without benefit of clergy.

And thus stands the law at this day; which, notwithstanding the repeated endeavours of the legislature, experience shews us, is incapable of removing this deplorable evil from the society.

The principal defect seems, to me, to lie in the extreme difficulty of convicting the offender; for,

1. Where the thief can be taken, you are not at liberty to prosecute for the misdemeanour.

2. The thief himself, who must be convicted before the accessary is to be tried, cannot be a witness.

3. Without such evidence it is very difficult to convict of the knowledge, that the goods were stolen; which, in this case, can appear from circumstances only. Such are principally, 1. Buying goods of value, of persons very unlikely to be the lawful proprietors. *2dly,* Buying them for much less than their real value. *3dly,* Buying them, or selling them again, in a clandestine manner, concealing them, *etc.* None of these are commonly liable to be proved; and I have known a man acquitted, where most of these circumstances have appeared against him.

What then is to be done, to extirpate this stubborn mischief? to prove the pernicious consequence of which, I need, I think, only appeal to the sense of Parliament, testified in so many repeated Acts, and very strongly expressed in their preambles.

First, Might it not be proper to put an effectual stop to the present scandalous method of compounding felony, by public advertisements in the news papers? Might not the inserting such advertisements be rendered highly criminal in the authors of them, and in the printers themselves, unless they discover such authors?

2dly, Is it impossible to find any means of regulating brokers and pawnbrokers? If so, What arguments are there against extirpating entirely a set of miscreants, which, like other vermin, harbour only about the poor, and grow fat by sucking their blood?

3*dly*, Why should not the receiving stolen goods, knowing them to be stolen, be made an original offence? by which means the thief, who is often a paultry offender in comparison of the receiver, and sometimes his pupil, might, in little felonies, be made a witness against him: for thus the trial of the receiver would in no case depend on the trial or conviction of the thief.

4*thly*, Why may not the bare buying or taking to pawn stolen goods, above a certain value, be made evidence of receiving with knowledge, *etc.* unless the goods were bought in market overt, (no broker's or pawnbroker's shop to be reputed such market overt) or unless the defendant could prove, by a credible witness to the transaction, that he had good cause to regard the seller or pawner of the goods to be the real owner. If 20 *s.* was the value limited, it would answer all the purposes contended for; and would in nowise interfere with the honest trade (if indeed it ever be so) between the pawnbroker and the poor.

If none of these methods be thought possible or proper, I hope better will be found out. Something ought to be done, to put an end to the present practice, of which I see daily the most pernicious consequences; many of the younger thieves appearing plainly to be taught, encouraged and employed by the receivers.

|| Prefaces to *Malefactor's Register* (1779) and Knapp
|| and Baldwin's *Newgate Calendar* (1826)

These prefaces show the new self-consciousness of the attitude to crime. At the start of the eighteenth century, crime was considered an unpleasant fact of life, and criminals were a nuisance to be eradicated, rather than people who needed help. A hundred years later, the idea of correctional punishment was coming into vogue, and the Newgate Calendars, *as well as works of fiction (by Dickens, Ainsworth and*

Thackeray), highlighted the plight of the poor and criminal classes, and helped draw public attention to the need for changes in the ways in which criminals were treated. (Both entries are given in full.)

In an age abandoned to dissipation, and when the ties of religion and morality fail to have their accustomed influence on the mind, the publication of a work of this nature makes its appearance with peculiar propriety.

It has not been unusual, of late years, to complain of the sanguinary complection of our laws; and if there were any reason to expect that the practice of felony would be lessened by the institution of any laws less sanguinary than those now in force, it would be a good argument for the enacting of such laws.

Wise and virtuous legislators can wish nothing more ardently than the general welfare of the community; and those who have from time to time given birth to the laws of England, have indisputably done it with a view to this general welfare. But as the wisest productions of the human mind are liable to error, and as there is visibly an encreasing depravity in the manners of the age, it is no wonder that our laws are found, in some instances, inadequate to the purposes for which they were enacted: and, perhaps, if, in a few instances they were made more, and in others less severe than they are at present, the happiest consequences might result to the public.

It is with the utmost deference to the wisdom of their superiors, that the editors of this work offer the following hints for the improvement of the police of this country, and the security of the lives and properties of the subject: and,

1st. If his majesty would be graciously pleased to let the law operate in its *full force* against every convicted housebreaker, it would probably greatly lessen the number of those atrocious offenders; and consequently add to the repose of every family of property in the kingdom. What can be conceived more dreadful than a band of ruffians drawing the curtains of the bed at midnight, and presenting the drawn dagger, and the loaded pistol? The imagination will paint the terrors of such a situation, in a light more striking than language can display them.

2dly. If the same royal prerogative was exerted for the punishment of women convicts, it would indisputably produce very happy effects. It is to the low and abandoned women that hundreds of young fellows owe their destruction. They rob, they plunder, to support these wretches. Let it not seem cruel that we make one remark, of which we are convinced experience would justify the propriety. The execution of *ten* women would do more public service than that of a *hundred* men; for, exclusive of the force of example, it would perhaps tend to the preservation of more than a hundred.

3dly. Notorious defrauds, by gambling or otherwise, should be rendered capital felonies by a statute; for, as the law now stands, after a temporary punishment, the common cheat is turned loose to make fresh depredations on the public.

4thly. Forgery, enormous as the crime is, in a commercial state, might perhaps be more effectually punished and prevented than at present, by dooming the convict to *labour for life* on board the ballast-lighters.[1] Forgerers are seldom among the low and abandoned part of mankind. Forgery is very often the last dreadful refuge to which the distressed tradesman flies. These people then are sensible of shame, and perpetual infamy would be abundantly more terrible to such men than the mere dread of death.

5thly. Highwaymen, we conceive, might with propriety be punished by labouring on the highway, chained by the legs, agreeable to a design we have given in a plate in this work. Many a young fellow is hardened enough to think of taking a purse on the highway, to supply his extravagancies, who would be terrified from the practice, if he knew he could not ride half a dozen miles out of London, without seeing a number of highwaymen working together, under the ignominious circumstances above-mentioned.

With regard to murderers, and persons convicted of unnatural crimes, we cannot think of altering the present mode of punishment. 'Him that sheddeth man's blood, by man shall his blood be shed':[2]

---

[1] flat-bottomed boats used to take ballast out to ships.
[2] Genesis 9.6.

as to the other wretches, it is only to be lamented that their deaths cannot be aggravated by every species of torment!

Having said thus much, we submit our labours to the candid revision of the public, nothing doubting that, on a careful perusal, they will be found to answer the purpose of guarding the minds of youth against the approaches of vice; and, in consequence, of advancing the happiness of the community.

The penal laws of the British empire are, by foreign writers, charged with being too sanguinary in the cases of lesser offences. They hold that the punishment of death ought to be inflicted only for crimes of the highest magnitude; and philanthropists of our own nation have accorded with their opinion. Such persons as have had no opportunity of inquiring into the subject will hardly credit the assertion that there are above one hundred and sixty offences punished by death, or, as it is denominated, without benefit of clergy. The multiplicity of punishments, it is argued, in many instances defeat their own ends; for the object is alone the prevention of crimes.

The Roman empire never flourished so much as during the era of the Portian law, which abrogated the punishment of death; and it fell soon after the revival of the utmost severity of its penal laws. But Rome was not a nation of commerce, or it never could, under such an abrogation, have so long remained the mistress of Europe. In the present state of society it has become indispensably necessary that offences which, in their nature, are highly injurious to the community, and where no precept will avail, should be punished with the forfeiture of life: but those dreadful examples should be exhibited as seldom as possible; for while, on the one hand, such punishment often proves inadequate to its intended effect, by not being carried into execution; so, on the other, by being often repeated, the minds of the multitude are rendered callous to the dreadful example.

The punishment awaiting the crime of murder, from the earliest ages of civilized nations, has been the same as that inflicted by the

33

laws of the British empire, varying alone in the mode of putting the sentence into execution. We find the murderer punished by death in the ancient laws of the Jews, the Romans and the Athenians; in nations of heathens and idolaters. The Persians, worshipping the sun as their deity, press murderers to death between two stones. Throughout the Chinese empire, and the vast dominions of the East, they are beheaded; a death in England esteemed the least dishonourable, but there considered the most ignominious. Mahometans impale them alive, where they long writhe in agony before death comes to their relief. In Roman Catholic countries the murderer expiated his crime upon the rack.

Several writers on crimes and punishments deny the right of man to take away life, given to us by God alone; but a crime of the dreadful nature of that now before us, however sanguinary they may find our laws in regard to lesser offences, unquestionably calls loudly for death. 'Whosoever sheddeth man's blood, by man shall his blood be shed,' saith Holy Writ; but with the life of the murderer should the crime be fully expiated? The English law on this head goes still further: the effects of the murderer revert to the State – thus, as it were, carrying punishment beyond the grave, and involving in its consequences the utter ruin of many a virtuous widow and innocent children, who had looked up alone to it for support. Yet we may be thankful for laws, the dread of which affords us such ample security for our lives and property, and which we find administered with rigorous impartiality, awarding the same punishment for the same offence, whether the culprit be rich or poor, humble in life or exalted in rank. In proof of this we need only refer our readers to the cases of Laurence Earl Ferrers, Doctor Dodd, the Perreaus, Ryland[1] and many others, whose lives are recorded in these pages.

It is the opinion of an able commentator on our criminal laws that punishment should succeed the crime as immediately as possible, if we intend that, in the rude minds of the multitude, the picture of

[1] Daniel and Robert Perreau, brothers who were forgers, executed in 1776, and William Ryland, executed for forgery in 1782.

the crime shall instantly awaken the attendant idea of punishment: delaying which, serves only to separate these two ideas; and thus affects the minds of the spectators rather as a terrible sight than the necessary consequences of a crime. The horror should contribute to heighten the idea of the punishment.

Next to the necessary example of punishment to offenders is to record examples, in order that such as are unhappily moved with the sordid passion of acquiring wealth by violence, or stimulated by the heinous sin of revenge to shed the blood of a fellow-creature, may have before them a picture of the torment of mind and bodily sufferings of such offenders. In this light THE NEWGATE CALENDAR must prove highly acceptable to all ranks and conditions of men; for we shall find, in the course of these volumes, that crime has always been followed by punishment; and that, in many instances, the most artful secrecy could not screen the offenders from detection, nor the utmost ingenuity shield them from the strong arm of impartial justice.

2

Murderers

DR THEODORE FABRICIUS *Tried for the murder of Grace Shaw in 1721; convicted of manslaughter and his hand burned* From the 1764 *Select Trials*

This case recalls that of the Cock Lane Ghost in 1762 (see William Bristow, The Mystery Revealed; Bristow, 1742), where local politics and infighting influenced the course of a trial. The principal witnesses against Fabricius hoped to see him convicted because he had blocked up a passage which had formerly been a public right of way; their testimonies were clearly influenced by personal resentment. The complication, to modern eyes, is the harsh treatment accorded servants as a matter of course: the severe beatings Shaw received at Fabricius's hands may not have caused her death directly but they would today be considered a grave crime in their own right; in the eighteenth century they were thought as part of a servant's unhappy lot. (The complete entry is given here.)

THEODORE CHRISTOPHER FABRICIUS, *FOR* MURDER, *JULY* 1721

Theodore Christopher Fabricius, of St *Leonard*, *Shoreditch*, Gent. was indicted for the murder of *Grace Shaw*, by striking, wounding and bruising her, with a wooden staff, on the head, face, neck, back and belly, on the 18th of *June* 1721, of which striking, wounding and bruising, she languish'd till the 26th of the same month, and then dy'd. He was a second time indicted on the coroner's inquest for the said murder.

Elizabeth Wilson. I liv'd next door to the prisoner, who is a mad doctor, and the deceased liv'd with him as a servant; but I can't tell whether she was under cure, or not; but thus much I know, that I have often heard her shriek out, and have seen the Doctor beat her several times a day, and even upon *Sundays* too; sometimes with his fist, and sometimes with a whip; and above all I remember, that, upon the 18th of *June* last, he us'd her very barbarously, for which I took him to task; but he up and told me, *That it was no business of mine, and he'd make me hold my tongue, that he would.*

Sarah Morris. I saw the prisoner beat the deceased severely in the garden—I think it was with a whip, and then he took and shov'd her in a doors [i.e. indoors], and I heard him give her some strokes in the house—This was on the 24th of *June.*

Benjamin Green. About seven or eight weeks ago I went into the prisoner's house, with a couch-bed, and was lock'd in a room with the deceas'd. She was black about the eyes, and told me, that her master did it, and that he would be the death of her before he had done.

Katherine Green. I did not *see* the prisoner strike the deceas'd, but (as I verily believe) *I heard* him almost every day, for two months together, and particularly on the *Sunday* before her death, I heard a great noise of beating and crying, and then I saw the deceas'd run out from the Doctor.

Mary Cowell. My house looks into the Doctor's garden, and as *Grace Shaw* was weeding in it, about three weeks before her death, I saw the Doctor go to her, pull off her headcloaths and strike her with his hand, seven or eight times upon her head.

Elizabeth Ward. On the 20th of *May,* I saw the deceas'd wheeling a barrow in the garden, and the prisoner go to her, and give her about a dozen blows with a broomstick, beat her hat and headcloaths off, and almost choak'd her with the strings of her hat.

John Deval. Between eleven and twelve o'clock, on a *Sunday* morning (about five weeks before the death of the deceas'd) I heard a dismal cry in the Doctor's house, and by and by the deceas'd came running out o'doors, all over bloody, and crying, *For the Lord's sake beat me no more, for I cannot bear it.*

Francis Frampton. The *Thursday* before the deceas'd dy'd, she cry'd out murder, and ran out of the kitchen, into another room, all bloody, with her cap in her hand.

Susannah Smithiman. I saw the prisoner beat the deceas'd three times; once he struck her down with his hand in the garden, another time when she let him in, he beat her from the gate into the house, and the last time that I remember was on the *Sunday* seven-night before her death.

Mr *Troughton*. I often visited the Doctor, and once I saw him beat the deceas'd with a stick or a whip, I cannot be certain which, but if it was a stick, it was a small one, and he did not misuse it at that time. Another time he beat her about the head, because she had killed a hen with feeding it. I have often saw him beat her about the face, and every where else with his hand. She had an imposthume[1] in her ear, and being in the kitchen one *Sunday*, between eleven and twelve o'clock, the Doctor broke it with a blow of his hand, so that the blood and matter ran out. He was not then in a passion, but what he did was, as I thought, only with a design to open the imposthume; she cry'd out indeed, but did not run away. He was very angry with her the *Sunday* evening before her death. She would not work except she was forc'd to it. She was not in her right senses, and I have seen him use her both roughly and gently.

Margaret Pike. I went to lay the deceas'd out, and found that she had black places on her head, face, arms, neck, shoulders, back and legs, she had a sad[2] ear, and her cap was bloody; I said that she had been us'd barbarously, but they told me, that those bruises were occasioned by a fall.

William Hobbs. I was the prisoner's gardiner. I have often seen him strike the deceas'd over the shoulders, and the small of the back, with his walking cane, and sometimes in the face with his fist, when I could see no manner of occasion for it. Once he beat her with the thick end of a stick, and, she crying out, he said, *Damn ye, do ye cry out?* and thrust the other end of the stick into her mouth, so that the blood ran out. Another time, as she was weeding in the garden, he came up to her and said, *Damn ye, can't ye kneel?* and then struck her down with his fist and stamp'd upon her.

Elizabeth Knighting. The prisoner frequently used to beat the deceased. I knew her voice, and have often heard her shriek. And when I have look'd out to see what was the matter, the prisoner has put up his window-shutters. He made her one day set up a very heavy ladder, and he went up it, in order to feed his pidgeons, and

[1] cyst.   [2] dark, swollen.

called her to bring him a bowl of water; she accordingly went five or six steps up the ladder, gave the bowl into his hand, and he at the same time kick'd her down again. I cannot indeed say that I saw his foot touch her, but I saw it push'd out when she fell from the ladder, and besides, he beat her intolerably on the same day.

Mr Fremoult. I went to view the deceas'd, and found her head, her temporal muscles and her ear contus'd. She had a bruise too betwixt her shoulders, a small wound on her lip, and had lost a tooth. 'Tis my opinion that those wounds and bruises were the occasion of her death.

Prisoner. Did you see any single wound or bruise about her that was mortal?

F. I cannot say that.

Prisoner. Had not she an imposthume in her ear?

F. Yes.

P. And might not that alone have prov'd the cause of her death?

F. I can't say but it might.—'Tis true, that her temporal muscles were much contused, but then I found no fracture.

Prisoner. Of what shape are the temporal muscles? – To this the witness made no answer.

Robert Baker. I saw the body in the coffin, but view'd the head only. One of the fore teeth of the upper jaw was wanting, there was a wound on the inner part of the lip, and another small one on the scalp. I believe the cartilage of the nose was broke; but there was no wound that was mortal.

Mr Wallis. The deceas'd dy'd on a *Monday*, and I saw the body on the *Thursday* following. I found two contusions under her ear, her nose was broke and her temporal muscles were bruised, but I cannot say, that she had any wound that was mortal.

Mr Fletcher. I found several contusions in her face, the cartilage of her nose was broke, a tooth was out and her ear and temporal muscles bruis'd, but I cannot say that any of these were the cause of her death.

The Prisoner's defence.

He said that the deceas'd was brought to him as a lunatick, and he was to have her service for her cure; that she had liv'd with him some time; that she was bruis'd by falling down stairs upon her face; that if he did but hold up a stick, she would cry out murder, and that she was subject to fits, in which she used to fall down and beat herself very much.—Then he call'd his witnesses.

Jane Grover. The mother of the deceas'd desir'd me to speak to the Doctor to take her daughter in, and let her have her cure for what service he found her capable of doing. She had often assaulted her mother in bed, and beat her so, that her life was in danger from her. One morning she ran away from the Doctor's to her brother's, from whence her mother brought her to me, that I might go with her once more to her master's, but while we were talking, the Doctor himself came in, to enquire after her, and she went to him again willingly. She had some black marks on her nose, and other parts of her face, and a swelling in her ear. I ask'd her how she came by them, and sometimes she said by a fall, and sometimes by a blast.[1] I acquainted her mother with it, and she went next day to the Doctor, and told him she was willing that her daughter should continue with him, but desir'd him to correct her moderately, and not strike her in the face. The deceas'd told me that she fell down a ladder, but made no complaint of her master. She was ill and had a purging upon her for four or five days before her death. On *Sunday* I went to see her at her master's house; she was sitting with her head leaning on a chair, and said that she was not well. I left her a-while, and coming in again, I found her a reading to her master. The next day I was sent for in haste, and when I came she was dead. The Doctor then told me, that she had had two convulsion fits, that he recover'd her from the first, but that she died in the other. He sent me to call her mother, and said that she should not be mov'd till her friends came.

Prisoner. Did you never hear her say, that she had another fall before that from the ladder?

[1] blow.

J.G. Yes, but she did not tell me how it happen'd.

Prisoner. I desire E. *Knighting* may be ask'd, if I did not stop up a passage in my house, that had been a thorough-fair?

Elizabeth Knighting, again. Yes, the house, the Doctor lives in, had been a public house before, and the neighbours had a passage thro' it; but now that passage is stopp'd up, and they are forc'd to go a great way about.

Prisoner. And therefore several of the neighbours have bore me ill ever since.

Alice Rogers. I saw the Deceas'd fall off the ladder, and when the Doctor took the bowl from her, he did not stir his foot; my eye was intent upon them, and, if he had kick'd her, I must have seen it.

Anne Grover. The deceas'd was put to the prisoner to be cur'd, for which he was to have nothing but her service. She was so stubborn and stomachful at home, that her mother told me she was forc'd to put her into the workhouse.

Mr *Seadon.* The deceas'd had several inconsiderable bruises on her face, head and neck; that on the ear was bad, but whether or no it was from an imposthume I cannot be certain. There was no fracture in her skull, nor any wound that affected her life.

Mr *Tanner.* I and the surgeons on the King's side were present at the same time. – There were some slight bruises on her face, two stripes across her shoulders, which might have been made by a whip, or rattan. Her temporal muscles were not contused, her lips not swelled nor black, there was no bruise on her nose, nor any thing that appear'd fatal or injurious.

Mr *Simmons.* I was present with Mr *Tanner,* and the other surgeons, and am of the same opinion with him.

Henry Grutchman. I used to visit the Doctor, and was at his house when the maid was dead, and both he and I receiv'd very ill usage from the neighbours.

Thomas Braithwait. I went to the Doctor's house and saw the steps of the ladder, they were not three foot perpendicular. I saw a whip which was a very slight one, and a small stick, which the neighbours told me, the Doctor us'd about his patients; they were extreamly enrag'd against him, said that he had shut up the passage; that he was a conjuring rogue, and dealt with the Devil. *Elizabeth Knighting* in particular rail'd at him excessively.

Joseph Reeves. I was formerly under the misfortune of lunacy, the Doctor cur'd me effectually, since which I have been conversant with him at his house, and I never saw any thing misbecoming, nor did I ever hear the deceas'd make any complaint of ill usage.

Charles Deering. I heard *John Deval* express himself very hotly and maliciously against the Doctor, and complain'd of the stopping up the passage, which made them go a great way about.

The prisoner call'd several others to his reputation, who gave him the character of a mild, well-temper'd man, and mention'd several cures that he had performed.

The jury found him guilty of manslaughter. *Burnt in the Hand.*

SARAH MALCOLM *Convicted of the murders of Lydia Duncombe, Elizabeth Harrison and Anne Price, and hanged in 1733* From *St James's Evening Post* (February and March 1733)

Called 'A Lady MacBeth in Low Life', the 22-year-old Sarah Malcolm strangled Duncombe, her eighty-year-old former employer; Harrison, Duncombe's companion; and slit the throat of Price, their seventeen-year-old maid. Her case made the headlines because she so cold-bloodedly insisted on her innocence up until she was hanged, testifying in court that the blood-stains on her shift (the main evidence against her) were menstrual, not the result of this crime — although the amount of blood on the dress belied her claim. William Hogarth visited her at Newgate as she awaited execution, and sketched her for a popular engraving: 'I see by this woman's face that she is capable of any wickedness.' She was hanged at Mitre Court, near the scene of her crime, and her body was dissected by the Royal College of Surgeons.

45

Yesterday came on at the Old Bailey, the trial of Sarah Malcolm, for the murder of Mrs Duncombe, Elizabeth Harrison and Anne Price, in the Temple, and also for breaking open the chambers of Mrs Duncombe, and stealing several things of great value. The first evidence was her master Mr Carroll, who gave an account of his finding plate and linen in a close-stool in his chambers, which she acknowledged to be her's, pretending they were taken out of pawn; upon which, and hearing of the murder, he caused her to be secured. Mrs Love, who was invited to dine with Mrs Duncombe on the Sunday, deposed, that the plate found was Mrs Duncombe's. Roger Johnson, an apothecary, and several other witnesses were examined, who corroborated the fact; and after a trial of about five hours, the jury brought her in guilty. She behav'd in a very extraordinary manner on her trial, oftentimes requesting the court for the witnesses to speak louder, and spoke upwards of half an hour in her own defence, but in a trifling manner. She confessed she was guilty of the robbery, but not of the murder, only standing on the stairs.

———

Sarah Malcolm is order'd to be executed to-morrow se'nnight in Fleet-street, facing Mitre-Court, which leads down to the King's Bench Walks; and the other eight are order'd to be executed on Monday next at Tyburn; and on Saturday night the dead warrant came down to Newgate accordingly. She is remov'd out of the Old Condemn'd Hold into a room in the Picts-Yard; and yesterday she declared herself a Roman Catholick, but desir'd however that she may take the sacrament to-morrow se'nnight, the day of her execution, from a minister of the Church of England, in confirmation of her assertion that she was no actress in that horrid tragedy, but that it was done by the two Alexanders and Mary Tracy; we hear that she has bespoke a shroud to be made for her, declaring that she intends to go to the place of execution in no other dress.

———

Yesterday Sarah Malcolm was executed on a gibbet erected over-against Mitre-Court in Fleet-Street. We don't hear that she made any confession of her being guilty of the murder of Mrs Duncombe and her maids; but just before she was turn'd off,[1] she deliver'd a paper, written with her own hand, to the Rev. Mr Piddington, minister of Little St Bartholomew's, which she said contained something that was necessary for her to acquaint the world with; and desir'd, that as the same had been seal'd up in Newgate, in the presence of several gentlemen, it might also be open'd before them and the Sheriffs. She receiv'd the sacrament in the morning, and declar'd at the place of execution that she died a Protestant. She was very desirous to see her master Mr Carrol, and looked about for him, whom she acquitted of all manner of aspersions or imputations laid on him at her tryal; but confess'd nothing concerning the murther. After she had talked some time with the ministers, as she was going to be turn'd off, she fainted away, and was some time before she was brought to her senses; but being afterwards recover'd, after a short stay she was executed. She was cut down after she had hung somewhat more than half an hour; and her body was carried back to Newgate under a strong guard of the mob. Several of the nobility, and other persons of distinction, saw the execution from the neighbouring houses; and there was as great a concourse of common people as ever was seen on the like occasion. Many of the spectators were hurt by the breaking down of a scaffold; and very few of the ladies and gentlemen but had their pockets either pick'd or cut off.

The same afternoon, about four o'clock, the Rev. Dr Middleton, the Rev. Mr Piddington and Mr Ingram, waited on the Lord Mayor, in order to break open the confession of the said Sarah Malcolm before his lordship, which shall be inserted as soon as made publick.

———

In the copy of the paper deliver'd by Sarah Malcolm[2] the night before her execution to the Reverend Mr Piddington, Lecturer of St Bartholomew the Great, declares, That on Sunday the 28th of January, after her master, Mr Carrol, was gone to commons, Mary

[1] was hanged.
[2] Spelled 'Malcom' throughout this piece; also 'Carrol' and 'Kerrol', 'Tracy' and 'Tracey', and 'Duncombe' and 'Duncomb'.

Tracy came to her and drank tea, and then it was she gave consent to that unhappy act of robbing Mrs Duncombe, but declares she did not know of the murder. On Saturday the 3d of February being the time appointed, they came about 10 o'clock at night, and Mary Tracy came to Mr Carrol's chambers, and they all four went to Mrs Duncombe's, and on the stairs Sarah Malcolm met Mrs Duncombe's maid, who ask'd her, whether she was going to the old maid, she answer'd Yes; and as soon as she thought the maid had got down stairs, would have gone in herself, but thought that would give some suspicion, and so ask'd which would go in, and James Alexander replied, he would, and the door being left open for the maid, against her return, she gave James Alexander directions to lie under the maid's bed, and desired Mary Tracy and Thomas Alexander to go and stay for her at her master's door until her return, which they did accordingly, and when she came, desired they would go and stay for her at Mrs Duncombe's stairs, who, on her return found them there, and there they waited till after two o'clock on the Sunday morning, which was the 4th of February, and then Sarah Malcolm would have gone in, but Thomas Alexander and Mary Tracy interrupted her, and said, if you go in, and they awake, they will know you, and if you stay on the stairs, it may be that some one will come up and see you; but she made answer, that no one lives up so high but Madam Duncombe.

At length it was concluded that Mary Tracy, and the other Alexander should go in, and shut the door, and accordingly they did, and Sarah Malcolm remained until between four and five o'clock, when they came out, and said Hip, and when she came higher up, they ask'd which way they should shut the door; and she told them to run the bolt back, and it would spring into its place, and accordingly they did, and when they came down, they asked where they should divide what they had got; she asked how much that was; they said, about three hundred pounds in goods and money, but said they were forced to gag them all.

She desired to know, where they had found it; they said, that fifty guineas of it was in the old maid's pocket, in a leathern purse, besides silver, that they said was loose; and above 150 l. [£] in a drawer, besides the money that they had out of a box, and the tankard, and one silver spoon, and a rug which was looped with thread, and one square piece of plate, one pair of sheets, and two pillow-beers[1] and five shifts, which they divided near Fig-Tree-Court, after which Mary Tracy and the Alexanders said to Sarah Malcolm, be sure that you bury the cole and plate under ground, until the robbery is over; for if you be seen flush of cole, you will be suspected.

WILLIAM DUELL *Convicted of the murder of Sarah Griffin in 1740; hanged and then transported*
From Knapp and Baldwin's *Newgate Calendar*

This case is interesting not because of the crime, but because Duell survived the punishment, coming back to life as the students at Surgeons' Hall prepared to dissect his body. The use of cadavers was recognized as being essential to the training of doctors at this period, and the bodies of malefactors were frequently given to the surgeons for this purpose. This practice, known as 'anatomization', both horrified the superstitious populus, who believed the dead bodies of criminals should not be thus desecrated, and created a demand for cadavers that could not be satisfied by the supply of criminals alone and was increasingly filled by grave-robbers (see Holmes and Wilson in 'A Miscellany'). (The complete entry is printed here.)

WILLIAM DUELL,

EXECUTED FOR MURDER, WHO CAME TO LIFE AGAIN WHILE PREPARING FOR DISSECTION IN SURGEONS' HALL

This man met a better fate than a criminal in a similar situation in Germany. The body of a notorious malefactor was stretched out upon the table, before an assembly of German surgeons, for dissection. The

[1] pillow cases.

operator, in placing it in a proper position, felt life in it; whereupon he thus addressed his brethren of the faculty, met to witness the operation:

'I am pretty certain, gentlemen, from the warmth of the subject, and the flexibility of the limbs, that by a proper degree of attention and care the vital heat would return, and life in consequence take place. But when it is considered what a rascal we should again have among us, that he was hanged for so cruel a murder, and that, should we restore him to life, he would probably kill somebody else: – I say, gentlemen, all these things considered, it is my opinion that we had better proceed in the dissection.' Whether this harangue, or the fear of being disappointed in so sumptuous a surgical banquet, operated on their consciences, we cannot tell; but, certain it is, they nodded accordance; and the operator, on the signal, plunged his knife into the breast of the culprit, thereby at once precluding all dread of future assassinations – all hopes of future repentance.

Duell was convicted of occasioning the death of Sarah Griffin, at Acton, by robbing and ill-treating her. Having suffered November 24 1740, at Tyburn, his body was brought to Surgeons' Hall to be anatomised; but, after it was stripped and laid on the board, and while one of the servants was washing him, in order to be cut, he perceived life in him, and found his breath to come quicker and quicker, on which a surgeon took some ounces of blood from him; in two hours he was able to sit up in his chair, and in the evening was committed to Newgate; and his sentence (which might have been again inflicted) was changed to transportation.

EARL FERRERS *Convicted of murder, and hanged in 1760*
From Jackson's *Newgate Calendar* (1795)

Lord Ferrers (b. 1720) was a violent man, especially when drunk, whose wife had procured a legal separation and generous maintenance from him on the grounds of his 'unwarrantable cruelty' – a very unusual move in the eighteenth century. Ferrers once kicked a servant so hard in the groin that he was unable to retain urine for many years thereafter, because the servant would not swear that a delivery-boy had not delivered bad oysters to Ferrers on purpose.

In 1760, Ferrers became convinced that his steward, Johnson, had contrived with Ferrers's trustees to deprive him of a lucrative coal-mining contract (which was not true) and summoned him to his house, Staunton, near Ashby-de-la-Zouch. Ferrers sent away from the house his mistress, their children and the servants; and when Johnson arrived, made him kneel down, and then shot him. Ferrers sent for the doctor, and said to him, 'I intended to have shot him dead, but since he is still alive, you must do what you can for him.' Despite the ministrations of the doctor, Johnson died the following morning; Ferrers was arrested by a small band of locals headed by the doctor, and taken to Ashby where he was convicted of murder. His sentence was confirmed by the House of Lords, and he was condemned to death. Ferrers's own cross-examination of the witnesses showed, said the Newgate Calendar, *the sanity of his mind 'of which some doubt had been entertained'. He petitioned the King to allow him to be beheaded in the Tower, a privilege until this time accorded to noble convicts, but the King refused, and Ferrers became the first peer to be hanged at Tyburn as a common criminal.*

About nine o'clock, the sheriffs attended at the Tower-gate; and Lord Ferrers being told that they were come, requested that he might go in his own landau, instead of a mourning-coach, which had been prepared for him. No objection being made to this request, he entered the landau, attended by the Rev. J. Mumphries, chaplain of the

Tower. His Lordship was dressed in a white suit richly embroidered with silver, and when he put it on, he said, This is the suit in which I was married, and in which I will die.

Mr Sheriff Vaillant joined them at the Tower-gate, and taking his seat in the landau, told his Lordship how disagreeable it was to wait on him on so awful an occasion, but that he would endeavour to render his situation as little irksome as possible.

The procession now moved slowly through an immense crowd of spectators. On their way, Lord Ferrers asked Mr Vaillant, if ever he had seen such a crowd? the Sheriff answered in the negative: to which the unhappy peer replied, I suppose it is because they never saw a Lord hanged before.

The chaplain observing that the public would be naturally inquisitive about his Lordship's religious opinion; he replied, that he did not think himself accountable to the world for his sentiments on religion; but that he always believed in one God, the maker of all things; that whatever were his religious notions, he had never propagated them; that all countries had a form of religion, by which the people were governed, and whoever disturbed them in it, he considered them as an enemy to society: that he thought Lord Bolingbroke[1] to blame, for permitting his sentiments on religion to be published to the world. And he made other observations of a like nature.

Respecting the death of Mr Johnson, he said, he was under particular circumstances, and had met with so many crosses and vexations, that he scarce knew what he did; but declared that he had no malice against the unfortunate man.

So immense was the crowd, that it was near three hours before the procession reached the place of execution, on the way to which Lord Ferrers desired to stop to have a glass of wine and water; but the sheriff observing that it would only draw a greater crowd about him, he replied, That is true, I say no more; let us by no means stop. He likewise observed that the preliminary apparatus of death produced more terror than death itself.

[1] (1678–1751), Tory leader of the opposition to Sir Robert Walpole.

At the place of execution, he expressed a wish to take a final leave of Mrs Clifford;[1] but the Sheriff advised him to decline it, as it would disarm him of the fortitude he possessed; to which he answered, If you, Sir, think I am wrong, I submit; after which he gave the sheriff a pocket-book, containing a bank note, with a ring and a purse of guineas; which were afterwards delivered to the unhappy woman.

The procession was attended by a party of horse-grenadiers, and foot-guards, and at the place of execution was met by another party of horse, which formed a circle round the gallows.

His Lordship walked up the steps of the scaffold with great composure, and having joined with the chaplain in repeating the Lord's Prayer, which he called a fine composition, he spoke the following words with great fervency, 'O God, forgive me all my errors! pardon all my sins!'

He gave five guineas to the executioner's assistant by mistake, instead of giving it to himself. The master demanding the money, a dispute arose between the parties, which might have discomposed the dying man, had not the Sheriff exerted his authority to put an end to it.

The executioner now proceeded to do his duty. Lord Ferrers's neck cloth was taken off, a white cap, which he had brought in his pocket put on his head, his arms secured with a black sash and the halter put round his neck. He then ascended the raised part of the scaffold, and the cap being pulled over his face, the Sheriff gave a signal, on which the raised scaffold was struck, and remained level with the rest.

After hanging an hour and five minutes, the body was put into a coffin lined with white satin, and conveyed to surgeon's hall, where an incision was made from the neck to the bottom of the breast, and the bowels were taken out: on inspection of which, the surgeons declared that they had never beheld greater signs of long life in any subject who had come under their notice.

[1] Ferrers's housekeeper and mistress.

ELIZABETH BROWNRIGG *Convicted of the murder of*
Mary Clifford, and hanged in 1767
From *British Chronicle* (September 1767)

The torture Brownrigg inflicted on her parish apprentice girls was
considered shocking even by eighteenth-century standards. Parish
apprentices, orphans let out from the workhouse to earn their keep,
were the most vulnerable section of society, with no one to protect their
interests or fight for their cause. These girls had no recourse when
their mistress turned on them; their deaths had a tragic inevitability
which brought the predicament of other parish apprentices to the
attention of the public, and were influential in changing the way they
were treated by society and the government.

It appears from the sessions paper, which was published this morning,
and contains the whole trial of James, Elizabeth and John Brownrigg,
for the murder of Mary Clifford, that the deceased at the time of her
death was about fifteen years old; that while she was on liking she
had a bed to lie on, and was well used; but that afterwards she lay
on the boards in the parlour and passage, and often in the cellar
without any covering; that the deceased having one night broke open
the cupboard for victuals, her mistress made her strip herself naked,
and go to washing, during which she frequently beat her with a
stump of a riding whip; that she afterwards used to be tied up naked
to a water pipe in the kitchen, at other times to a hook and at other
times fastened by a jack chain[1] round her neck to the yard door; that
they [Mary Clifford and Mary Mitchell] were several times lock'd up
under the stairs from Saturday night to Sunday night, while the
family were at Islington, and were allowed only a bit of bread; that
the deceased, the last time she was whipped, went naked all the rest
of the day, and that she was frequently charged by her mistress not
to put on her cloaths. The apprentice John Benham never saw the

[1] a chain, of which each link is a double loop of wire.

deceased beaten till two months after he was bound, and then not at the times she was tied up and stripped; but had often seen her cap bloody. Mary Mitchell the surviving apprentice saw the deceased beat by her master with a hearth broom once, but the apprentice never saw him strike her, and has seen him push her out of the room when she was going to be beat by her mistress. A few days before the last whipping the deceased fell down stairs with a saucepan and hurt herself; but the wounds of the last whipping appearing to be the cause of her death, Elizabeth Brownrigg was found guilty, and the other two prisoners were acquitted. The latter were detained to be tried for assaulting Mary Mitchell.

To this account of the trial, it may not be improper to add, that the morning before Mrs Brownrigg's execution, she seemed resigned and joined in prayer. Afterwards she, together with her husband and son, received the Holy Sacrament in the chapel. After which she prayed with great fervency, crying 'Lord deliver me from blood-guiltiness. I have nothing to plead or recommend me to thee but my misery; but thy beloved Son died for sinners, therefore on his merits I rely and depend for pardon.' She was now quite resigned, and prayed with her husband and son upwards of two hours, when she took leave of them, which exhibited a scene too affecting to be described, and which drew tears from all present. On her husband's assuring her that he would take care to maintain their two younger children, when he should be released from confinement, she begged him to seek a release from the prison of sin; and as for her children, God was all-sufficient, and hoped he would not suffer them to be used as she had treated the unhappy girls put under her care. Her son fell on his knees, and begged his mother's blessing: on which she fell on his face and kissed him, while her husband fell on his knees on the other side, praying to God to have mercy on her soul. Which occasioned her to say, 'Dear James, I beg that God, for Christ's sake, will be reconciled, and that he will not leave nor forsake me in the hour of death, and in the day of judgment.' She took her last farewel of them, and was soon after carried to the place of execution. At Tyburn she composedly assisted in prayer; and desired the Ordinary to acquaint the spectators, that she acknowledged her guilt, and the justice of the sentence. And her last words were, 'Lord Jesus, receive my spirit.'

She repeatedly, before her death, declared her husband innocent of ill-treating the girls, and that the son never did so, but by her order.

HANNAH WEBLEY *Convicted of the murder of her infant son, and hanged in 1794*
From Knapp and Baldwin's *Newgate Calendar*

Unmarried young women of the lower classes who became pregnant were often unable to find work if they were known to have a child, and so this crime — the murder or more often the abandonment of a fatherless new-born baby — was heartbreakingly common in the eighteenth century. (The entry is given in full.)

HANNAH WEBLEY,

EXECUTED FOR THE MURDER OF HER BASTARD CHILD

At the same assizes, August 1794, came on the trial of Hannah Webley, who was charged with the murder of her male bastard child, at Hinton, in the parish of Berkeley.

Hannah Chair, a girl of sixteen years of age, deposed that the prisoner was a single woman; that she was taken ill on the 1st and 2d of June; she slept with the prisoner, who was a servant with Mr James Pick, and was awaked in the night by the noise and crying of a child: it was dark; she could only observe that the prisoner was leaning over the bed-side; she heard her curse the child; after that she heard two blows (after which the child did not cry), and the prisoner said, 'Damn thee, thou *bist*[1] done for now.' She then took

---

[1] art, i.e. are.

her petticoat off the bed, and went down stairs: the witness now went and told her master. The prisoner returned in a few minutes after she had called her master, and brought the child back again: it was between two and three in the morning; she was afraid to speak to her: the prisoner had provided no child-bed linen.

Mr Pick, the master, corroborated what Hannah Chair said; he also deposed that the prisoner never acknowledged that she was with child: he saw the child, which lived till noon the same day; he had it baptized.

John Cornelius Hends, a man-midwife, said that he was sent for to Mr Pick's on the 2d of June, to look at a child, which was alive, and a male: a woman had it on her lap; he observed a depression or fracture of the skull. There was only one fracture, which appeared to have been done with great violence; there was a discharge of blood from the right ear. He said the fracture might possibly have been occasioned by the child's falling on the floor, but he never knew an instance of such a thing happening on delivery.

The prisoner, in her defence, made the following declaration: –

'I was taken very ill, was used to have the colic: my pains came on – I walked backward and forward – the child fell down with great violence: I said "Lord have mercy upon me, I am afraid thou art done for." I went down, thinking to take the child to my intended husband at Newport.'

The jury, after a little consultation, brought in the prisoner guilty.

The following sentence was then passed by Mr Justice Heath: –

'Hannah Webley, you have been convicted of a most cruel and unnatural murder. So far was you led on by the fear of a discovery of your shame, as first to curse and then deprive an helpless infant of life: by this wicked act your own life is forfeited to the injured laws of your country. You must now suffer a severe punishment for your crime, even the loss of life: and I hope the punishment, dreadful as it is, will be an instructive lesson to the female part of the creation, and convince them that those who swerve from the paths of virtue will be tempted to the commission of the worst of crimes. I also hope that your punishment will be a lesson to those young men who artfully endeavour to seduce young women from the paths of virtue, and that your sad end will be a monitor to them, and especially to him, who, though at present unknown, except to yourself, inveigled you into the paths of infamy and disgrace. It remains with me to pass that terrible sentence of the law, which is, that on Saturday next you be taken to the place of execution, and there to be hanged by the neck till you are dead, and that your body be delivered to be dissected, and may the Lord have mercy on your soul!'

Applications were made to his lordship for a respite for this unhappy female; but his lordship declared that he was so much convinced of her guilt that she must suffer, and her execution took place accordingly.

3

Prostitutes

SARAH PRIDDEN *Convicted of assault in 1722, fined £100 and sentenced to a year's imprisonment*
From Anon, *The Genuine History of Mrs. Sarah Pridden, usually called Sally Salisbury, and her Gallants* (1723), and de Saussure, *A Foreign View of England*

Pridden, who called herself Sally Salisbury after the name of one of her lovers, was born into poverty in 1692, and spent her childhood working on the streets of St Giles, the poorest area of London. At different seasons she shelled 'beans and peas, cried nose-gays and newspapers, peeled walnuts, made matches, turned hunter [whore] etc., well knowing that a wagging hand always gets a penny'. At the age of fourteen (although the anonymous biography says seventeen), she had already been abandoned by her first lover, the notorious Colonel Charteris (see 'Sexual Offenders'). Salisbury went on to become a highly paid courtesan at the most expensive and exclusive bordello in London. It belonged to Mother Wisebourne who was noted for keeping a chaplain in her establishment who read prayers to her 'girls' twice daily. Salisbury's lovers included two Secretaries of State. Her demise came about when, as de Saussure describes, she stabbed one of her admirers in a fit of rage (he had complimented her sister in front of her); although he did not die, and pleaded vehemently for her release, she was convicted of assault, and sentenced to a year's imprisonment. She died while still at Newgate of 'brain fever' – probably syphilis – in 1723. Her unhappy life served as the model for Hogarth's Harlot and John Cleland's Fanny Hill.

But there was a different person, upon whom Mrs *Sally* had cast her eyes and heart; he was a *Collonel*[1] under his grace the late D. of *Marlborough*, whose name I need not repeat after that of Mrs *Salisbury*:

[1] Colonel Charteris.

his air was lively and pleasant, his shape compleat, tho' his face not handsome; he had several times took occasion to speak soft things to *Sally*, but thought her too unripe a beauty to have an intrigue with, having others at his devotion of fuller and superior charms. After one of those, he posted to the *Bath*, his equipage of grandeur glistering about him; not dreaming that he was carrying little *Sally*'s heart away with him. But she soon got intelligence whither he was gone; and soon she followed him; but tho' she frequently saw him, and met him in publick places, she was scarce in appearance well enough to hope for his regard or observance; so that this prov'd a greater uneasiness to her, than if she had been distant from him; for she every day saw him surrounded with the smiles and graces of finer women, whom she thought infinitely happy in the circle of his observation. However she ne'er desponded; and as Fortune favours the bold, it favour'd her.

All the blooming flower of beauty was *Sally* now adorn'd with, and her blood beat love thro' her eager veins; when the sprightliness of her nature was transported with the less sprightly voices of drums and trumpets: but when she found that they beat to strife and war, not that of the arms, but of the feet; and that the cleverest lasses were to dance for a smock; she thought this a lively opportunity, to change the dull and heavy scene before her, into gaiety observance and conversation; accordingly she cloth'd her self in her softest airs, and pluck'd up all her charms; resolving to appear brilliant in the eyes of those gallant men that would attend that match of dancing: several competitors appear'd upon the stage, who delighted, tho' faintly, the eyes of the gentlemen gazers; while the *smock*, the noble object of their efforts was expanded full in view, adorn'd with ribbons, and enrich'd with the finest lace. But immediatly upon *Sally*'s entering the list's in a party-colour'd petticoat, and lovely shift, the spectators were ravished with the sweet assurance of her air, and the symmetrical proportion of her limbs; her leg and foot having powers to excite, like the face and voice of others. When the rivals disputed who should dance first, she refus'd not, like the rest; but pertly told them *she'd dance first and last*. Whereupon, the *beau monde* gave her a universal clap, and she began the wandering contest, like a midnight unctuous fire, bright, but uncertain, that leads uncautious men into bogs and watry places.

No sooner had her heels perform'd their weary task, but applauding sounds repeatedly shook the buildings. The other rivals seeing the hearts of the judges in their looks, retir'd from the stage, leaving Miss *Sally* sole heiress of the praise and linnen. For the abovenam'd *Collonel*, having his former kind sentiments of *Sally* now almost ripen'd into love, had made so strong a party in her favour among the gentlemen that 'twas impossible to oppose them.

By this means, the dancing was taken from the sight of several, who would willingly have seen it longer; but by the same means, a dancing was left in the breasts of some, who would willingly have had it absent: for as *Sally* had carry'd off the holland prize, so her self, a softer prize, was carry'd off by the *Collonel* and two other gentlemen: they engros'd her to themselves, even smock and all, leaving a hundred hearts to sigh; and to hold her theirs but in mocking dreams and delusive visions.

But this glitter of a sunshine was not long without its intercepting clouds; for certain ladies, I know not who, took occasion to lessen *Sally*, and to represent her as a worthless girl, a strouling vagabond, *etc*. So that, to continue the opinion those ladies had of him, he diminished that he had entertain'd of *Sally*. So that she grew uneasy at that perplexing *place*; where one goes to win new hearts, another to lose her own; whither one lady repairs for her health, which dear health makes many hundreds sick; while *Damons* and *Strephons*[1] appear, or to get spouses, or be freed from those they have at home.

When the heroine of our history arrived at *London*, after two or three days, she showed her self to her mother who guessing what tricks she had been playing with her bodily powers, striped her of all the presents, *etc*. that adorn'd her features; thinking thereby to prevent her running again into the same gay vices: tho' the report

---

[1] Stock names from pastoral romances: Damon was the goatherd in Virgil's *Eclogues*, Strephon the swain in Sir Philip Sydney's *Arcadia*.

of the ill-natured *town*, is, that her mother did it for the profit of her apparel, that she might partake of *the wages of sin*, which is wholly false and fictitious: nor is it well in her three sisters, to relate such stories, but to look at home, and consider whither their own conduct is wholly unblemish'd. Some there are, who are of opinion, that to be a woman of pleasure is to be a giant of mischief; and in the frequency of her gay extravagances, I am assured by those who know, that *Sally* does no way come up to her own relations.

But the unfortunate young lady, being thus stript of her peacock-feathers, the gaiety of her soul disappear'd with that of her cloaths; she look'd to her self, like a pick'd goose, sent naked to shew it self upon a *Lincolnshire* common. This was the more grievous to her, as she was just in the sweet blossom of youth (being seventeen years of age) and as her blood had so lately learn'd to glide, with love and victory.

Now it was, that being unable to exist a single hour out of the bustle of people, and the sight of the active world, she bethought her of an employment, that was easy to attain to, yet seem'd to her polite: accordingly, she got a budget full of plays, pamphlets and other papers, and stood to dispose of them, or her self, at the corner of *Pope*'s-head *Alley* in *Cornhill*, and at the corner of another alley opposite to the *Royal-Exchange*: she had not long been scituated on that advantageous ground, before she became the talk of all the apprentices and young lads of those parts; but seeming like a very girl, and being but mean in apparel, she escaped the notice of gentlemen. I remember still, as I went that way to school, I was told there was the beautifullest wench, who sold papers about *Cornhill*, that ever appear'd on a sunny day; and that several boys had given her half a crown, for an hour of her love; that being her usual price: and indeed she appear'd to the eye, to be then, compar'd with what she is now, like the soft beauty of the morning blush of light, compar'd with the full heat of the mid-day sun; but the beauty of conversation, which is the only valuable beauty, was at that time greatly inferiour to her present sharpened wit.

Some short time after this, she met with a wealthy *Dutchman*, who took her and wholly new rig'd her; promising her to make her his wife, if she could love him, and no other; which she assured him of for several days; and had the management of a good part of his gold, about 20 pounds of which she made over to her self, and carried it to a place of security. This ancient kisser believ'd, from the mean appearance that he found her in, that she had never tasted of the pleasures of sense, and carressed her as an untouch'd innocent. But one day, as he kiss'd her unseasonably, and ask'd her a hundred times if she could love him, and him alone, she unluckily cry'd, *D— you, and your broken tongue, can I love rotten teeth and stinking fifty?* And so flew off his knee. The *master of a ship*, finding he had *caught a* tartar *by the tail*,[1] look'd with as much care, as if the main-mast had crack'd in the mid way, between *Gravenhague*[2] and *Gravesend*.

But however, the jilting beauty, after this broad-side, got safe away, with all her rigging and new tackling, and enough of wealth about her. Her impatient aim, was to find out, and engage the *Collonel* we mentioned before: and this she so successfully did, I know not by what means, that he took her and kept her a considerable time; expressing a great tenderness and affection for her; and she, having now her charms more full at her command, studied to employ them to the best advantage. It is unlucky, that when people strive to please the most, they are commonly then, the most unable to do it. So wandering was his mind, so accustom'd to change, that with all her insinuations she could not fix him: she showed him she was fortunate, by winning from him, four times, all his money; she shewed him she was lik'd by others, by puting him once upon defending her with his sword, in a famous skirmish that happen'd in *Southampton Buildings*, where his adversary, being in liquor, unfortunately lost the use of one of his arms, and died about four years afterwards: but he had (as it is reported) after that time, very frequently satisfaction of *Sally*, in a house of pleasure, for the damage sustain'd.

[1] To get hold of something that unexpectedly proves difficult to control.
[2] A port in Holland, therefore the author means stranded in the middle of the Channel.

Being dismist from the *Collonel's* arms and keeping, she went and took a lodging at a *distiller's* in *New-street*, by St *Martin*'s Lane; and there, (if they tell true) she made her self extreamly common and generally had gally-pots[1] and phial to adorn her chamber window: from whence we may gather, she did not proceed so well fledg'd from the *Collonel's* house as from the *sea-man's*.

After some continuance here, a violent quarrel happen'd, insomuch, that Mrs *Salisbury* affirm'd that she had been wrong'd; and her landlady asserted, that she it was that had been so used; and having many in the house of her side, Mrs SALLY was decently conveyed to the house of *Justice S*—'s, and oath being there made, that she had given them the carriage of certain goods, and that she was a person of light behaviour *etc.* she was as decently conveyed thence to confinement, but immediately got bail, to prevent her becoming *the fair captive*, and as soon as she could went to her adversaries, and put her hand pretty deep into her purse, to prevent her holding it up at *Hicks's-Hall*.

At the time of this fatal accident, her relations say, that she was frequently invited to go home and live with her friends; but that, instead of it, she took up the name of *Salisbury*, which name she dearly lov'd; giving her parents (as they say) but ill language, and telling them, *she was not sprung from their scoundrel impotent bodies, but from the illustrious loins of a nobleman, who sent her to them for milk and pancakes.* Tho' to compose the foregoing breaches, she had wholly exhausted her pocket, and was also again grown mean in habit; such are the vicissitudes of fortune!

———

Some time ago a courtesan, of the name of Sally Salsbury [sic], famed for her rare and wonderful beauty, her wit and fun, became the fashion in London, and was favoured by distinguished personages. One night, at a wine supper, one of her admirers having displeased her by some uncomplimentary speech, she seized a knife and plunged it into his body. Next morning she was conveyed a prisoner to Newgate. You will suppose her lovers abandoned her in her distress. They did no

[1] apothecaries' bottles.

such thing, but crowded into the prison, presenting her with every comfort and luxury possible. As soon as the wounded man[1] – who, by the way, belongs to one of the best-known English families – was sufficiently recovered, he asked for her discharge, but Sally Salsbury died of brain fever, brought on by debauch, before she was able to leave the prison.

You will, no doubt, be surprised to hear of so much corruption, but many causes contribute to this. The liberty and leniency of the government, the impunity of vice, the by no means considerable education which the young men receive and the easy and frequent temptations of a big town are the sources of the extraordinary licentiousness that reigns openly in London. I do not mean to say that it is a general vice. God forbid! I should be most unjust towards a number of well-conducted, reserved and respectable persons, whom the public, recognising their merits, term 'civil and sober gentlemen'.

PRISONERS AT BRIDEWELL
de Saussure, *A Foreign View of England*

These two women show the penalty meted out for prostitution (at a time when the man paying the prostitute incurred neither punishment nor blame) at Bridewell, the prison for vagrant women (where Mary Toft, the 'Rabbit Lady' (see 'Confidence Tricksters'), was also imprisoned for a short time, as was Sally Salisbury). The fact that the second woman is later observed by de Saussure looking like a duchess at the theatre illustrates the heights to which a prostitute might rise as well as the depths to which she could fall.

One of my friends, on the pretext of drinking a bottle of beer, asked me to go one day with him to Tottlefields [Tothillfields] Bridewell. We entered a big court, on one side of which was a low building

---

[1] John Finch, son of the Countess of Winchelsea.

containing about thirty or forty robbers, pickpockets, etc., male and female, occupied in beating out flax. Each of these unfortunate wretches was seated in front of a large block of wood, on which he beat the flax with a large and heavy wooden mallet. On one side of this room were the men, on the other the women, and between these two lines walked the inspector, or Captain Whip'em. This man had a surly, repulsive countenance; he held a long cane in his hand about the thickness of my little finger, and whenever one of these ladies was fatigued and ceased working he would rap them on the arms, and in no gentle fashion, I can assure you . . . In the women's part we saw a fine, tall, handsome and well-dressed creature. Her linen was of the finest and so was her lace, and she wore a magnificent silk dress brocaded with flowers. The captain took great heed of her; he had made her arms quite red with the little raps he gave her with his cane. The girl received these attentions most haughtily and with great indifference. It was a most curious contrast, this handsome girl or woman in rich clothes, looking like a queen and having a mallet in her hand, with which she was forced to beat out hemp, and that in such a way that she was covered with large drops of perspiration, all this being accompanied with raps from the cane. I confess that this sight made me quite unhappy. I could not help thinking that such a handsome, proud, queenly woman should be at least spared the blows. We were told that she had been sent here the day before because she had stolen a gold watch from her lover, and that it was not her first visit, for she always stole everything she could lay hands on. At the opposite end of the room we remarked a young girl from fifteen to sixteen years of age, extremely beautiful; she seemed a mere child, and was touching to look at. We asked her why she was in this place. 'Alas,' said she, 'because of my tender heart!' She informed us that she was a prisoner through having helped one of her comrades to steal some guineas from one of her lovers; that the comrade had run away with the spoil, whilst she had been seized and brought to Bridewell; that her imprisonment should only have lasted a fortnight, but that she had now been three weeks in this place of misery, and that, as she could not pay the crown she owed for extra food, she expected never to leave it. She went on to tell us that she had eaten nothing but dry bread, the prisoners' food, for three days past. The girl related all this sad history with tears and in such a touching way that I was sorry for her, and gave her a shilling. This did not escape Captain Whip'em's eye, for he fell on her, snatched the shilling from her, rapping her at the same time with his cane to make her resume her work. Indignant at this piece of injustice, I ordered him to give the girl back the coin I had just given her, but he explained that the custom of the prison was that no money should be given to any prisoners, male or female, unless he was allowed to keep half of it for himself, and he thereupon returned the prisoner sixpence. My friend was so shocked and indignant at this treatment that without any hesitation he pulled a crown out of his pocket, so that she might be liberated at once from this house of horrors. The poor creature was so touched, so thankful for my friend's generosity, that she threw herself at his feet, shedding tears of joy and scarcely able to speak for emotion. We exhorted her to lead a better life, and she vowed she would do so; but a couple of months later, being at the play, I saw this little creature in one of the principal boxes, dressed like a duchess and more beautiful than ever. Do not be surprised at this, for every night at the comedy or opera you see women of this class and profession occupying the best places.

CORINNA
Jonathan Swift, 'A Beautiful Young Nymph Going to Bed'
(1732)

Corinna, the nymph of the title of this mock-heroic poem, is an invention of the satirist Swift; but her story illustrates better than any true-life writing the fate of so many of London's prostitutes: poverty and need from youth and premature old age, with nothing more to look forward to than a lonely, diseased death.

Corinna, pride of Drury Lane,[1]
For whom no shepherd sighs in vain;
Never did Covent Garden boast
So bright a battered, strolling toast;
No drunken rake to pick her up,
No cellar where on tick to sup;
Returning at the midnight hour;
Four storeys climbing to her bower;
Then, seated on a three-legged chair,
Takes off her artificial hair:
Now, picking out a crystal eye,
She wipes it clean, and lays it by.
Her eyebrows from a mouse's hide,
Stuck on with art on either side,
Pulls off with care, and first displays 'em,
Then in a play-book smoothly lays 'em.
Now dexterously her plumpers draws,
That serve to fill her hollow jaws.
Untwists a wire; and from her gums
A set of teeth completely comes.
Pulls out the rags contrived to prop
Her flabby dugs, and down they drop.
Proceeding on, the lovely goddess
Unlaces next her steel-ribbed bodice;
Which by the operator's skill,
Press down the lumps, the hollows fill.
Up goes her hand, and off she slips
The bolsters that supply her hips.
With gentlest touch, she next explores
Her shankers,[2] issues, running sores;
Effects of many a sad disaster,

[1] Notorious for prostitutes. (Poem is subtitled: WRITTEN FOR THE HONOUR OF THE FAIR SEX.)
[2] chancres or venereal ulcers.

And then to each applies a plaster.
But must, before she goes to bed,
Rub off the daubs of white and red.
And smooth the furrows in her front,
With greasy paper stuck upon't.
She takes a bolus e'er she sleeps;
And then between two blankets creeps.
With pains of love tormented lies;
Or if she chance to close her eyes,
Of Bridewell and the compter dreams,
And feels the lash, and faintly screams.
Or, by a faithless bully drawn,
At some hedge-tavern lies in pawn.
Or to Jamaica seems transported,
Alone, and by no planter courted;
Or, near Fleet Ditch's oozy brinks,
Surrounded with a hundred stinks,
Belated, seems on watch to lie,
And snap some cully passing by;
Or, struck with fear, her fancy runs
On watchmen, constables and duns,
From whom she meets with frequent rubs;
But, never from religious clubs;
Whose favour she is sure to find,
Because she pays them all in kind.

Corinna wakes. A dreadful sight!
Behold the ruins of the night!
A wicked rat her plaster stole,
Half ate, and dragged it to his hole.
The crystal eye, alas, was missed;
And Puss had on her plumpers pissed.
A pigeon picked her issue-peas,
And Shock her tresses filled with fleas.

The nymph, though in this mangled plight,
Must every morn her limbs unite.
But how shall I describe her arts
To recollect the scattered parts?
Or show the anguish, toil and pain,
Of gathering up herself again?
The bashful muse will never bear
In such a scene to interfere.
Corinna in the morning dizened,
Who sees, will spew; who smells, be poisoned.

AN ANONYMOUS MALE PROSTITUTE
From *London Chronicle* (1757)

This man illustrates the homosexual underworld of London in a way like that of Wild's account of Charles Hitchin (see 'Sexual Offenders'). The fact that he had previously written letters similar to that to Lord Tankerville, presumably successfully, shows that this combination of prostitution and blackmail could be a profitable pursuit. The meeting-place he chose, St James's Park, was a well-known point of assignation for homosexuals – 'this all sin-sheltering grove', the poet Rochester called it the century before – one of many in London including Moorfields, known as 'Sodomites' Walk'. There were certain recognized signs that homosexual men in search of a partner would use to signal their availability to each other, including wearing a white handkerchief in the pleats of the coat-skirt or sticking their thumbs into their waistcoat.

On Wednesday last a person, who, as it since appears, got his livelihood by prostituting himself, sent a letter of assignation to the Rt Hon. the Earl of Tankerville, appointing a place where his Lordship should send his answer; who ordered his porter to go every day to the said place, with a piece of paper in the form of a letter, till he met with the man; which he did last Monday night, took him into custody, and carried him before Mr Justice Fielding,[1] who committed him to prison, and the next morning he was examined at that magistrate's, in the presence of his Lordship: and as this vilest of all prostitutes had no other excuse for the writing of this letter but his impudence, he was delivered over to the commissioners for impressing men, who sent him immediately to the Savoy. It appeared on his examination, that Kensington Gardens, and some of the more obscure places in Hyde Park, were the places of rendezvous for these monsters in human nature. He had in his pocket-book, directions to numbers of people of all degrees, and some fair copies of the same stamp with that above mentioned, beginning with 'My Lord' but without directions. On enquiring at the place where he lodged, it appeared that he lay in bed every day till after 12; that he constantly breakfasted in bed, wore a bed-gown and a woman's cap and knot:[2] his paint and patch-boxes were found on his toilet. In a word, he is the completest Gomorrean[3] that has been met with for some time; tho' from some papers found in his pocket, it is no less certain than shocking, that there are many clones of these animals now in town, who, it is hoped, will soon be exposed to public view. It is remarkable, that this man was so great a stranger to Lord Tankerville's person, that he could not have told him from any man in the world; but his letters are so contrived, that they may either pass for a begging letter of a man in distress, or to offer his person for the basest purposes.

HARRIETTE WILSON
From her *Memoirs* (1825)

Harriette Wilson (1789–1846) was the most celebrated of three courtesan sisters known as the 'Three Graces' at the end of the eighteenth

---

[1] Sir John Fielding, QC at Bow Street after the retirement of his brother Henry in 1754.
[2] bow. [2] sodomite.

century. For nearly twenty years she revelled in all the luxuries Regency London could offer, unhampered by the constraints of convention that bound the wives of the men who kept her. She lived in the grandest houses, threw the best parties, wore the most extravagant dresses and jewels and head-dresses – and never had to preside over her husband's tenants' Christmas party or distribute alms to the poor. 'A fifty pound note is as good as an introduction,' she used to say. Her lovers included the Marquis of Worcester, whose father the Duke of Beaufort paid her off not to marry his heir, and Leinster, Argyle and Wellington – just to mention the dukes. At the end of her career, desperately in need of the money she had squandered so freely in the past, she wrote her memoirs and sent a copy of the unexpurgated version to each of her lovers with a note demanding '£200 by return of post, to be left out'; Wellington was one of the few who dared brazen it out, scrawling 'Publish and be damned' on the manuscript before sending it back; that is, perhaps, why this portrait of him is so unflattering. It is not known where she died.

I was getting into debt, as well as my sister Amy, when it so came to pass, as I have since heard say, that the – immortal!!! No; that's common; a very outlandish distinction, fitter for a lady in a balloon. The terrific!!! that will do better. I have seen His Grace in his cotton nightcap. Well, then, the terrific Duke of Wellington!!!¹ the wonder of the world!! Having six feet from the tail to the head, and – but there is a certain technicality in the expressions of the gentleman at Exeter 'Change, when he has occasion to show off a wild beast, which it would be vanity in me to presume to imitate; so leaving out his dimensions, etc. etc., it was even the Duke of Wellington, whose laurels, like those of the giant in the *Vicar of Wakefield*,² had been hardly earned by the sweat of his little dwarfs' brows, and the loss of their little legs, arms and eyes; who, feeling himself amorously given – it was in summer – one sultry evening, ordered his coachman

¹ (1769–1852), victor of Napoleon and Prime Minister in 1827 and 1834.
² 1766 novel by Oliver Goldsmith.

to set him down at the White Horse Cellar, in Piccadilly, whence he sallied forth, on foot, to No. 2 or 3, in Berkeley Street, and rapped hastily at the door, which was immediately opened by the tawdry, well-roughed housekeeper of Mrs Porter,[1] who, with a significant nod of recognition, led him into her mistress's boudoir, and then hurried away, simpering, to acquaint the good Mrs Porter with the arrival of one of her oldest customers.

Mrs Porter, on entering her boudoir, bowed low; but she had bowed lower still to His Grace, who had paid but shabbily for the last *bonne fortune* she had contrived to procure him.

'Is it not charming weather?' said Mrs Porter, by way of managing business with something like decency.

'There is a beautiful girl just come out,' said His Grace, without answering her question; 'a very fine creature; they call her Harriette, and—'

'My Lord,' exclaimed Mrs Porter, interrupting him, 'I have had three applications this very month for the girl they call Harriette, and I have already introduced myself to her.'

This was a fact, which happened while I was in Somerstown, and which I have forgotten to relate.

'It was,' continued Mrs Porter, 'at the very earnest request of General Walpole.[2] She is the wildest creature I ever saw. She did not affect modesty, nor appear in the least offended at my intrusion. Her first question was, is your man handsome? I answered frankly, that the General was more than sixty years of age; and at which account she laughed heartily; and then, seeming to recollect herself, she said, she really was over head and ears in debt, and therefore must muster up courage to receive one visit from her antiquated admirer, at my house.'

'Well?' interrupted Wellington, half jealous, half disgusted.

'Well, my Lord,' continued Mrs Porter, 'the appointment was made for eight o'clock on the following evening, at which hour the

---

[1] A procuress.
[2] (1758–1835), nephew of Sir Robert Walpole.

old General was punctual, and fidgeted about the room over this, my Lord, for more than three-quarters of an hour. At last, he rang the bell violently: I answered it; and he told me, in a fury, he would not thus be trifled with. I was beginning very earnest protestations, when we heard a loud rap at the street door, and, immediately afterwards, my housekeeper entered, to inform me that a lady, whose face was covered with a thick black veil, had just arrived in a hackney-coach, and she had shown her into the best room.'

'She came then?' inquired Wellington impatiently, and blowing his nose.

'You shall hear, my Lord,' continued Mrs Porter. 'The old General, in a state of perfect ecstasy, took me by the hand, and begged me to pardon his testy humour, assuring me, that he had been for more than a year following Harriette, and therefore, that this disappointment had been too much for his stock of patience.

'I led the way to the room, where we expected to find Harriette. The black veil did not surprise us. She was too young to be expected to enter my house, void of shame. Judge our astonishment, my Lord, when the incognita, throwing back her veil with much affectation, discovered a wrinkled face, which had weathered at least sixty summers, aye, and winters too! "The Lord defend me!" said I. "Who the devil are you?" said the General. "A charming creature," replied the hag, "if you did but know me. A widow, too, dear General, very much at your disposal; for my dear good man has been dead these sixty years." "You are a set of—" The General was interrupted by his fair incognita, with – "Here is gallantry! here is treatment of the soft sex! No, Mr General, not the worst of your insinuations shall ever make me think the less of myself!"

'The General, at this moment, beginning to feel a little ashamed, and completely furious, contrived to gain the street, declaring that he would never enter my house again. His fair one insisted on following him; and all I could say or do would not prevent her. I know not what became of them both.'

'My good woman,' said Wellington, without making any remarks on her story, 'my time is precious. One hundred guineas are yours, and as much Harriette's, if you can induce her to give me the meeting.'

'My dear Lord,' said Mrs Porter, quite subdued, 'what would I not do to serve you? I will pay Harriette a visit early tomorrow morning; although, my Lord, to tell you the truth, I was never half so afraid of any woman in my life. She is so wild, and appears so perfectly independent and careless of her own interests and welfare, that I really do not know what is likely to move her.'

'Nonsense!' said Wellington, 'it is very well known that the Marquis of Lorne[1] is her lover.'

'Lord Lorne may have gained Harriette's heart,' said Mrs Porter, just as if she understood the game of hearts! 'However,' added she, 'I will not give up the business till I have had an interview with Harriette.'

'And make haste about it,' said Wellington, taking up his hat; 'I shall call for your answer in two days. In the meantime, if you have anything like good news to communicate, address a line to Thomas's Hotel, Berkeley Square.' . . .

The next morning I received another visit from Mrs Porter, who informed me that she had just had an interview with my new lover, and had reported to him all I had desired her to say.

'Since you object to meet a stranger,' continued Mrs Porter, 'His Grace desires me to say, he hopes you can keep a secret, and to inform you, that it is the Duke of Wellington who so anxiously desires to make your acquaintance.'

'I have heard of His Grace often,' said I, in a tone of deep disappointment: for I had been indulging a kind of hope about the stranger with the great Newfoundland dog,[2] with whose appearance I had been so unusually struck as to have sought for him every day, and I thought of him every hour.

'His Grace,' Mrs Porter proceeded, 'only entreats to be allowed to make your acquaintance. His situation, you know, prevents the possibility of his getting regularly introduced to you.'

---

[1] The Marquess of Lorne, later the Duke of Argyle; Wilson refers to him as both Lorne and Argyle.
[2] Lord Ponsonby, see below.

'It will never do,' said I, shaking my head.

'Be assured,' said Mrs Porter, 'he is a remarkably fine-looking man, and, if you are afraid of my house, promise to receive him in your own, at any hour when he may be certain to find you alone.'

Well, thought I, with a sigh; I suppose he must come. I do not understand economy, and am frightened to death at debts. Argyle is going to Scotland; and I shall want a steady sort of friend, of some kind, in case a bailiff should get hold of me.

'What shall I say to His Grace?' Mrs Porter inquired, growing impatient.

'Well then,' said I, 'since it must be so, tell His Grace that I will receive him tomorrow at three; but mind, only as a common acquaintance!'

Away winged Wellington's Mercury, as an old woman wings it at sixty; and most punctual to my appointment, at three on the following day, Wellington made his appearance. He bowed first, then said –

'How do you do?' then thanked me for having given him permission to call on me; and then wanted to take hold of my hand.

'Really,' said I, withdrawing my hand, 'for such a renowned hero you have very little to say for yourself.'

'Beautiful creature!' uttered Wellington, 'where is Lorne?'

'Good gracious,' said I, out of all patience at his stupidity – 'what come you here for, Duke?'

'Beautiful eyes, yours!' reiterated Wellington.

'Aye, man! they are greater conquerors than ever Wellington shall be; but, to be serious, I understand you came here to try to make yourself agreeable?'

'What, child! do you think that I have nothing better to do than to make speeches to please ladies?' said Wellington.

'*Après avoir dépeuplé la terre, vous devez faire tout pour la repeupler,*'[1] I replied.

'You should see me where I shine,' Wellington observed, laughing.

---

[1] After having cleared the ground of people, you have to do all you can to bring people back again.

'Where's that, in God's name?'

'In a field of battle,' answered the hero.

'*Battez-vous, donc, et qu'un autre me fasse la cour!*[1] said I.

But love scenes, or even love quarrels, seldom tend to amuse the reader, so, to be brief, what was a mere man, even though it were the handsome Duke of Argyle, to a Wellington!!!!

Argyle grew jealous of Wellington's frequent visits, and, hiding himself in his native woods, wrote me the following very pathetic letter:

I am not quite sure whether I do or do not love you – I am afraid I did too much; – but, as long as you find pleasure in the society of another, and a hero too, I am well contented to be a mere common mortal, a monkey or what you will. I too have my heroines waiting for me, in all the woods about here. Here is the woodcutter's daughter, and the gardener's maid always waiting for my gracious presence, and to which of them I shall throw the handkerchief I know not. How then can I remain constant to your inconstant charms? I could have been a little romantic about you, it is true; but I always take people as I find them, '*et j'ai ici beau jeu*'.[2] Adieu.

I am very fond of you still, for all this.

ARGYLE

This was my answer:

Indeed you are, as yet, the only man who has ever had the least influence over me, therefore, I entreat you, do not forget me! I wish I were the woodcutter's daughter, awaiting your gracious presence in the woods for days! weeks! months! so that, at last, you would reward me with the benevolent smile of peace and forgiveness; or that illumined, beautiful expression of more ardent feeling, such as I have often inspired and shall remember for ever, come what may, and whether your fancy changes, or mine. You say you take people as you find them; therefore, you must and you shall love me still, with all my imperfections on my foolish head, and that dearly.

HARRIETTE

[1] Go and get on with it, and leave others to work on my heart!

[2] and I'm having a good time here.

Wellington was now my constant visitor – a most unentertaining one, Heaven knows! and, in the evenings, when he wore his broad red ribbon,[1] he looked very like a rat-catcher.

'Do you know,' said I to him one day, 'do you know the world talks about hanging you?'

'Eh?' said Wellington.

'They say you will be hanged, in spite of all your brother Wellesley can say in your defence.'

'Ha!!' said Wellington, very seriously, 'what paper do you read?'

'It is the common talk of the day,' I replied.

'They must not work me in such another campaign,' Wellington said, smiling, 'or my weight will never hang me.'

'Why, you look a little like the apothecary in Romeo already,' I said . . .

Wellington called on me the next morning before I had finished my breakfast. I tried him on every subject I could muster. On all, he was most impenetrably taciturn. At last he started an original idea of his own; actual copyright, as Stockdale[2] would call it.

'I wonder you do not get married, Harriette!'

(By the by, ignorant people are always wondering.)

'Why so?'

Wellington, however, gives no reason for anything unconnected with fighting, at least since the convention of Cintra;[3] and he, therefore, again became silent. Another burst of attic sentiment blazed forth.

'I was thinking of you last night, after I got into bed,' resumed Wellington.

'How very polite to the Duchess,' I observed. '*Apropos* to marriage, Duke, how do you like it?'

Wellington, who seems to make a point of never answering one,

---

[1] The insignia of the Order of Bath.

[2] Percival Stockdale (1736–1811), prolific man of letters.

[3] Peace in Portugal between England and France, 1808, negotiated by Wellington.

continued, 'I was thinking – I was thinking that you will get into some scrape, when I go to Spain.'

'Nothing so serious as marriage neither, I hope!'

'I must come again tomorrow, to give you a little advice,' continued Wellington.

'Oh, let us have it all out now, and have done with it.'

'I cannot,' said Wellington, putting on his gloves and taking a hasty leave of me.

I am glad he is off, thought I, for this is indeed very uphill work. This is worse than Lord Craven.

As soon as he was gone, I hastened to Curzon Street. The window-shutters of Lord Ponsonby's[1] house were all closed. How disappointed and low-spirited I felt at the idea that His Lordship had left town! Suspense was insufferable; so I ventured to send my servant to inquire when the family were expected in London.

In about a month, was the answer. I must forget this man, thought I, it is far too great a bore; and yet I felt that to forget him was impossible . . .

Some short time after this the Duke of Wellington, who, I presume, had discovered the tough qualities of his heart, which contributed to obtain him such renown in the field of battle, possessed no more merit for home service, or ladies' uses, than did his good digestion, betook himself again to the wars. He called to take a hasty leave of me, a few hours before his departure.

'I am off for Spain directly,' said Wellington.

I know not how it was, but I grew melancholy. Wellington had relieved me from many duns, which else had given me vast uneasiness. I saw him there, perhaps for the last time in my life. Ponsonby was nothing to me, and out of town; in fact, I had been in bad spirits all the morning, and strange, but very true, and he remembers it still, when I was about to say, God bless you, Wellington! I burst into tears. They appeared to afford rather an unusual unction to his soul, and his astonishment seemed to me not quite unmixed with gratitude.

---

[1] (c. 1770–1855), diplomat and the handsomest man of his generation.

'If you change your home,' said Wellington, kissing my cheek, 'let me find your address at Thomas's Hotel, as soon as I come to England; and, if you want anything in the meantime, write to Spain; and do not cry; and take care of yourself; and do not cut me when I come back.

'Do you hear?' said Wellington, first wiping away some of my tears with my handkerchief; and then, kissing my eyes, he said, 'God bless you!' and hurried away.

4

Thieves

JACK SHEPPARD *Convicted of burglary, and hanged in 1724*
From Daniel Defoe, *A Narrative of all the Robberies, Escapes,*
&c. of John Sheppard (1724)

Jack Sheppard (b. 1702) was the model for William Hogarth's idle
apprentice: the talented wastrel, who turns his wits to crime with the
inevitable end at the gallows. His incredible escapes from various prisons
in London, including most spectacularly two from Newgate, made him
the most famous man in London for a few heady weeks in 1724 before
his dramatic execution. The road to Tyburn was lined with weeping
girls dressed in white, throwing flowers at Sheppard in his cart as he
passed by. When he was 'turned off', as the expression went, the crowd
surged forward to tug at his legs, a method of ensuring a fast and
painless death – but which foiled the plan Sheppard had hatched with
Defoe and Applebee, the ghost-writer and publisher (respectively) of
his autobiography, for his hanged body to be whisked away after the
fifteen allotted minutes had elapsed and efforts made to revive him. It
was possible to survive hanging – as the case of William Duell shows;
but the crowd were so determined to prevent their hero from being
anatomized that there was a scuffle over the body when Applebee's men
tried to spirit it away. Later in the day there were riots when attempts
were made to remove the corpse for burial but he was interred that
night in the graveyard of St Martin's-in-the-Fields. As well as serving
as an inspiration for Hogarth, Sheppard was also the model for John
Gay's Macheath and Dickens's Artful Dodger.

Defoe's biography (given in full) is notable for the moralizing
ideas he attributes to Sheppard, despite Sheppard's own lack of interest
in conventional rights and wrongs. Although Defoe tries throughout
to use Sheppard as an example of why crime is bad – Defoe disapproved
of the glamorization of such criminals – Sheppard's irrepressible sense
of individuality and humour defy attempts to fit him into a predetermined
mould.

As my unhappy life and actions have afforded matter of much amusement to the world; and various pamphlets, papers and pictures relating thereunto are gone abroad, most or all of them misrepresenting my affairs; 'tis necessary that I should say something for my self, and set certain intricate matters in a true light; every subject, how unfortunate or unworthy soever, having the liberty of publishing his case. And it will be no small satisfaction to me to think that I have thoroughly purg'd my conscience before I leave the world, and made reparation to the many persons injur'd by me, as far as is in my poor power.

If my birth, parentage or education will prove of service or satisfaction to mankind, I was born in Stepney Parish, the year Queen Anne came to the crown; my father a carpenter by trade, and an honest industrious man by character, and my mother bore and deserved the same. She being left a widow in the early part of my life, continued the business, and kept my self, together with another unfortunate son, and a daughter, at Mr Garrett's school near great St Hellen's in Bishopsgate parish, till Mr Kneebone a woollen-draper in the Strand, an acquaintance, regarding the slender circumstances of our family, took me under his care, and improv'd me in my writing and accompts,[1] himself setting me copies with his own hand; and he being desirous to settle me to a trade, and to make my mother easy in that respect, agreed with Mr Owen Wood, a carpenter in Drury-Lane, to take me apprentice[2] for seven years, upon condition that Mr Kneebone should procure Mr Wood to be employ'd in performing the carpenter's work, etc. at a house at Hampstead, which he did accordingly, and upon that and no other consideration was I bound to Mr Wood.

We went on together for about six years, there happening in that time what is too common with most families in low life, as frequent quarrels and bickerings. I am far from presuming to say that I was one of the best of servants, but I believe if less liberty had been allow'd me then, I should scarce have had so much sorrow and

---

[1] accounts.

[2] This system of indenture was a way for lower-class children, especially boys, to learn a trade while living with the family of their master.

confinement after. My master and mistress with their children were strict observers of the Sabbath, but 'tis too well known in the neighbourhood that I had too great a loose given to my evil inclinations, and spent the Lord's Day as I thought convenient. It has been said in print that I did beat and bruise my master Mr Wood in a most barbarous and shameful manner at Mr Britt's, the Sun ale-house at Islington, and that I damn'd my mistress's blood, and beat her to the ground, etc. These stories have been greatly improved to my disadvantage. Mr Wood cannot but remember how hard I wrought for him that day at Islington, what refreshment was offer'd to my fellow-servant and my self; the cause of that unhappy quarrel is still fresh in my memory: and as for that of my mistress, when Elizabeth Lyon and her husband, a soldier, were quarrelling together in Mr Wood's yard, I bid them be gone, and threw a small lath at Lyon, which might fall on my mistress, but she received no harm as I know of, and if she did, I am sorry for it.

After all I may justly lay the blame of my temporal and (without God's great mercies) my eternal ruin on Joseph Hind, a button-mould maker, who formerly kept the Black Lyon ale-house in Drury-Lane; the frequenting of this wicked house brought me acquainted with Elizabeth Lyon, and with a train of vices, as before I was altogether a stranger to. Hind is now a lamentable instance of God's divine vengeance, he being a wretched object about the streets; and I am still far more miserable than him.

It has been said in the History of my Life,[1] that the first robbery I ever committed was in the house of Mr Bains, a piece-broker in White-Horse Yard; to my sorrow and shame I must acknowledge my guilt of a felony before that, which was my stealing two silver spoons from the Rummer Tavern at Charing-Cross, when I was doing a jobb there for my master: for which I ask pardon of God, and the persons who were wrongfully charg'd and injur'd by that my crime.

Unhappy wretch! I was now commenced thief, and soon after

[1] At the height of Sheppard's fame cheap biographies of him abounded; the best one, *The History of the Life of Jack Sheppard*, is also by Defoe.

house-breaker; growing gradually wicked, 'twas about the latter end of July 1723, that I was sent by my master to do a jobb at the house of Mr Bains aforesaid, I there stole a roll of fustian[1] containing 24 yards, from amongst many others, and Mr Bains not missing it, had consequently no suspicion. I offer'd it to sale among the young lads in our neighbourhood at 12d. per yard, but meeting with no purchasers I concealed the fustian in my trunk.

On the 1st of August following, I again wrought in Mr Bains's shop, and that night at about 12 of the clock I came and took up the wooden bars over the cellar-window, so enter'd and came up into the house, and took away goods to the value of fourteen pounds, besides seven pounds in money out of the till, then nail'd down the bars again and went off. The next day I came to the house to finish the shutters for the shop, when Mr Bains and his wife were in great trouble for their loss, saying to me they suspected a woman their lodger had let the rogues in, for that they were assured the house had not been broken; the poor people little dreaming they were telling their story to the thief, I condoling with them, and pretending great sorrow for their misfortune. Not long afterwards my fellow-prentice Thomas acquainted Mr Wood that he had observed a quantity of fustian in my trunk. My master and I had broke measures, and I begging absent from home and hearing Thomas had tattled, in the night-time I broke through a neighbour's house and into my master's and so carried off the fustian, to prevent the consequences of a discovery. Mr Wood rightly concluding I had stolen it from Mr Bains, sent him word of what had happen'd, who upon overlooking his goods soon found his loss, and threaten'd to prosecute me for the robbery. I thought it was adviseable to meet the danger; and therefore went to Mr Bains, bullied and menac'd him, and bid him be careful how he sullied my reputation, lest he might be brought to repent of it. But this was not sufficient to avert the danger. Mr Bains resolving to proceed upon the circumstances he was already furnished with; I thought of another expedient, and acknowledg'd that I had a piece

[1] heavy cotton cloth.

of fustian which my mother had bought for me in Spittle-Fields of a weaver; and she, poor woman, willing to screen her wicked son, confirm'd the story, and was a whole day together with Mr Bains in Spittle-Fields to find out the pretended weaver. In the end, I was forc'd to send back about 19 yards of the fustian to Mr Bains, and then the storm blew over. I related all these particulars to Mr Bains when he came to me in the Castle Room, as well to wipe off the suspicion from the poor innocent woman Mr Bains's lodger, as for his own satisfaction.

I abruptly quitted Mr Wood's service almost a year before the expiration of my apprenticeship, and went to Fulham, and there wrought as a journey-man[1] to a Master Carpenter, telling the man that I had served out my apprenticeship in Smithfield. Elizabeth Lyon cohabiting with me as my wife, I kept her in a lodging at Parson's-Green; but Mr Wood's brother being an inhabitant in the town discover'd me, and my master with Justice Newton's warrant brought me to London, and confin'd me in St Clement's Round-house all night: the next day I was carried to Guild-Hall to have gone before the Chamberlain, but he being gone, I agreed with Mr Wood, and making matters easy got clear of him, and then fell to robbing almost every one that stood in my way. The robbery at Mr Charles's house in May-Fair I have confess'd in a particular manner to Mr Wagstaffe, and to many others.

The robberies of Mr Bains, Mr Barton and Mr Kneebone, together with the robbery of Mr Pargiter and two others on the Hampstead Road, along with Joseph Blake, alias Blewskin,[2] I did amply confess before Justice Blackerby, Mr Bains and Mr Kneebone being present,

---

[1] A qualified mechanic or artisan who has not yet set up his own business; one who has finished his apprenticeship but still works for a master. These young men, like apprentices, were considered rowdy and inclined to petty crime.

[2] Sheppard's closest friend was 'Blueskin Blake' (so-called for his dark countenance) who had been born on the streets and brought up to a life of crime by Jonathan Wild. Wild later betrayed him in court, prompting Blake to attack him from the stand with a rusty knife. Afterwards he said he was 'only sorry that he had not done it, for never did such a rogue as Wild live, and go unpunished so long'.

and did make all the reparation that was in my power, by telling them where the goods were sold, part whereof has been recovered by those means to the owners.

I declare upon the word of a dying man, that Will Field was not concerned with Blueskin and my self in the breaking and robbing of Mr Kneebone's house, altho' he has sworn the same at our respective tryals; and I have been inform'd that by certain circumstances which Field swore to, Mr Kneebone himself is of opinion that he was not concerned in the fact: but he has done the work for his master,[1] who in the end no doubt will reward him, as he has done all his other servants. I wish Field may repent and amend his wicked life, for a greater villain there is not breathing. Blueskin and my self, after we had robb'd Mr Kneebone's house, lodg'd the goods at my warehouse, a little stable at Westminster Horse-ferry, which I had hired for such purposes. I was so cautious of suffering any one to be acquainted with it, that even Elizabeth Lyon was out of the secret; but hearing of a lock or fence in Bishopsgate to dispose of the cloth to, Blueskin carried the pack, and I follow'd to guard him, and met the chap at an alehouse; a small quantity we got off at a very low price, which was always not ours, but is the constant fate of all other robbers; for I declare that when goods (the intrinsick value whereof has been 50 £.) have been in my hands, I have never made more than ten pounds of them clear money; such a discount and disadvantage attends always the sale of such unlawful acquirements. Field lodging with Blueskin's mother in Rosemary-Lane, we all became acquainted, and being all of a piece made no secret of Mr Kneebone's robbery; we told him the manner of it, the booty, etc. and withal carried him down to the warehouse at Westminster, he pretending to buy the goods. In a day or two after, to the great surprize of Blueskin and my self, we found the warehouse broke open, the cloth gone and only a wrapper or two of no value left; we concluded, as it appeared after, that Field had plaid at rob-thief with us, for he produc'd some of Mr Kneebone's cloth at my tryal, of which he became possess'd by no

[1] Jonathan Wild, who sent Field to frame Sheppard.

other means than those I have related. I must add this to what relates to Mr Kneebone's robbery, that I was near a fortnight, by intervals, in cutting the two oaken bars that went over the back part of his house in Little Drury-Lane. I heartily ask his pardon for injuring him my kind patron and benefactor in that manner, and desire his prayers to God for the forgiveness of that as of all my other enormous crimes.

I have been at times confin'd in all the round-houses belonging to the respective parishes within the liberty of Westminster; Elizabeth Lyon has been a prisoner in many of them also: I have sometimes procur'd her liberty, and she at others has done her utmost to obtain mine, and at other times she has again betray'd me into the hands of justice. When I was formerly in St Anne's Round-house, she brought me the spike of an halbert, with the help whereof I did break open the same, but was discover'd before I could get off, and was put into the dungeon of the place fetter'd and manacled; and that was the first time that I had any irons put upon me. I in return rescu'd her from St Giles's Round-house soon after; but the manner of my own escape from St Giles's Round-house may be worthy of notice. Having in confederacy with my brother Thomas a Sea-faring person, and Elizabeth Lyon committed several robberies about Clare Market and Thomas being in Newgate for them, impeach'd me and Lyon; and the prosecutors being in close pursuit of us, I kept up as much as possible; 'till being one day at the Queens-Head ale-house in King street, Westminster, an acquaintance call'd Sykes (alias Hell and Fury),[1] a chairman, desir'd me to go thence to an ale-house at the Seven Dials, saying he knew two chubs[2] that we might make a penny of at skettles, we being good players: I went with him; a third person he soon procur'd, and said the fourth should not be long wanting, and truly he prov'd to be a constable of St Giles's parish. In short, Sykes charg'd him with me, saying I stood impeach'd of several robberies. Justice Parry sent me to St Giles's Round-house for that

---

[1] Bill Sykes, ex-footman of the rake-hell Duke of Wharton.
[2] fools.

night, with orders to the constable to bring me before him again the next morning for farther examination. I had nothing but an old razor in my pocket, and was confin'd in the upper part of the place, being two stories from the ground; with my razor I cut out the stretcher of a chair, and began to make a breach in the roof, laying the feather-bed under it to prevent any noise by the falling of the rubbish on the floor. It being about nine at night, people were passing and repassing in the street, and a tile or brick happening to fall, struck a man on the head, who rais'd the whole place; the people calling aloud that the prisoners were breaking out of the round-house. I found there was no time then to be lost, therefore made a bold push thro' the breach, throwing a whole load of bricks, tiles, etc. upon the people in the street; and before the beadle and assistance came up I had dropt into the church-yard, and got over the lower end of the wall, and came amidst the crowd, who were all staring up, some crying, there's his head, there he goes behind the chimney, etc. I was well enough diverted with the adventure, and then went off about my business.

The methods by which I escap'd from New-Prison, and the condemn'd hold of Newgate, have been printed in so many books and papers, that it would be ridiculous to repeat them; only it must be remember'd that my escaping from New-Prison, and carrying with me Elizabeth Lyon over the wall of Bridewell yard, was not so wonderful as has been reported, because Captain Geary and his servants cannot but know, that by my opening the great gate I got Lyon upon the top of the wall without the help of a scaling ladder, otherwise it must have been impracticable to have procur'd her redemption. She indeed rewarded me as well for it, in betraying me to Jonathan Wild so soon after. I wish she may reform her life: a more wicked, deceitful and lascivious wretch there is not living in England. She has prov'd my bane. God forgive her: I do; and die in charity with all the rest of mankind.

Blueskin has atton'd for his offences. I am now following, being just on the brink of eternity, much unprepar'd to appear before the face of an angry God. Blueskin had been a much older offender than my self, having been guilty of numberless robberies, and had formerly convicted four of his accomplices, who were put to death. He was concern'd along with me in the three robberies on the Hampstead Road, besides that of Mr Kneebone, and one other. Tho' he was an able-bodied man and capable of any crime, even murder, he was never master of a courage or conduct suitable to our enterprizes; and I am of opinion, that neither of us had so soon met our fate, if he would have suffer'd himself to have been directed by me; he always wanting resolution, when our affairs requir'd it most. The last summer, I hired two horses for us at an inn in Piccadilly, and being arm'd with pistols, etc. we went upon Enfield-Chace, where a coach pass'd us with two footmen and four young ladies, who had with them their gold watches, tweezer cases and other things of value; I declar'd immediately for attacking them, but Blueskin's courage dropt him, saying that he would first refresh his horse and then follow, but he designedly delayed till we had quite lost the coach and hopes of the booty. In short, he was a worthless companion, a sorry thief, and nothing but the cutting of Jonathan Wild's throat could have made him considerable.

I have often lamented the scandalous practice of thief-catching, as it is call'd, and the publick manner of offering rewards for stoln goods, in defiance of two several Acts of Parliament; the thief-catcher living sumptuously, and keeping publick Offices of Intelligence: these who forfeit their lives every day they breathe, and deserve the gallows as richly as any of the thieves, send us as their representatives to Tyburn once a month: thus they hang by proxy, while we do it fairly in person.

I never corresponded with any of them. I was indeed twice at a thief-catcher's levee,[1] and must confess the man treated me civilly; he complimented me on my successes, said he heard that I had both an hand and head admirably well turn'd to business, and that I and my friends should be always welcome to him: but caring not for his acquaintance, I never troubled him, nor had we any dealings together.

As my last escape from Newgate out of the strong room call'd the Castle, has made a greater noise in the world than any other action

---

[1] Probably Jonathan Wild's.

of my life, I shall relate every minute circumstance thereof as far as I am able to remember: intending thereby to satisfie the curious and do justice to the innocent. After I had been made a publick spectacle of for many days together, with my legs chain'd together, loaded with heavy irons, and stapled down to the floor, I thought it was not altogether impracticable to escape, if I could but be furnished with proper implements; but as every person that came near me was carefully watch'd, there was no possibility of any such assistance; till one day in the absence of my jaylors, being looking about the floor, I spy'd a small nail within reach, and with that, after a little practice, I found the great horse padlock that went from the chain to the staple in the floor might be unlock'd, which I did afterward at pleasure; and was frequently about the room, and have several times slept on the barracks, when the keepers imagin'd I had not been out of my chair. But being unable to pass up the chimney, and void of tools, I remain'd where I was; till being detected in these practices by the keepers, who surpriz'd me one day before I could fix my self to the staple in the manner as they had left me, I shew'd Mr Pitt, Mr Rouse and Mr Parry my art, and before their faces unlockt the padlock with the nail; and though people have made such an outcry about it, there is scarce a smith in London but what may easily do the same thing. However this call'd for a farther security of me; and till now I had remain'd without hand-cuffs, and a jolly pair was provided for me. Mr Kneebone was present when they were put on: I with tears begg'd his intercession to the keepers to preserve me from those dreadful manacles, telling him, my heart was broken, and that I should be much more miserable than before. Mr Kneebone could not refrain from shedding tears, and did use his good offices with the keepers to keep me from them, but all to no purpose; on they went, though at the same time I despis'd them, and well knew that with my teeth only I could take them off at pleasure: but this was to lull them into a firm belief, that they had effectually frustrated all attempts to escape for the future. I was still far from despairing. The turnkey and Mr Kneebone had not been gone down stairs an hour, ere I made an experiment, and got off my hand-cuffs, and before they visited me again, I put them on, and industriously rubb'd and fretted the skin on my wrists, making them very bloody, as thinking (if such a thing was possible to be done) to move the turnkeys to compassion, but rather to confirm them in their opinion; but though this had no effect upon them, it wrought much upon the spectators, and drew down from them not only much pity, but quantities of silver and copper: but I wanted still a more useful metal, a crow,[1] a chissel, a file and a saw or two, those weapons being more useful to me than all the mines of Mexico; but there was no expecting any such utensils in my circumstances.

Wednesday the 14th of October the sessions beginning, I found there was not a moment to be lost; and the affair of Jonathan Wild's throat, together with the business at the Old Baily, having sufficiently engag'd the attention of the keepers, I thought then was the time to push. Thursday the 15th at about two in the afternoon Austin my old attendant came to bring my necessaries, and brought up four persons, viz. the Keeper of Clerkenwell-Bridewell, the clerk of Westminster Gate-house, and two others. Austin, as it was his usual custom, examin'd the irons and hand-cuffs, and found all safe and firm, and then left me; and he may remember that I ask'd him to come again to me the same evening, but I neither expected or desired his company; and happy was it for the poor man that he did not interfere, while I had the large iron bar in my hand, though I once had a design to have barricaded him, or any others from coming into the room while I was at work: but then considering that such a project would be useless, I let fall that resolution.

As near as can be remember'd, just before three in the afternoon I went to work, taking off first my hand-cuffs; next with main strength I twisted a small iron link of the chain between my legs asunder; and the broken pieces prov'd extream useful to me in my design; the fett-locks I drew up to the calves of my leggs, taking off before that my stockings, and with my garters made them firm to my body, to prevent their shackling. I then proceeded to make a hole in the

---

[1] crowbar.

chimney of the Castle about three foot wide, and six foot high from the floor, and with the help of the broken links aforesaid wrench'd an iron bar out of the chimney, of about two feet and an half in length, and an inch square: a most notable implement. I immediately enter'd the Red Room directly over the Castle, where some of the Preston rebels[1] had been kept a long time agone; and as the keepers say the door had not been unlock'd for seven years; but I intended not to be seven years in opening it, though they had: I went to work upon the nut of the lock, and with little difficulty got it off, and made the door fly before me; in this room I found a large nail, which prov'd of great use in my farther progress. The door of the entry between the Red Room and the Chapel prov'd an hard task, it being a laborious piece of work; for here I was forc'd to break away the wall, and dislodge the bolt which was fasten'd on the other side. This occasion'd much noise, and I was very fearful of being heard by the master-side debtors. Being got to the chapel, I climb'd over the iron spikes, and with ease broke one of them off for my further purposes, and open'd the door on the inside. The door going out of the chapel to the leads, I stripp'd the nut from off the lock, as I had done before from that of the Red Room, and then got into the entry between the chapel and the leads; and came to another strong door, which being fasten'd by a very strong lock, there I had like to have stopt, and it being full dark, my spirits began to fail me, as greatly doubting of succeeding; but cheering up, I wrought on with great diligence, and in less than half an hour, with the main help of the nail from the Red Room, and the spike from the chapel, wrench'd the box off, and so made the door my humble servant.

A little farther in my passage another stout door stood in my way; and this was a difficulty with a witness; being guarded with more bolts, bars and locks than any I had hitherto met with: I had by this time great encouragement, as hoping soon to be rewarded for all this toil and labour. The clock at St Sepulchre's was now going the eighth hour, and this prov'd a very useful hint to me soon after. I went first

---

[1] Jacobite rebels, imprisoned in Newgate after their surrender in 1715.

upon the box and the nut, but found it labour in vain; and then proceeded to attack the fillet of the door; this succeeded beyond expectation, for the box of the lock came off with it from the main post. I found my work was near finish'd, and that my fate soon would be determined.

I was got to a door opening in the lower leads, which being only bolted on the inside, I open'd it with ease, and then clambered from the top of it to the higher leads, and went over the wall. I saw the streets were lighted, the shops being still open, and therefore began to consider what was necessary to be further done, as knowing that the smallest accident would still spoil the whole workmanship, and was doubtful on which of the houses I should alight. I found I must go back for the blanket which had been my covering a-nights in the Castle, which I accordingly did, and endeavoured to fasten my stockings and that together, to lessen my descent, but wanted necessaries so to do, and was therefore forc'd to make use of the blanket alone. I fixt the same with the chappel spike into the wall of Newgate, and dropt from it on the Turner's leads, a house adjoyning to the prison; 'twas then about nine of the clock, and the shops not yet shut in. It fortunately happen'd, that the garret door on the leads was open. I stole softly down about two pair of stairs, and then heard company talking in a room; the door open. My irons gave a small clink, which made a woman cry, Lord, what noise is that? A man reply'd, Perhaps the dog or cat; and so it went off. I return'd up to the garret, and laid my self down, being terribly fatigu'd; and continu'd there for about two hours, and then crept down once more to the room where the company were, and heard a gentleman taking his Leave, being very importunate to be gone, saying he had disappointed friends by not going home sooner. In about three quarters more the gentleman took leave, and went, being lighted down stairs by the maid, who, when she return'd shut the chamber-door; I then resolv'd at all hazards to follow, and slipt down stairs, but made a stumble against a chamber-door. I was instantly in the entry and out at the street door, which I was so unmannerly as not to shut after me. I was once more, contrary to my own expectation and that of all mankind, a freeman.

I pass'd directly by St Sepulchre's watch-house, bidding them Good-morrow, it being after twelve, and down Snow-hill, up Holborn, leaving St Andrew's Watch on my left, and then again pass'd the watch-house at Holborn Bars, and made down Gray's-Inn Lane into the fields, and at two in the morning came to Tottenham Court, and there got into an old house in the fields, where cows had some time been kept, and laid me down to rest, and slept well for three hours. My legs were swell'd and bruis'd intollerably, which gave me great uneasiness; and having my fetters still on, I dreaded the approach of the day, fearing then I should be discovered. I began to examine my pockets, and found my self master of between forty and fifty Shillings. I had no friend in the world that I could send to, or trust with my condition. About seven on Friday morning it began raining, and continued so the whole day, insomuch that not one creature was to be seen in the fields. I would freely have parted with my right hand for an hammer, a chisel and a punch. I kept snug in my retreat till the evening, when after dark I ventur'd into Tottenham, and got to a little blind chandler's shop, and there furnish'd my self with cheese and bread, small-beer and other necessaries, hiding my irons with a great coat as much as possible. I ask'd the woman for an hammer, but there was none to be had; so I went very quietly back to my dormitory, and rested pretty well that night, and continued there all Saturday. At night I went again to the chandler's shop and got provisions, and slept till about six the next day, which being Sunday, I began with a stone to batter the basils of the fetters in order to beat them into a large oval, and then to slip my heels through. In the afternoon the master of the shed, or house, came in, and seeing my irons asked me, For God's sake, who are you? I told him, 'an unfortunate young man, who had been sent to Bridewell about a bastard-child, as not being able to give security to the parish, and had made my escape'. The man reply'd, If that was the case it was a small fault indeed, for he had been guilty of the same things himself formerly; and withal said, however, he did not like my looks, and cared not how soon I was gone.

After he was gone, observing a poor-looking man like a joiner, I made up to him and repeated the same story, assuring him that 20s. should be at his service, if he could furnish me with a smith's hammer, and a punch. The man prov'd a shoe-maker by trade, but willing to obtain the reward, immediately borrow'd the tools of a black-smith his neighbour, and likewise gave me great assistance, and before five that evening I had entirely got rid of those troublesome companions my fetters, which I gave to the fellow, besides his twenty shillings, if he thought fit to make use of them.

That night I came to a cellar at Charing-Cross, and refresh'd very comfortably with roast veal, etc. where about a dozen people were all discoursing about Sheppard, and nothing else was talk'd on whilst I staid amongst them. I had tyed an handkerchief about my head, tore my woollen cap in many places, as likewise my coat and stockings, and look'd exactly like what I designed to represent, a beggar-fellow.

The next day I took shelter at an ale-house of little or no trade, in Rupert-Street, near Piccadilly. The woman and I discours'd much about Sheppard. I assur'd her it was impossible for him to escape out of the kingdom, and that the keepers would have him again in a few days. The woman wish'd that a curse might fall on those who should betray him. I continued there till the evening, when I stept towards the Hay-market, and mixt with a crowd about two ballad-singers; the subject being about Sheppard. And I remember the company was very merry about the matter.

On Tuesday I hired a garret for my lodging at a poor house in Newport-Market, and sent for a sober young woman,[1] who for a long time past had been the real mistress of my affections, who came to me, and render'd all the assistance she was capable of affording. I made her the messenger to my mother, who lodg'd in Clare-street. She likewise visited me in a day or two after, begging on her bended knees of me to make the best of my way out of the kingdom, which

---

[1] Kate Keys, whose testimony at her trial in December 1725 shows her to be anything but. 'With a vulgar double entendre,' states the trial record, she added 'that she was Jack Sheppard's washer-woman, and had many a time washed his three pieces betwixt her legs.'

I faithfully promis'd; but I cannot say it was in my intentions heartily so to do.

I was oftentimes in Spittle-fields, Drury-lane, Lewkenors-lane, Parkers-lane, St Thomas-Street, etc. those having been the chief scenes of my rambles and pleasures.

I had once form'd a design to have open'd a shop or two in Monmouth-street for some necessaries, but let that drop, and came to a resolution of breaking the house of the two Mr Rawlins's brothers and pawn-broker in Drury-lane, which accordingly I put in execution, and succeeded; they both hearing me rifling their goods as they lay in bed together in the next room. And though there were none others to assist me, I pretended there was, by loudly giving our directions for shooting the first person through the head that presum'd to stir: which effectually quieted them, while I carried off my booty; with part whereof on the fatal Saturday following, being the 31st of October, I made an extraordinary appearance; and from a carpenter and butcher was now transform'd into a perfect gentleman; and in company with my sweetheart aforesaid, and another young woman her acquaintance, went into the City, and were very merry together at a publick house not far from the place of my old confinement. At four that same afternoon we all pass'd under Newgate in a hackney coach, the windows drawn up, and in the evening I sent for my mother to the Sheers ale-house in Maypole Alley near Clare-Market, and with her drank three quarterns[1] of brandy; and after leaving her I drank in one place or other about the neighbourhood all the evening, till the evil hour of twelve, having been seen and known by many of my acquaintance; all of them cautioning of me, and wondering at my presumption to appear in that manner. At length my senses were quite overcome with the quantities and variety of liquors I had all the day been drinking of, which pav'd the way for my fate to meet me; and when apprehended, I do protest, I was altogether incapable of resisting, and scarce knew what they were doing to me, and had but two second-hand pistols scarce worth carrying about me.

[1] ¾ pint.

A clear and ample account have I now given of the most material transactions of my life, and do hope the same will prove a warning to all young men.

There nothing now remains. But I return my hearty thanks to the Reverend Dr Bennet, the Reverend Mr Purney, the Reverend Mr Wagstaffe, the Reverend Mr Hawkins, the Reverend Mr Flood and the Reverend Mr Edwards, for their charitable visits and assistances to me; as also my thanks to those worthy gentlemen who so generously contributed towards my support in prison.

I hope none will be so cruel as to reflect on my poor distressed mother, the unhappy parent of two miserable wretches, my self and brother; the last gone to America for his crimes, and my self going to the grave for mine; the weight of which misfortune is sufficient surely to satisfy the malice of her enemies.

I beseech the Infinite Divine Being of Beings to pardon my numberless and enormous crimes, and to have mercy on my poor departing soul.

Middle-Stone-Room in
Newgate, Novem. 10.
1724.   John Sheppard

POSTSCRIPT

After I had escap'd from the Castle, concluding that Blueskin would have certainly been decreed for death, I did fully resolve and purpose to have gone and cut down the gallows the night before his execution.

MARY YOUNG (JENNY DIVER) *Convicted of robbery, and hanged in 1740*
From Knapp and Baldwin's *Newgate Calendar*

Mary Young, or Jenny Diver as she was more commonly known, was the most skilled pickpocket of her generation. Gay used her name for one of Macheath's loose women in The Beggar's Opera; *'diver' was also a cant word for a prostitute. She enjoyed a long career, twice returning from North America where she had been transported as punishment instead of execution, before eventually being arrested for trying to rob a woman on the street of thirteen shillings and a penny – her intended victim felt Diver's hand in her pocket and was able to grab her gown. She was taken to Tyburn in a coach instead of a wagon, an unusual mark of respect, and died repentant and newly religious.*

MARY YOUNG, *ALIAS* JENNY DIVER, EXECUTED FOR STREET ROBBERY

We cannot expect to present to our readers a character more skilled in the various arts of imposition and robbery than that of Mary Young. Her depredations, executed with the courage of a man and the softer deceptions of an artful female, surpass any thing which we have as yet come to, in our researches into crimes and punishments.

Mary Young was born in the north of Ireland: her parents were in indigent circumstances; and they dying while she was in a state of infancy, she had no recollection of them.

At about ten years of age she was taken into the family of an ancient gentlewoman, who had known her father and mother, and who caused her to be instructed in reading, writing and needle-work; and in the latter she attained to a proficiency unusual to girls of her age.

Soon after she had arrived at her fifteenth year, a young man, servant to a gentleman who lived in the same neighborhood, made pretensions of love to her; but the old lady, being apprized of his views, declared that she would not consent to their marriage, and positively forbade him to repeat his visits at her house.

Notwithstanding the great care and tenderness with which she was treated, Mary formed the resolution of deserting her generous benefactor, and of directing her course towards the metropolis of England; and the only obstacle to this design was the want of money for her support till she could follow some honest means of earning a subsistence.

She had no strong prepossession in favour of the young man who had made a declaration of love to her; but, determining to make his passion subservient to the purpose she had conceived, promised to marry him on condition of his taking her to London. He joyfully embraced this proposal, and immediately engaged for a passage in a vessel bound for Liverpool.

A short time before the vessel was to sail the young man robbed his master of a gold watch and eighty guineas, and then joined the companion of his flight, who was already on board the ship, vainly imagining that his infamously acquired booty would contribute to the happiness he should enjoy with his expected bride. The ship arrived at the destined port in two days; and Mary being indisposed in consequence of her voyage, her companion hired a lodging in the least frequented part of the town, where they lived a short time in the character of man and wife, but avoiding all intercourse with their neighbours, the man being apprehensive that measures would be pursued for rendering him amenable to justice.

Mary being restored to health, they agreed for a passage in a waggon that was to set out for London in a few days. On the day preceding that fixed for their departure they accidentally called at a public house, and the man being observed by a messenger dispatched in pursuit of him from Ireland, he was immediately taken into custody. Mary, who, a few hours before his apprehension, had received ten guineas from him, voluntarily accompanied him to the mayor's house, where he acknowledged himself guilty of the crime alleged against him, but without giving the least intimation that she was an accessary in his guilt. He being committed to prison, Mary sent him all his clothes, and part of the money she had received from him, and the next day took her place in the waggon for London. In a short time her companion was sent to Ireland, where he was tried, and condemned to suffer death; but his sentence was changed to that of transportation.

Soon after her arrival in London Mary contracted an acquaintance with one of her countrywomen, named Anne Murphy, by whom she was invited to partake of a lodging in Long Acre. Here she endeavored to obtain a livelihood by her needle; but, not being able to procure sufficient employment, in a little time her situation became truly deplorable.

Murphy intimated to her that she could introduce her to a mode of life that would prove exceedingly lucrative; adding, that the most profound secrecy was required. The other expressed an anxious desire of learning the means of extricating herself from the difficulties under which she labored, and made a solemn declaration that she would never divulge what Murphy should communicate. In the evening, Murphy introduced her to a number of men and women, assembled in a kind of club, near St Giles's. These people gained their living by cutting off women's pockets, and stealing watches, etc. from men, in the avenues of the theatres, and at other places of public resort; and, on the recommendation of Murphy, they admitted Mary a member of the society.

After Mary's admission they dispersed, in order to pursue their illegal occupation; and the booty obtained that night consisted of eighty pounds in cash, and a valuable gold watch. As Mary was not yet acquainted with the art of thieving, she was not admitted to an equal share of the night's produce; but it was agreed that she should have ten guineas. She now regularly applied two hours every day in qualifying herself for an expert thief, by attending to the instructions of experienced practitioners; and, in a short time, she was distinguished as the most ingenious and successful adventurer of the whole gang.

A young fellow of genteel appearance, who was a member of the club, was singled out by Mary as the partner of her bed; and they cohabited for a considerable time as husband and wife.

In a few months our heroine became so expert in her profession as to acquire great consequence among her associates, who, as we conceive, distinguished her by the appellation of Jenny Diver on account of her remarkable dexterity; and by that name we shall call her in the succeeding pages of this narrative.

Jenny, accompanied by one of her female accomplices, joined the crowd at the entrance of a place of worship in the Old Jewry, where a popular divine was to preach, and, observing a young gentleman with a diamond ring on his finger, she held out her hand, which he kindly received in order to assist her: at this juncture she contrived to get possession of the ring without the knowledge of the owner; after which she slipped behind her companion, and heard the gentleman say, that, as there was no probability of gaining admittance, he would return. Upon his leaving the meeting he missed his ring, and mentioned his loss to the persons who were near him, adding that he suspected it to be stolen by a woman whom he had endeavoured to assist in the crowd; but, as the thief was unknown, she escaped.

The above robbery was considered as such an extraordinary proof of Jenny's superior address, that her associates determined to allow her an equal share of all their booties, even though she was not present when they were obtained.

In a short time after the above exploit she procured a pair of false hands and arms to be made, and concealed her real ones under her clothes; she then, putting something beneath her stays to make herself appear as if in a state of pregnancy, repaired on a Sunday evening to the place of worship above mentioned in a sedan chair, one of the gang going before to procure a seat among the genteeler part of the congregation, and another attending in the character of a footman.

Jenny being seated between two elderly ladies, each of whom had a gold watch by her side, she conducted herself with great seeming devotion; but, the service being nearly concluded, she seized the opportunity, when the ladies were standing up, of stealing their watches, which she delivered to an accomplice in an adjoining pew. The devotions being ended, the congregation were preparing to depart, when the ladies discovered their loss, and a violent clamour ensued. One of the injured parties exclaimed 'That her watch must have been taken either by the devil or the pregnant woman!' on which the other said, 'She could vindicate the pregnant lady, whose hands she was sure had not been removed from her lap during the whole time of her being in the pew.'

Flushed with the success of the above adventure, our heroine determined to pursue her good fortune; and, as another sermon was to be preached the same evening, she adjourned to an adjacent public house, where, without either pain or difficulty, she soon reduced the protuberance of her waist, and, having entirely changed her dress, she returned to the meeting, where she had not remained long before she picked a gentleman's pocket of a gold watch, with which she escaped unsuspected.

Her accomplices also were industrious and successful; for, on a division of the booty obtained this evening, they each received thirty guineas. Jenny had now obtained an ascendency over the whole gang, who, conscious of her superior skill in the arts of thieving, came to a resolution of yielding an exact obedience to her directions.

Jenny again assumed the appearance of a pregnant woman, and, attended by an accomplice as a footman, went towards St James's Park on a day when the king was going to the House of Lords; and, there being a great number of persons between the Park and Spring Gardens, she purposely slipped down, and was instantly surrounded by many of both sexes, who were emulous to afford her assistance; but, affecting to be in violent pain, she intimated to them that she was desirous of remaining on the ground till she should be somewhat recovered. As she expected, the crowd increased, and her pretended footman, and a female accomplice, were so industrious as to obtain two diamond girdle-buckles, a gold watch, a gold snuff-box and two purses, containing together upwards of forty guineas.

The girdle-buckles, watch and snuff-box, were the following day advertised, a considerable reward was offered, and a promise given that no questions should be asked the party who should restore the property. Anne Murphy offered to carry the things to the place mentioned in the advertisement, saying the reward offered exceeded what they would produce by sale: but to this Jenny objected, observing that she might be traced, and the association utterly ruined. She called a meeting of the whole gang, and informed them that she was of opinion that it would be more prudent to sell the things, even at one half of their real value, than to return them to the owners for the sake of the reward; as, if they pursued the latter measure, they would subject themselves to great hazard of being apprehended. Her associates coincided entirely in Jenny's sentiments, and the property was taken to Duke's Place,[1] and there sold to a Jew.

Two of the gang being confined to their lodgings by illness, Jenny, and the man with whom she cohabited, generally went in company in search of adventures. They went together to Burr Street, Wapping, and, observing a genteel house, the man, who acted as Jenny's footman, knocked at the door, and, saying that his mistress was on a sudden taken extremely ill, begged she might be admitted: this was readily complied with, and, while the mistress of the house and her maid-servant were gone up stairs for such things as they imagined would afford relief to the supposed sick woman, she opened a drawer, and stole sixty guineas; and after this, while the mistress was holding a smelling-bottle to her nose, she picked her pocket of a purse, which, however, did not contain money to any considerable amount. In the mean time the pretended footman, who had been ordered into the kitchen, stole six silver table-spoons, a pepper-box and a salt-cellar. Jenny, pretending to be somewhat recovered, expressed the most grateful acknowledgments to the lady, and, saying she was the wife of a capital merchant in Thames Street, invited her in the most pressing terms to dinner on an appointed day, and then went away in a hackney-coach, which, by her order, had been called to the door by her pretended servant.

She practised a variety of felonies of a similar nature in different parts of the metropolis and its environs; but the particulars of the above transaction being inserted in the newspapers, people were so effectually cautioned, that our adventurer was under the necessity of employing her invention upon the discovery of other methods of committing depredations on the public.

The parties whose illness we have mentioned being recovered, it was resolved that the whole gang should go to Bristol, in search of adventures, during the fair which is held in that city every summer; but, being unacquainted with the place, they deemed it good policy

---

[1] A poor area on the site of the ruined old Holy Trinity Place in the City.

to admit into their society a man who had long subsisted there by villainous practices.

Being arrived at the place of destination, Jenny and Murphy assumed the characters of merchants' wives, the new member and another of the gang appeared as country traders and our heroine's favorite retained his former character of footman. They took lodgings at different inns, and agreed that, if any of them should be apprehended, the others should endeavor to procure their release by appearing to their characters, and representing them as people of reputation in London. They had arrived at such a proficiency in their illegal occupation, that they were almost certain of accomplishing every scheme they suggested; and, when it was inconvenient to make use of words, they were able to convey their meaning to each other by winks, nods and other intimations.

Being one day in the fair, they observed a west-country clothier giving a sum of money to his servant, and heard him direct the man to deposit it in a bureau. They followed the servant, and one of them fell down before him, expecting that he would also fall, and that, as there was a great crowd, the money might be easily secured. Though the man fell into the snare, they were not able to obtain their expected booty, and therefore had recourse to the following stratagem: one of the gang asked whether his master had not lately ordered him to carry home a sum of money; to which the other replied in the affirmative: the sharper[1] then told him he must return to his master, who had purchased some goods, and waited to pay for them.

The countryman followed him to Jenny's lodging, and, being introduced to her, she desired him to be seated, saying his master was gone on some business in the neighborhood, but had left orders for him to wait till his return. She urged him to drink a glass of wine, but the poor fellow repeatedly declined her offers with awkward simplicity, the pretended footman having taught him to believe her a woman of great wealth and consequence. However, her encouraging solicitations conquered his bashfulness, and he drank till he became intoxicated. Being

[1] con man.

conducted into another apartment, he was soon fast locked in the arms of sleep, and, while in that situation, he was robbed of the money he had received from his master, which proved to be a hundred pounds. They were no sooner in possession of the cash, than they discharged the demand of the innkeeper, and set out in the first stage for London.

Soon after their return to town Jenny and her associates went to London Bridge in the dusk of the evening, and, observing a lady standing at a door to avoid the carriages, a number of which were passing, one of the men went up to her, and, under pretence of giving her assistance, seized both her hands, which he held till his accomplices had rifled her pockets of a gold snuff-box, a silver case containing a set of instruments and thirty guineas in cash.

On the following day, as Jenny, and an accomplice, in the character of a footman, were walking through Change Alley, she picked a gentleman's pocket of a bank-note for two hundred pounds, for which she received one hundred and thirty from a Jew, with whom the gang had very extensive connexions.

Our heroine now hired a real footman; and her favorite, who had long acted in that character, assumed the appearance of a gentleman. She hired lodgings in the neighborhood of Covent Garden, that she might more conveniently attend the theatres. She proposed to her associates to reserve a tenth part of the general produce for the support of such of the gang as might, through illness, be rendered incapable of following their iniquitous occupations; and to this they readily assented.

Jenny dressed herself in an elegant manner, and went to the theatre one evening when the king was to be present; and, during the performance, she attracted the particular attention of a young gentleman of fortune from Yorkshire, who declared, in the most passionate terms, that she had made an absolute conquest of his heart, and earnestly solicited the favour of attending her home. She at first declined a compliance, saying she was newly married, and that the appearance of a stranger might alarm her husband. At length she yielded to his entreaty, and they went together in a hackney-coach, which set the young gentleman down in the neighborhood where

Jenny lodged, after he had obtained an appointment to visit her in a few days, when she said her husband would be out of town.

Upon Jenny's joining her companions, she informed them that while she remained at the play-house she was only able to steal a gold snuff-box, and they appeared to be much dissatisfied on account of her ill success; but their good humour returned upon learning the circumstances of the adventure with the young gentleman, which they had no doubt would prove exceedingly profitable.

The day of appointment being arrived, two of the gang appeared equipped in elegant liveries, and Anne Murphy acted as waiting-maid. The gentleman came in the evening, having a gold-headed cane in his hand, a sword with a gold hilt by his side, and wearing a gold watch in his pocket, and a diamond ring on his finger.

Being introduced to her bed-chamber, she contrived to steal her lover's ring; and he had not been many minutes undressed before Anne Murphy rapped at the door, which being opened, she said, with an appearance of the utmost consternation, that her master was returned from the country. Jenny, affecting to be under a violent agitation of spirits, desired the gentleman to cover himself entirely with the bed-clothes, saying she would convey his apparel into another room, so that, if her husband came there, nothing would appear to awaken his suspicion; adding, that under pretence of indisposition she would prevail upon her husband to sleep in another bed, and then return to the arms of her lover.

The clothes being removed, a consultation was held, when it was agreed by the gang that they should immediately pack up all their moveables, and decamp with their booty, which, exclusive of the cane, watch, sword and ring, amounted to a hundred guineas.

The amorous youth waited in a state of the utmost impatience till morning, when he rang the bell, which brought the people of the house to the chamber-door; but they could not gain admittance, the fair fugitive having turned the lock, and taken away the key; but, the door being forced open, an eclaircissement[1] ensued. The gentleman

---

[1] an enlightening explanation.

represented in what manner he had been treated; but the people of the house were deaf to his expostulations, and threatened to circulate the adventure throughout the town unless he would indemnify them for the loss they had sustained. Rather than hazard the exposure of his character he agreed to discharge the debt Jenny had contracted; and dispatched a messenger for clothes and money, that he might take leave of a house of which he had sufficient reason to regret having been a temporary inhabitant.

Our heroine's share of the produce of the above adventure amounted to seventy pounds. This infamous association was now become so notorious a pest to society, that they judged it necessary to leave the metropolis, where they were apprehensive they could not long remain concealed from justice. They practised a variety of stratagems with great success in different parts of the country; but, upon re-visiting London, Jenny was committed to Newgate on a charge of having picked a gentleman's pocket; for which she was sentenced to transportation.

She remained in the above prison nearly four months, during which time she employed a considerable sum in the purchase of stolen effects. When she went on board the transport-vessel, she shipped a quantity of goods nearly sufficient to load a waggon. The property she possessed ensured her great respect, and every possible convenience and accommodation during the voyage; and, on her arrival in Virginia, she disposed of her goods, and for some time lived in great splendour and elegance.

She soon found that America was a country where she could expect but little emolument from the practices she had so successfully followed in England; and therefore she employed every art she was mistress of to ingratiate herself into the esteem of a young gentleman who was preparing to embark on board a vessel bound for the port of London. He became much enamoured of her, and brought her to England; but, while the ship lay at Gravesend, she robbed him of all the property she could get into her possession, and, pretending indisposition, intimated a desire of going on shore, in which her admirer acquiesced; but she was no sooner on land than she made a precipitate retreat.

‖ ANN FLYNN *Convicted of robbery, and fined in 1750*
‖ From Knapp and Baldwin's *Newgate Calendar*

This is one of the few cases in which the judge and jury act with compassion, interpreting the law leniently to be merciful to a pitiful defendant. (The entry is given in full.)

Ann Flynn was indicted at the Old Bailey, for stealing from a butcher in Whitechapel, a shoulder of mutton. It appeared in evidence, that the prosecutor being busy with his customers, on a Saturday night, the prisoner availed herself of that opportunity, and carried away the shoulder of mutton. She was, however, soon seized and brought back; and, an officer being sent for, she was carried before a Magistrate, and committed for trial. These facts being proved, the prisoner was called upon for her defence; and she told a tale of woe, that penetrated every heart: she acknowledged the robbery; but solemnly declared, she was urged to it by the most afflicting distress. Her husband had been ill, and unable to earn a shilling for twelve weeks; and she was driven to the last extremity, with two infant children. In that deplorable situation, continued the unfortunate woman, while the tears ran down her wan cheeks, she desperately snatched the shoulder of mutton, and for which she had already been confined five weeks.

The jury found her guilty, with a faultering accent; and the Recorder immediately replied, 'Gentlemen, I understand you'; and he sentenced her to be fined only one shilling and discharged, which the jury themselves paid, but the officer of the prison gave it to her.

This case, if the extremity of the law had been resorted to, was felony.

As soon as she was taken away, the prosecutor addressed the Court, and said, that the constable had done him more injury than the thief! for though Sir William Parsons, the magistrate that committed her, had ordered him to take care of the shoulder of mutton, *he thought fit to cook it for his own dinner, and to sit down and eat it.*

[This new complaint, as might naturally be supposed, excited, not a little, the risible muscles of the Court.]

The constable was immediately called upon to account for his conduct, who said, 'My Lord, I did take care of it, as ordered; I kept it whilst it was worth keeping, and if my wife and I had not eat it, the dogs must have dined on it.'

WILLIAM COX *Convicted of robbery, and hanged in 1773*
From Knapp and Baldwin's *Newgate Calendar*

Cox's innovative methods of stealing recall Jenny Diver's false arms and fake pregnancy. The express association of Cox's fate with that of his father, also a thief, and the emphasis on a childhood without parental support, show an early awareness of the importance of upbringing in forming criminals but without any sense of the need for social change to bring down crime rates. (The entry is given in full.)

WILLIAM COX,
EXECUTED FOR PRIVATELY STEALING

This most expert thief was initiated into all the arts of plunder and deception, at a very early period of life, by his own father!

The elder Cox had long been a robber in all the various degrees and characters assumed for that purpose. He had been transported, and for returning before the expiration of his sentence he was executed.

Of the old sinner we shall here adduce but one instance of his depravity towards his son, the immediate subject of this memoir.

The father and his son passing through Grosvenor Street, the former observed a silver tankard in a window, and attempted to steal it; but, being prevented by the iron rails of the area, he lifted the boy over them, ordering him to take the tankard, which he immediately handed to his father, who lifted him back into the street.

The father, as we have already observed, having been transported, young Cox was left to depredate on his own account; and, as usual, with other wicked habits, he began by picking pockets; but was soon apprehended, and committed to Bridewell, where he was reduced to a most miserable degree of poverty; but he no sooner obtained his liberty than he procured decent apparel, and was from that time remarkably clean and neat in his appearance.

Cox lived some years at the house of his uncle, West, in Feathers' Court, High Holborn, who encouraged him to pursue those illegal courses which led to his destruction.

He got unperceived into a grocer's, the corner of Long Lane, in Aldersgate Street, and stole a silver-hilted sword from a room on the first floor. Returning through the shop with his booty, he was asked some questions; on which he said he had been playing with Master Billy, which he had informed himself was the name of the grocer's son; but on going out of the shop the sword struck against the steps, and he was taken into custody, and brought to trial, but it was his fortune to escape conviction.

Being provided with a tame sparrow, he let the bird fly into a window of a house in Hanover Street, and, the door happening to be open, he went in, and concealed plate to a considerable amount. Hearing some person walking towards the room, he sought refuge in the area, where being perceived by an elderly gentlewoman, who was the only person in the house, he burst into tears, and, saying his sparrow had flown into the window, requested he might be allowed to catch it. The old lady complied, and he soon found an opportunity of decamping with his booty.

It was the common practice of Cox to play at marbles and other games with young gentlemen before the doors of their parents, and he seldom suffered an opportunity to escape of getting into and robbing the houses. He had a very remarkable boyish appearance; and on a variety of occasions that circumstance greatly assisted him in pursuit of his felonious designs.

So childish, in fact, was his appearance (for he was very short and slender for his years), that sometimes he provided himself with marbles, and, dressing himself like young master, he would ask to play with gentlemen's children, whom he might observe, in the environs of London, amusing themselves in their father's court-yard. Thus he would insidiously get every information from the innocent and unsuspicious boys, and repay their little acts of hospitality by plundering the houses of their parents.

Cox was connected with a notorious thief, who called himself Captain Davis; and, by means of the most artful stratagems that could be suggested, these accomplices perpetrated a surprising number of robberies. Davis was at length apprehended, and sentenced to suffer death; but he was reprieved on condition of transportation.

About the middle of the summer, 1773, the apartments of Mr Kendrick, in Oxford Street, were privately entered, and a bureau was opened, and three bank-notes, of a hundred pounds each, and a hundred and thirty guineas and a silver watch, were stolen, to the amount of four hundred and forty pounds. Soon after Mr Kendrick's robbery Cox and William Claxton went together to Reading, in Berkshire, and there purchased three horses, for which Claxton paid with one of the notes stolen from Mr Kendrick, receiving in part of change a fifty-pound bank-note, which he afterwards changed at the bank for notes of smaller value, two of which were found in the possession of West, Cox's uncle. On the first examination of these offenders at the public office in Bow Street, which was on Wednesday, the 11th day of August, West said he received the notes of his wife on the day preceding that of her decease, which was about the time of Mr Kendrick's robbery; but, on the following Wednesday, he assured the magistrates that the notes had been in his possession three years. In contradiction to this it was proved that the notes had not been many days issued from the bank.

Mr Knapp and Mr White, of Reading, appeared, and the fifty-pound note, given in part of change of that of a hundred, was regularly traced from the hands of Claxton to the bank, where he had changed it for others of smaller value. West was discharged, the receiving of notes, which are the produce of other notes feloniously obtained, not coming under the description of the law; and Claxton was admitted as evidence against Cox, who was committed for trial at the ensuing sessions at the Old Bailey.

The evidence against Cox was chiefly circumstantial; but it was of such a nature as to be almost as strong as positive proof, and on that evidence he was capitally convicted.

Finding the end of his career fast approaching, Cox began to prepare himself for eternity. He was executed, as we have already stated, at Tyburn, October the 27th, 1773, along with four more unhappy men, who excited much commiseration from the spectators.

GEORGE BARRINGTON *Convicted of theft, and sentenced to five years' hard labour in 1773*
From Knapp and Baldwin's *Newgate Calendar*

Barrington was unusual in that he was an educated, middle-class man – a surgeon – convicted of theft. He seems to have realized that his genteel bearing made him unthreatening, and this combined with the poker-face required to front out stealing from people in places like the House of Commons made him a successful thief. Barrington's appearance benefited him after he was arrested too – he was able to persuade the court to transmute his sentence from hanging to transportation to hard labour. (The entry is given in full.)

AN ACCOUNT OF THAT REMARKABLE OFFENDER, GEORGE BARRINGTON, WHO WAS CONVICTED OF STEALING A METAL WATCH FROM THE PERSON OF ELIZABETH IRONMONGER, ON THE 15TH OF MARCH 1778

Barrington was convicted of stealing a watch from a lady in the pit of one of the theatres, and sentenced to labour three years on the

Thames. When about a year of the time had expired, he procured a petition to be presented to the court, praying that the remaining part of his sentence might be remitted: and the officers of the Justitia hulk made so favourable a report of his behaviour, that, some time after, an order was sent to Mr Campbell for his releasement.

A few days after Barrington's releasement, he went to St Sepulchre's church, when Doctor Mylne was to preach a sermon for the benefit of the society for the recovery of persons apparently drowned. William Payne, a constable, saw him put his hand into a lady's pocket in the south aisle, and presently after followed him out of the church, and took him into custody near the end of Cock-lane upon Snow-hill. Having taken the prisoner to St Sepulchre's watch-house, and found a gold watch and some other articles in his possession; Payne returned to the church, and spoke to the lady whom he had seen the prisoner attempt to rob; and she informed him that she had lost nothing, for, expecting the church to be much crowded, she had taken the precaution of emptying her pockets before leaving her house.

Upon Payne's return to the watch-house, a gentleman advised that the prisoner might be more strictly searched. He was desired to take off his hat, and, raising his left arm, he cautiously removed his hat from his head, when a metal watch dropped upon the floor. He was now obliged to pull off the greatest part of his cloaths. He wore three pairs of breeches, in one of the pockets of which was found a purse, containing thirteen guineas, and a bank-note for £10, made payable to himself.

In consequence of an advertisement inserted the next day in the newspapers, Mrs Ironmonger came to Payne's house, and described the watch she had lost; and it proved to be that which had been concealed in Barrington's hair, and dropped on the floor when he took off his hat. She attended the examination of the prisoner, and, having sworn that the watch produced by Payne was her property, was bound over to prosecute.

Upon his trial, Barrington made a long, an artful and a plausible defence. He said that, upon leaving the church, he perceived the watch mentioned in the indictment laying upon the ground, and took it up, intending to advertise it the next day; that he was followed to Snow-hill by Payne and another constable, who apprehended him, and had, in all probability, seen him take up the watch. 'I reflected (said he) that how innocently soever I might have obtained the article in question, yet it might cause some censure; and no man would wonder, considering the unhappy predicament I stood in,[1] that I should conceal it as much as possible.'

The jury having pronounced the prisoner guilty, he addressed the court, earnestly supplicating that he might be permitted to enter into his majesty's service, and promising to discharge his trust with fidelity and attention; or, if he could not be indulged in that request, he wished that his sentence might be banishment for life from his majesty's dominions. The court informed him, that, by an application to the throne, he might obtain a mitigation of his sentence, if his case was attended by such circumstances of extenuation as would justify him in humbly petitioning to be considered as an object of the royal favour. He requested that the money and bank-note might be returned. Hereupon the court observed, that, in consequence of his conviction, the property found on him when he was apprehended became vested in the hands of the sheriffs of the city of London, who had discretionary powers either to comply with, or reject, his request.

George Barrington was convicted to labour on the Thames for the space of five years, on Tuesday the 5th of April 1778.

Barrington was by profession a surgeon; and his education, abilities and address, were such, that, had they been properly employed, would certainly have introduced him to a genteel competency, and a reputable station in life. He was early attached to dissipation and extravagance, to which the earnings of honest industry proving greatly unequal, he had recourse to felonious practices, for the means of indulging his insatiable desire of engaging in scenes of gaiety and fashionable amusement. Barrington seems to have had a natural taste for dress, in which particular he was never beneath gentility, but frequently bordering upon elegance. His appearance gained him ready

[1] Having previously been convicted of theft.

admission to the most respectable public assemblies; and he was a frequent visitor in the galleries of both houses of parliament.

Count Orlow, the Russian minister, being in one of the boxes of Drury-lane play-house, was robbed of a gold snuff-box set with diamonds, estimated to be worth an immense sum; and one of the count's attendants, inspecting Barrington, seized him, and found the snuff-box in his possession. He was examined by Sir John Fielding, but the count, being in a foreign country, was influenced by motives of delicacy to decline a prosecution.

Some time after the above circumstance, a gentleman observed Barrington in the house of lords, and pointed him out to Philip Quarme Esquire, deputy usher of the black rod, who insisted upon his immediately quitting the house, assuring him that his attendance in parliament would, for the future, be dispensed with. We have not heard that he disputed Mr Quarme's power of expulsion, or that, after the disgrace he sustained from the strong arm of authority, he made any attempt to gain a seat in either house . . .

How strange is it that, after having experienced the intolerable severities to which offenders sentenced to labour on the Thames are exposed, Barrington should return to his former illegal courses! The horror he expressed upon being subjected to the same kind of punishment for a longer time, we hope will deter others from following his iniquitous example. To be deprived of all the comforts, conveniences and almost, the very necessaries of life – to be cut off from all communication with the rest of mankind – to be condemned to hard, and almost incessant labour – to be exposed, in the most degrading situation, to which human nature can possibly be reduced, to public curiosity and public reproach – is a punishment of such extreme severity, that the dread of feeling its complicated miseries we should think sufficient to enforce a due obedience to the laws.

SARAH STANLEY *Convicted of petty larceny, and released in 1796*
From Knapp and Baldwin's *Newgate Calendar*

Like Mary Read and Anne Bonny (see 'Pirates'), Sarah Stanley seems to have found more freedom living as a man. She was discharged honourably from the army, avoiding the unpleasantness and accusations that might have arisen from this situation, a testament to her ability to interact well with men as a man. As with the case of Ann Flynn, the court looked mercifully upon Stanley's predicament; women, considered the weaker sex, were treated gently more often than men. (The entry is given in full.)

SARAH PENELOPE STANLEY,
(The Female Trooper,)
CONVICTED AT THE OLD BAILEY, IN OCTOBER SESSIONS, 1796, OF PETTY LARCENY

This female warrior was born at Mercival-hall, in Warwickshire, the seat of Mr Stratford, to whom her father was steward, whose name was Brindley. She was put apprentice to a milliner at Lichfield, and married to a shoe-maker. Her husband being an idle dissolute fellow, they were reduced to very indigent circumstances. She left him to come to London. Having had a good education, and writing an excellent hand, she put on men's apparel, and for some time wrote for gentlemen in the Commons; but meeting with a recruiting serjeant at Westminster, she engaged to serve in a regiment of light horse, then raising, called the Ayrshire Fencible Cavalry. She served upwards of a year with great credit to herself, and was promoted to the rank of corporal; rode extremely well, and had the care of two horses; but was discovered at Carlisle to be a woman, when she was honourably discharged, after many marks of friendship shewn her, not only by Major Horsley, in whose troop she rode, but by the other officers, and many of the inhabitants of Carlisle. She came to town, was much reduced, and through mere necessity, stole the cloak for which she was tried and convicted. – She acknowledged her crime, said it was the first offence of the kind she had committed, and meant to make satisfaction. The court passed a slight sentence upon her, and she was discharged from Newgate. The two under-sheriffs, and the keeper, gave her some money to provide her a few necessaries, and she left the court, promising henceforward to seek an honest livelihood, in the proper habit of her sex. She was a masculine looking woman of about 30 years of age.

5

Pirates

WILLIAM KIDD *Convicted of piracy, and hanged in 1701*
From the trial records *The Trial of Captain Kidd*,
ed. G. Brooks (London, 1930), and 'Captain Kid's Farewel
to the Seas, or, the Famous Pirate's Lament, 1701',
W. H. Bonner, *Pirate Laureate* (New Brunswick, Maine,
1947)

Captain Kidd was a respected and respectable middle-aged family man making a successful living as a sea-captain in New York when he was hired by William III in 1695 as a government-commissioned privateer, and soon after authorized to seize 'pirates, free-booters and sea-rovers of what nature soever' in the name of the British government. The King referred to him as his 'beloved friend, William Kidd'. A year later, Kidd's ship, the Adventure, *committed its first act of piracy off the Malabar Coast of India; this was reported to the English government in November 1698, and a warrant was issued for Kidd's arrest. In July 1699, protesting his innocence, Kidd handed himself in to the British authorities in Boston, represented by the Earl of Bellomont – who had been a private backer of Kidd's expedition three years earlier. Kidd claimed that his men had mutinied and forced him to lead them in acts of piracy; his cause divided MPs and public opinion with many believing, as Kidd insisted, that there had been a miscarriage of justice. But although there were accusations that the Admiralty had suppressed evidence in Kidd's favour, and it was clear that the trial against Kidd in the House of Commons was intended to inculpate his important backers as well as him, Kidd's demeanour on the witness stand did him no favours. Said one MP: 'I had thought him only a knave. I now know him to be a fool as well.' He was convicted of murder (of one of his crew, William Moore) and piracy on 9 May 1701 and hanged at Execution Dock, Wapping, the usual place of death for pirates. The rope broke, and Kidd, still conscious but very drunk, fell to the ground before being strung up again amid the exhortations of the Ordinary for him to confess and repent.*

Testimony of Robert Bradinham, surgeon on board the Adventure
Galley, *the ship outfitted by Kidd with Bellomont &c's money, in the
House of Commons, on 9 May 1701, in the trial of Captain William
Kidd for piracy and robbery.*

Kidd's first acts of piracy:
Some time in the year 1696, about the beginning of May, I and others
were with Captain Kidd, and we sailed from Plymouth, designing for
New York. We went with Captain Kidd in the *Adventure Galley*, and
there were about 70 or 80 men aboard the ship, which had thirty
guns. Captain Kidd was the commander of this ship. In May 1696,
we left Plymouth, and went to New York, and on the way met with
the French ship, and took her. When we came to New York Captain
Kidd put up articles that if any men would enter themselves on board
his ship they should have their shares of what should be taken; and
he himself was to have forty shares. He carried away from New York
155 men. From New York we sailed to the Madeiras, from thence to
Bonavista, from thence to St Jago, from thence to Madagascar, from
thence to Johanna, from thence to Mohilla, from Mohilla to Johanna
again, and from thence to the Red Sea; and there we waited for the
Mocha fleet. They passed us one night, and we pursued them, and
went among them, but he found they were too strong for him, and
was fain to leave them. We lay in wait for that fleet for about a
fortnight or three weeks. As far as I know, Captain Kidd did not lie
in wait for any French effects in that fleet, but only for the Moorish
fleet. By the Moorish fleet I mean the natives of India, the Mahometans.
Kidd said he intended to make a voyage out of them. We lay in the
mouth of the Red Sea, where several sail of ships may lie. During the
first night there Captain Kidd sent his boat three times to Mocha,
to see if they could make any discovery. The two first times they
could make none; but the third time they brought word that
fourteen or fifteen ships were ready to sail. Accordingly they came,
and we sailed after them, and fell in with them, and Captain Kidd
fired at them. What colours the boats had I cannot tell. When Captain
Kidd had fetched them up, he found they were under convoy, and

so he left them. Captain Kidd fired divers guns at the Mocha fleet.

After we left the Mocha fleet we set sail for the Malabar coast, and on the way we took a ship that Captain Parker was commander of, between Carawar and the Red Sea. She was a Moorish ship; she came from Bombay, and Captain Parker was the master. Captain Kidd took out Parker, and a Portuguese for a linguister. By linguister I mean an interpreter. Kidd also took out of her a bale of coffee, a bale of pepper, about twenty pieces of Arabian gold, and ordered some men to be taken and hoisted up by their arms, and drubbed with a naked cutlace. He did this to make them confess what money they had. The men whom he treated thus were not Frenchmen, but Moors. While we were at Carawar the English factory sent for Captain Parker and the Portuguese, but Kidd denied that he had any such persons on board, for he kept them in the hold. Then we went to sea, and that night we met with a Portuguese man of war. The next morning we came up with her, and the Portuguese first fired at Captain Kidd, and he at him again; they fought four or five hours. Captain Kidd had ten men wounded.

We then went to the coast of Malabar, to one of the Malabar Islands for wood and water, and Captain Kidd went ashore, with several of his men. He plundered several boats, burnt several houses and ordered one of the natives to be tied to a tree, and one of his men to shoot him. One of Kidd's men, that was his cooper, had been ashore, and some of the natives had cut this man's throat, and that was the reason Kidd ordered his men to serve this man so. Then we came back again to the Malabar coast and cruised; and in October 1697, Kidd killed his gunner, William Moore. Some time in November Kidd took a Moorish ship belonging to Surat: there were two Dutchmen belonging to her, the rest were Moors. Captain Kidd chased this ship under French colours; and when the Dutchman saw that he put out French colours too. And Captain Kidd came up with them, and commanded them on board; and he ordered a Frenchman to come upon deck, and to pretend himself captain. So this commander comes aboard, and comes to this Monsieur Le Roy that was to pass for the captain, and he shows him a paper, and said it was a French pass. Captain Kidd said, 'By God, have I catched you? You are a free prize to England.' We took two horses, some quilts and other things, and the ship he carried to Madagascar.

In December 1697, he took a Moorish ketch; she was taken by the boat. We had one man wounded in taking of her. Our people took the vessel ashore, and Captain Kidd took out of her thirty tubs of sugar, a bale of coffee, and then he ordered the vessel to be turned adrift. On 20th January 1698, Captain Kidd took a Portuguese that came from Bengal; he took out of her two chests of opium, some East India goods and bags of rice. He kept this Portuguese ship about seven days; he kept her till he was chased by seven or eight sail of Dutch, and then he left her. Some time in January, Captain Kidd took the *Quedagh Merchant*; he gave her chase under French colours. He came up with her, and commanded the master aboard, and there came an old Frenchman in the boat. After he had been aboard a while he told Captain Kidd he was not the captain, but the gunner; and Captain Kidd sent for his captain on board his ship. He was an Englishman named Wright. He was sent for aboard, and he came; and Captain Kidd told him he was his prisoner. He ordered his men to go aboard and take possession of the ship, and disposed of the goods on that coast, to the value of £7000 or £8000. On board this ship there were Captain Wright, two Dutchmen, a Frenchman and some Armenians; the rest were Moors. Captain Kidd told the Armenians they should be ransomed if they made an offer that he liked of; so they offered him 20,000 rupees. He told them that was but a small parcel of money, and the cargo was worth a great deal more. I was informed by Captain Wright that the cargo belonged to these Armenians. Kidd sold some of the goods on the coast and shared the money out amongst the crew. Each of the prisoners at the bar had a share. Captain Wright came aboard Kidd's ship. I am sure that Captain Wright was an Englishman.

While Captain Kidd was off this part of the coast he boarded several ships, and took out of them what was for his turn. As to the people he traded with, some of them came aboard several times, and he traded with them; but some of them came aboard when he was going away, and he plundered them, and sent them ashore without any goods. These people were Mahometans. They had dealt with him before considerably. He took from them about 500 pieces of eight. I saw it told afterwards. We went to Madagascar afterwards, and by the way met with a Moorish ship, and took out of her several casks of butter, and other things . . .

When we came to Madagascar there came a canoe to us with some Englishmen in her; they were formerly acquainted with Captain Kidd, and they told him they had heard that he was come to take them and hang them. They belonged to the *Mocha Frigate*. Captain Culliford was the commander; and there were some white men in her that had formerly been acquainted with Captain Kidd. They heard that he was come to take them, and hang them. He told them it was no such thing, for he was as bad as they. They were pirates. Captain Kidd assured them it was no such thing; and afterwards went aboard with them, and swore to be true to them. He took a cup of bumbo[1] and swore to be true to them and assist them; and he assisted this Captain Culliford with guns, and an anchor, to fit him to sea again . . .

At Madagascar the goods were divided among us. When we came there Captain Kidd ordered the goods to be carried ashore, and shared; and he had forty shares himself.

> *Captain Kid's Farewel to the Seas,*
> *or,*
> *the Famous Pirate's Lament, 1701.*
>
> My name is Captain Kid, who has sail'd [who has sail'd],
> My name is Captain Kid, who has sail'd;
> My name is Captain Kid,
> What the laws did still forbid
> Unluckily I did while I sail'd [while I sail'd, etc.].
>
> Upon the ocean wide, when I sail'd, [when I sail'd],
> Upon the ocean wide, when I sail'd,

---

[1] drink of rum, water, sugar and nutmeg.

Upon the ocean wide
I robbed on every side,
With the most ambitious pride, when I sail'd.

My faults I will display while I sail'd, [while I sail'd],
My faults I will display while I sail'd,
My faults I will display,
Committed day by day
[*A line lost.*]

Many long leagues from shore when I sail'd, [when I sail'd],
Many long leagues from shore when I sail'd,
Many long leagues from shore
I murdered William Moore,
And laid him in his gore, when I sail'd.

Because a word he spoke when I sail'd, [when I sail'd],
Because a word he spoke when I sail'd,
Because a word he spoke,
I with a bucket broke
His scull at one sad stroke, when I sail'd.

I struck with a good will when I sail'd, [when I sail'd],
I struck with a good will when I sail'd,
I struck with a good will,
And did a gunner kill
As being cruel still when I sail'd.

A Quida merchant then while I sail'd, [while I sail'd],
A Quida merchant then while I sail'd,
A Quida merchant then
I robbed of hundreds ten,
Assisted by my men, while I sail'd.

A banker's ship of France, while I sail'd, [while I sail'd],
A banker's ship of France, while I sail'd,
A banker's ship of France

Before us did advance:
I seized her by chance, while I sailed.

Full fourteen ships I see when I sailed, [when I sailed],
Full fourteen ships I see when I sailed,
    Full fourteen ships I see
    Merchants of high degree;
They were too hard for me when I sailed.

We steered from sound to sound while we sailed, [while we sailed],
We steered from sound to sound while we sailed,
    We steered from sound to sound,
    A Moorish ship we found;
Her men we stripped and bound while we sailed.

Upon the ocean seas while we sailed, [while we sailed],
Upon the ocean seas while we sailed,
    Upon the ocean seas
    A warlike Portuguese
In sport did us displease, while we sailed.

At famous Malabar when we sailed, [when we sailed],
At famous Malabar when we sailed,
    At famous Malabar
    We went ashore, each tar,
And robbed the natives there, when we sailed.

Then after this we chased, while we sailed, [while we sailed],
Then after this we chased, while we sailed,
    Then after this we chased
    A rich Armenian, graced
With wealth, which we embraced, while we sailed.

Many Moorish ships we took while we sailed, [while we sailed],
Many Moorish ships we took while we sailed,
    Many Moorish ships we took;
    We did still for plunder look;

All conscience we forsook while we sailed.

I, Captain Culliford, while I sailed, [while I sailed],
I Captain Culliford, while I sailed,
    I, Captain Culliford,
    Did many merchants board,
Which did much wealth afford, while we sailed.

Two hundred bars of gold, while we sail'd, [while we sail'd],
Two hundred bars of gold, while we sail'd,
    Two hundred bars of gold
    And rix dollars manifold
We seized uncontrolled, while we sailed.

St *John*, a ship of fame, when we sailed, [when we sailed],
St *John*, a ship of fame, when we sailed,
    St *John*, a ship of fame
    We plundered when she came,
With more than I could name, when we sailed.

We taken was at last, and must die, [and must die],
We taken was at last, and must die,
    We taken were at last
    And into prison cast:
Now, sentence being past, we must die.

Tho' we have resigned while we must die, [while we must die],
Tho' we have resigned while we must die,
    Tho' we have resigned awhile,
    While fortune seemed to smile,
Now on the British isle we must die.

Farewel the ocean main, we must die, [we must die],
Farewel the ocean main, we must die,
    Farewel the ocean main:
    The coast of France or Spain
We ne'er shall see again; we must die.

From Newgate now in carts we must go, [we must go],
From Newgate now in carts we must go,
   From Newgate now in carts,
     With sad and heavy hearts,
To have our due deserts we must go.

Some thousands they will flock when we die, [when we die],
Some thousands they will flock when we die,
   Some thousands they will flock
     To Execution Dock,
Where we must stand the shock and must die.

EDWARD TEACH (BLACKBEARD) *Accused of piracy and killed in battle trying to escape arrest in 1718*
From Johnson's *Lives of the Pirates*

Edward Teach, or Blackbeard, as he was known, was the most notorious pirate of the eighteenth century who lived and died according to his own idiosyncratic rules. Born in Bristol, he sailed his ship around the Caribbean, taking sugar, rum and money from English trading boats as they headed home. The warrant for his arrest was issued in 1718 and Captain Maynard, in a boat called the Pearl, *commissioned by the Governor of North Carolina, engaged Blackbeard in a fierce battle in which Blackbeard preferred to die rather than be captured and tried.*

The 17th of *November* 1718, the Lieutenant sail'd from *Kicquetan*, in *James* River in *Virginia*, and, the 21st in the evening, came to the mouth of *Okerecock* Inlet, where he got sight of the pyrate. This expedition was made with all imaginable secrecy, and the officer manag'd with all the prudence that was necessary, stopping all boats and vessels he met with, in the river, from going up, and thereby preventing any intelligence from reaching *Black-Beard*, and receiving at the same time an account from them all, of the place where the pyrate was lurking; but notwithstanding this caution, *Black-Beard* had information of the design, from his Excellency of the province; and his secretary, Mr *Knight*, wrote him a letter, particularly concerning it, intimating, *That he had sent him four of his men, which were all he could meet with, in or about town, and so bid him be upon his guard.* These men belonged to *Black-Beard*, and were sent from *Bath-Town* to *Okerecock* Inlet, where the sloop lay, which is about twenty leagues.

Black-Beard had heard several reports, which happened not to be true, and so gave the less credit to this, nor was he convinced till he saw the sloops: whereupon he put his vessel in a posture of defence; he had no more than 25 men on board, tho' he gave out to all the vessels he spoke with, that he had 40. When he had prepared for battle, he set down and spent the night in drinking with the master of a trading sloop, who, 'twas thought, had more business with *Teach*, than he should have had.

Lieutenant *Maynard* came to an anchor, for the place being shoal, and the channel intricate, there was no getting in, where *Teach* lay, that night; but in the morning he weighed, and sent his boat a-head of the sloops to sound; and coming within gun-shot of the pyrate, received his fire; whereupon *Maynard* hoisted the King's colours, and stood directly towards him, with the best way that his sails and oars could make. *Black-Beard* cut his cable,[1] and endeavoured to make a running fight, keeping a continual fire at his enemies, with his guns; Mr *Maynard* not having any, kept a constant fire with small arms, while some of his men laboured at their oars. In a little time *Teach*'s sloop ran a-ground, and Mr *Maynard*'s drawing more water than that of the pyrate, he could not come near him; so he anchored within half gun-shot of the enemy, and, in order to lighten his vessel, that he might run him aboard, the Lieutenant ordered all his ballast to be thrown over-board, and all the water to be staved, and then weigh'd and stood for him; upon which *Black-Beard* hail'd him in this rude manner: *Damn you for villains, who are you? And, from whence came*

[1] the line to the anchor.

you? The Lieutenant made him answer, *You may see by our colours we are no pyrates*. *Black-Beard* bid him send his boat on board, that he might see who he was but Mr *Maynard* reply'd thus; *I cannot spare my boat, but I will come aboard of you as soon as I can, with my sloop*. Upon this, *Black-beard* took a glass of liquor, and drank to him with these words: *Damnation seize my soul if I give you quarters*,[1] or take any from you. In answer to which, Mr *Maynard* told him, *That he expected no quarters from him, nor should he give him any*.

By this time *Black-beard's* sloop fleeted,[2] as Mr *Maynard's* sloops were rowing towards him, which being not above a foot high in the waste, and consequently the men all exposed, as they came near together, (there being hitherto little or no execution done, on either side,) the pirate fir'd a broadside, charged with all manner of small shot. — a fatal stroke to them! the sloop the Lieutenant was in, having twenty men killed and wounded, and the other sloop 9: this could not be help'd, for there being no wind, they were oblig'd to keep to their oars, otherwise the pirate would have got away from him, which, it seems, the Lieutenant was resolute to prevent.

After this unlucky blow, *Black-beard's* sloop fell broadside to the shore; Mr *Maynard's* other sloop, which was call'd the *Ranger*, fell a-stern, being, for the present, disabl'd; so the Lieutenant finding his own sloop had way, and would soon be on board of *Teach*, he ordered all his men down, for fear of another broadside, which must have been their destruction, and the loss of their expedition. Mr *Maynard* was the only person that kept the deck, except the man at the Helm, whom he directed to lye down snug, and the men in the hold were ordered to get their pistols and their swords ready for close fighting, and to come up at his command; in order to which, two ladders were placed in the hatch-way for the more expedition. When the Lieutenant's sloop boarded the other, Captain *Teach's* men threw in several new fashioned sort of grenadoes, *viz*. case bottles filled with powder, and small shot, slugs and pieces of lead or iron, with a quick

[1] mercy in return for surrender.
[2] changed direction, tacked.

match in the mouth of it, which being lighted without side, presently runs into the bottle to the powder, and as it is instantly thrown on board, generally does great execution, besides putting all the crew into a confusion; but by good providence, they had not that effect here; the men being in the hold, and *Black-beard* seeing few or no hands aboard, told his men, *that they were all knock'd on the head, except 3 or 4; and therefore*, says he, *let's jump on board, and cut them to pieces.*

Whereupon, under the smoak of one of the bottles just mentioned, *Black-beard* enters with 14 men, over the bows of *Maynard*'s sloop, and were not seen by him till the air cleared; however, he just then gave a signal to his men, who all rose in an instant, and attacked the pyrates with as much bravery as ever was done upon such an occasion: *Black-beard* and the Lieutenant fired the first pistol at each other, by which the pirate receiv'd a wound, then engag'd with swords, till the Lieutenant's unluckily broke, and stepping back to cock a pistol, *Black-beard*, with his cutlash, was striking at that instant, that one of *Maynard*'s men gave him a terrible wound in the neck and throat, by which the Lieutenant came off with a small cut over the fingers.

They were now closely and warmly engaged, the Lieutenant and twelve men, against *Black-beard* and fourteen, till the sea was tinctur'd with blood round the vessel; *Black-beard* receiv'd a shot into his body from the pistol that Lieutenant *Maynard* discharg'd, yet he stood his ground, and fought with great fury, till he receiv'd five and 20 wounds, and 5 of them by shot. At length, as he was cocking another pistol, having fir'd several before, he fell down dead; by which time, 8 more out of the 14 dropp'd, and all the rest, much wounded, jumped over-board, and call'd out for quarters, which was granted, tho' it was only prolonging their lives for a few days. The sloop *Ranger* came up, and attack'd the men that remain'd in *Black-beard*'s sloop, with equal bravery, till they likewise cry'd for quarters.

Here was an end of that couragious brute, who might have passed in the world for a heroe, had he been employed in a good cause; his destruction, which was of such consequence to the plantations, was entirely owing to the conduct and bravery of Lieutenant *Maynard* and his men, who might have destroy'd him with much less loss, had they had a vessel with great guns; but they were obliged to use small vessels, because the holes and places he lurk'd in would not admit of others of greater draught; and 'twas no small difficulty for this gentleman to get to him, having grounded his vessel, at least, a hundred times, in getting up the river, besides other discouragements, enough to have turned back any gentleman without dishonour, who was less resolute and bold than this Lieutenant. The broadside that did so much mischief before they boarded, in all probability saved the rest from destruction; for before that *Teach* had little or no hopes of escaping, and therefore had posted a resolute fellow, a Negroe, whom he had bred up, with a lighted match, in the powder-room, with commands to blow up, when he should give him orders, which was as soon as the Lieutenant and his men could have enter'd, that so he might have destroy'd his conquerors: and when the Negro found how it went with *Black-beard*, he could hardly be perswaded from the rash action, by two prisoners that were then in the hold of the sloop.

What seems a little odd, is, that some of these men, who behaved so bravely against *Black-beard*, went afterwards a pyrating themselves, and 1 of them was taken along with *Roberts*; but I do not find that any of them were provided for, except one that was hanged; but this is a digression.

The Lieutenant caused *Black-beard*'s head to be severed from his body, and hung up at the boltsprit end, then he sailed to *Bath-Town*, to get relief for his wounded men . . .

After the wounded men were pretty well recover'd, the Lieutenant sailed back to the men of war in *James River*, in *Virginia*, with *Black-beard*'s head still hanging at the bolt-sprit end, and 15 prisoners, thirteen of whom were hang'd, it appearing upon tryal, that 1 of them, *viz. Samuel Odell*, was taken out of the trading sloop, but the night before the engagement. This poor fellow was a little unlucky at his first entering upon his new trade, there appearing no less than 70 wounds upon him after the action, notwithstanding which, he lived, and was cured of them all. The other person that escaped the gallows, was one *Israel Hands*, the master of *Black-beard*'s sloop, and formerly captain of the same, before the *Queen Anne's Revenge* was lost in *Topsail* Inlet.

The aforesaid *Hands* happened not to be in the fight, but was taken afterwards ashore at *Bath-Town*, having been sometime before disabled by *Black-beard*, in one of his savage humours, after the following manner. – One night drinking in his cabin, with *Hands*, the pilot and another man; *Black-beard* without any provocation privately draws out a small pair of pistols, and cocks them under the table, which being perceiv'd by the man, he withdrew and went on deck, leaving *Hands*, the pilot and the Captain together. When the pistols were ready, he blew out the candle, and crossing his hands, discharged them at his company; *Hands*, the master, was shot thro' the knee, and lam'd for life; the other pistol did no execution. – Being asked the meaning of this, he only answered, by damming them, that *if he did not now and then kill one of them, they would forget who he was.*

Hands being taken, was try'd and condemned, but just as he was about to be executed, a ship arrives at *Virginia* with a proclamation for prolonging the time of His Majesty's pardon, to such of the pyrates as should surrender by a limited time therein expressed: notwithstanding the sentence, *Hands* pleaded the pardon, and was allowed the benefit of it, and is alive at this time in *London*, begging his bread.

Now that we have given some account of *Teach's* life and actions, it will not be amiss, that we speak of his beard, since it did not a little contribute towards making his name so terrible in those parts . . .

This beard was black, which he suffered to grow of an extravagant length; as to breadth, it came up to his eyes; he was accustom'd to twist it with ribbons, in small tails, after the manner of our Ramilies wiggs,[1] and turn them about his ears: in time of action, he wore a sling over his shoulders, with three brace of pistols, hanging in holsters like bandaliers; and stuck lighted matches under his hat, which appearing on each side of his face, his eyes naturally looking fierce and wild, made him altogether such a figure, that imagination

[1] wig, with ringlets.

cannot form an idea of a Fury, from Hell, to look more frightful.

If he had the look of a Fury, his humours and passions were suitable to it; we shall relate two or three more of his extravagancies, which we omitted in the body of his history, by which it will appear, to what a pitch of wickedness, human nature may arrive, if its passions are not checked.

In the commonwealth of pyrates, he who goes the greatest length of wickedness, is looked upon with a kind of envy amongst them, as a person of a more extraordinary gallantry, and is thereby entitled to be distinguished by some post, and if such a one has but courage, he must certainly be a great man. The hero of whom we are writing, was thoroughly accomplished this way, and some of his frolicks of wickedness, were so extravagant, as if he aimed at making his men believe he was a devil incarnate; for being one day at sea, and a little flushed with drink: – *Come*, says he, *let us make a hell of our own, and try how long we can bear it*; accordingly he, with two or three others, went down into the hold, and closing up all the hatches, filled several pots full of brimstone, and other combustible matter, and set it on fire, and so continued till they were almost suffocated, when some of the men cried out for air; at length he opened the hatches, not a little pleased that he held out the longest.

The night before he was kill'd, he set up and drank till the morning, with some of his own men, and the master of a merchant-man, and having had intelligence of the 2 sloops coming to attack him, as has been before observ'd; 1 of his men ask'd him, in case anything should happen to him in the engagement with the sloops, whether his wife knew where he had buried his money? He answered, that nobody but himself and the Devil, knew where it was, and the longest liver should take it all.

ANNE BONNY AND MARY READ *Convicted of piracy in 1720: Bonny disappeared from prison; Read died there, of natural causes*
From Anonymous, The Lives and Adventures of the German Princess &c. (1760)

Anne Bonny was the daughter of an Irish lawyer who emigrated to Charleston, North Carolina. When she married a sailor against her father's wishes, he cut her off, and she went to the Bahamas with her new husband, where, in 1719, she met Captain John 'Calico Jack' Rackham. Within a year she was fighting and leading parties boarding ships they attacked throughout the Caribbean.

Mary Read had lived most of her life disguised as a boy so it was no great hardship for her to remain in disguise when she joined Rackham's crew soon after Bonny went to sea with him. His ship was taken by the authorities in 1720, and the entire crew was arrested and tried for piracy – Rackham was hanged.

[Anne Bonny] was of a fierce and couragious temper, wherefore when she lay under condemnation, several stories were reported of her much to her disadvantage; as, that she had kill'd an *English* servant-maid once in her passion, with a case-knife, while she look'd after her father's house; but upon further enquiry, we found this story to be groundless: 'tis certain, she was so robust, that once, when a young fellow would have lain with her against her will, she beat him so that he lay ill of it a considerable time.

While she liv'd with her father, she was look'd upon as one that would be a considerable fortune; wherefore it was thought her father design'd a good match for her; but she spoil'd all, for, without his consent, she married a young fellow who belong'd to the sea, and was not worth a groat. This provok'd her father to such a degree, that he turn'd her out of doors; upon which, the young fellow who married her, finding himself disappointed in his expectation, shipp'd himself and his wife for the island of *Providence*, expecting employment there.

Here she became acquainted with *Rackam* the pyrate, who, making courtship to her, soon found means of withdrawing her affections from her husband, so that she consented to elope from him, and go to sea with *Rackam* in mens cloaths. She was as good as her word, and after she had been at sea some time, she prov'd with child. When she began to grow big, *Rackam* landed her on the island of *Cuba*; and, recommended her there to some friends of his: they took care of her till she was brought to bed. When she was up, and well again, he sent for her to bear him company in his future expeditions.

The King's proclamation for pardoning of pyrates being out, he took the benefit of it, and surrender'd. Afterwards, being sent upon the privateering account, he return'd to his old trade, as has been already hinted in the story of *Mary Read*. In all these expeditions *Anne Bonny* bore him company, and, when any business was to be done in their way, no body was more forward or couragious than she; and, particularly, when they were taken; when she and *Mary Read*, with one more, were all the persons that durst keep the deck, as has been before hinted.

Her father was known to a great many gentlemen, planters of *Jamaica*, who had dealt with him, and among whom he had a good reputation; and some of them, who had been in *Carolina*, remember'd to have seen her in his house: this made them inclin'd to shew her favour, but the action of leaving her husband was an ugly circumstance against her. The day that *Rackam* was executed, by special favour, he was admitted to see her; but all the comfort she gave him, was, *that she was sorry to see him there, but if he had fought like a man, he need not have been hang'd like a dog.*

She was continu'd in prison till the time of her lying-in, and afterwards repriev'd from time to time; but what is become of her since we cannot learn: only this we know, that she never was executed.

Here [Mary Read's] mother lived three or four years, till what money she had was almost gone; then she thought of returning to *London*; and considering that her husband's mother was in good circumstances, she did not doubt but to prevail upon her to provide for the child, if she could but pass it upon her for the same; but the changing a girl into a boy seemed a difficult piece of work, and how to deceive an experienced old woman, in such a point, was altogether impossible; however she ventured to dress it up as a boy, brought it to town and presented it to her mother in law, as her husband's son, the old woman would have taken it, to have bred it up, but the mother pretended it would break her heart to part with it; so it was agreed betwixt them, that the child should live with the mother, and the supposed grandmother should allow a crown a week for its maintenance.

Thus the mother gained her point; she bred up her daughter as a boy, and when she grew up to some sense, she thought proper to let her into the secret of her birth, to induce her to conceal her sex. It happened that the grandmother died, by which means the subsistance that came from that quarter, ceased, and they were more and more reduced in their circumstances: wherefore she was obliged to put her daughter out, to wait on a *French* lady, as a footboy, being now thirteen years of age: here she did not live long; for growing bold and strong, and having also a roving mind, she entered herself on board a man of war, where she served some time. At length, she quitted the sea service, went over into *Flanders* and carried arms in a regiment of foot, as a cadet; and though in all actions she behaved herself with a great deal of bravery, yet she could not get a commission, they being generally bought and sold; therefore she quitted the service, and took on in a regiment of horse: here she behaved so well in several engagements, that she got the esteem of all her officers; but her comrade, who was a *Fleming*, happening to be a handsome young fellow, she fell in love with him, and from that time grew a little more negligent in her duty; so that, it seems, *Mars* and *Venus* could not be served at the same time; her arms and accoutrements, which were always kept in the best order, were quite neglected: 'tis true, when her comrade was ordered out upon a party, she used to go without being commanded, and frequently run herself into danger, where she had no business, only to be near him. The rest of the troopers, little suspecting the secret cause which moved her to this behaviour, fancied her to be mad; and her comrade himself could not account for this strange alteration in her; but love is ingenious, and, as they lay in the same tent, and were constantly together, she found a way of letting him discover her sex, without appearing that it was done with design.

He was much surprised at what he found out, and not a little pleased; taking it for granted, that he should have a mistress solely to himself, which is an unusual thing in a camp, since there is scarce one of those campaign ladies that is ever true even to a troop or company; so that he thought of nothing but gratifying his passions with very little ceremony: but he found himself strangely mistaken, for she proved very reserved and modest, and resisted all his temptations; yet, at the same time, was so obliging and insinuating in her carriage, that she quite changed his purpose, and made him so far from thinking of making her his mistress, that he now courted her for a wife.

This was the utmost wish of her heart; in short, they exchanged promises, and when the campaign was over, and the regiment marched into winter quarters, they bought woman's apparel for her, with such money as they could make up betwixt them, and were publickly married.

The story of two troopers marrying each other made a great noise, and several officers were drawn by curiosity to assist at the ceremony; who agreed together, that every one of them should make a small present to the bride towards house-keeping, in consideration of her having been their fellow soldier. Thus being set up, they seemed to have a desire of quitting the service, and settling in the world; the adventure of their love and marriage had gained them so much favour, that they easily obtained their discharge, and they immediately set up an eating house or ordinary, with the sign of the *Three Horse Shoes*, near the castle of *Breda*,[1] where they soon got into a good trade, a great many officers eating with them constantly.

But this happiness lasted not long; for the husband soon died, and

[1] In Flanders.

the peace being concluded, there was no resort of officers to *Breda*, as usual; so that the widow, having little or no trade, was forced to give up house-keeping, and her substance being by degrees quite spent, she again assumes her man's apparel, and, going into *Holland*, there takes on in a regiment of foot, quartered in one of the frontier towns: here she did not remain long, for there was no likelihood of preferment in time of peace; therefore she took a resolution of seeking her fortune another way; and, withdrawing from the regiment, shipped herself on board of a vessel bound for the *West-Indies*.

It happened that this ship was taken by *English* pyrates, and *Mary Read* was the only *English* person on board; they kept her amongst them, and having plundered the ship, let it go again; after following this trade for some time, the King's proclamation came out, and was publish'd in all parts of the *West Indies*, for pardoning such pyrates, as should voluntarily surrender themselves by a certain day therein mentioned. The crew of *Mary Read* took the benefit of this proclamation, and, having surrendered, lived afterwards quietly on shore; but money beginning to grow short, and our adventuress hearing that Captain *Woods Rogers*, Governor of the island of *Providence*, was fitting out some privateers to cruise against the *Spaniards*, she, with several others, embarked for that island, in order to go upon the privateering account, being resolved to make her fortune one way or other.

These privateers were no sooner sailed out, but the crews of some of them, who had been pardoned, rose against their commanders, and turned themselves to their old trade: in this number was *Mary Read*. 'Tis true, she often declared, that the life of a pyrate was what she heartily abhorred, and went into it only upon compulsion, both this time and before, intending to quit it, whenever a fair opportunity should offer itself; yet some of the evidences against her, upon her tryal, who were forced men,[1] and had sailed with her, deposed upon oath, that, in times of action, no persons amongst them were more resolute, or ready to board, or undertake any thing that was hazardous,

---

[1] Men forced to testify.

than she and *Anne Bonny*; and particularly at the time they were attacked and taken, when they came to close quarters, none kept the deck except *Mary Read* and *Anne Bonny*, and one more; upon which, she (*Mary Read*) called to those under deck, to come up and fight like men, and, finding that they did not stir, fired her arms down the hold amongst them, killing one, and wounding others.

This was part of the evidence against her, which she denied; whether this was true or no, thus much is certain, that she did not want bravery; nor indeed, was she less remarkable for her modesty, according to her notions of virtue: her sex was not so much as suspected by any person on board, till *Anne Bonny* took her for a handsome young fellow, and, for some reasons best known to herself, first discovered her sex to *Mary Read*: *Mary Read* knowing what she would be at, and being very sensible of her own incapacity that way, was forced to come to a right understanding with her, and so, to the great disappointment of *Anne Bonny*, she let her know she was a woman also; but this intimacy so disturbed Captain *Rackam*, who was the lover and gallant of *Anne Bonny*, that he grew furiously jealous, so that he told *Anne Bonny*, he would cut her new lover's throat; whereupon, to quiet him, she let him into the secret also.

Captain *Rackam* (as he was enjoin'd) kept the thing a secret from all the ship's company; yet, notwithstanding all her cunning and reserve, love found her out in this disguise, and hindered her from forgetting her sex. In their cruize they took a great number of ships belonging to *Jamaica*, and other parts of the *West-Indies*, bound to and from *England*; and whenever they met any good artist, or other person that might be of any great use to their company, if he was not willing to enter, it was their custom to keep him by force. Among these was a young fellow of a most engaging behaviour, or at least he was so in the eyes of *Mary Read*, who became so smitten with his person and address, that she could not rest, either night or day; but as there is nothing more artful than love, it was no hard matter for her, who had before been practised in these wiles, to find a way to let him discover her sex: she first insinuated herself into his liking, by talking against the life of a pyrate, which he was altogether averse to; so that they became mess-mates and strict companions: when she found he had a friendship for her, as a man, she suffered the discovery to be made, by carelessly shewing her breasts, which were very white and swelling.

The young fellow, who, we may suppose, was made of flesh and blood, had his curiosity and desire so rais'd by this sight, that he never ceased importuning her, till she confessed what she was. Now begins the scene of love: as he had a liking and esteem for her, under her supposed character, it was now turned into fondness and desire; her passion was no less violent than his, and she expressed it by one of the most generous actions, perhaps, that ever love inspir'd. It happened that this young fellow had a quarrel with one of the pyrates, and their ship then lying at anchor, near one of the islands, they had appointed to go a-shore and fight, according to the custom of these people: *Mary Read* was to the last degree uneasy and anxious for the fate of her lover; she would not have had him refuse the challenge, because she could not bear the thoughts of his being branded with cowardice; on the other side, she dreaded the event, and apprehended the fellow might be too hard for him: when love once enters into the breast of a person who has any sparks of generosity, it stirs the heart up to the most noble actions. In this dilemma, she shew'd, that she feared more for his life than she did for her own; for she took a resolution of quarrelling with this fellow herself, and, having challenged him a-shore, she appointed the time two hours sooner than when he was to meet her lover, where she fought him at sword and pistol, and killed him upon the spot.

It is true, she had fought before, when she had been insulted by some of those fellows; but now it was altogether in her lover's cause, for she stood as it were betwixt him and death, as if she could not live without him. If he had no regard for her before, this action would have been enough to have bound him to her for ever; but there was no occasion for ties or obligations, his inclination towards her was sufficient; in fine, they ply'd their troth to each other, which *Mary Read* said, she look'd upon to be as good a marriage in conscience, as if it had been done by a minister in church; and to this was owing her great belly, which she pleaded at her trial to save her life.

She declared she had never committed adultery or fornication with any man; she commended the justice of the court, before which she was tried, for distinguishing the nature of their crimes; her husband, as she called him, with several others, being acquitted. When she was ask'd, who he was? she would not tell; but said he was an honest man, and had no inclination to such practices, and that they had both resolved to leave the pyrates the first opportunity, and apply themselves to some honest livelihood.

There is no doubt, but many had compassion for her; yet the court could not avoid finding her guilty; for, among other things, one of the evidences against her deposed, that being taken by *Rackam*, and detained some time on board, he fell accidentally into discourse with *Mary Read*; whom taking for a young man, he ask'd her what pleasure she could have in being concern'd in such enterprizes, where her life was continually in danger, by fire or sword; and not only so, but she must be sure of dying an ignominious death, if she should be taken alive?—She answer'd, that, as to hanging, she thought it no great hardship; for, were it not for that, every cowardly fellow would turn pyrate, and so infest the seas, that men of courage must starve:—that if it was put to the choice of the pyrates, they would not have the punishment less than death, the fear of which kept some dastardly rogues honest; that many of those who are now cheating the widows and orphans, and oppressing their poor neighbours, who have no money to obtain justice, would then rob at sea, and the ocean would be crowded with rogues, like the land, so that no merchant would venture out, and the trade, in a little time, would not be worth following.

Being found quick with child, as has been observed, her execution was respited, and it is possible she would have found favour, but that she was seiz'd with a violent fever, soon after her trial, of which she died in prison.

‖ JOHN LANCEY *Convicted of arson, and hanged in 1754*
‖ From the 1764 *Select Trials*

Lancey was a pirate of an altogether more modern type, who connived
to set fire to his ship in order to claim the insurance. His weakness is
in contrast to the fierce individuality and freedom-loving ethos of pirates
like Blackbeard, although his brave and dignified demeanour after his
arrest testifies to his sincere repentance.

John Lancey, aged 27, was born at *Biddeford*, in the county of *Devon*,
and descended from a reputable family in that neighbourhood. He
was a young man of good parts and understanding, improved by an
education suited to the course of life to which he was destined, which
was the sea. He always behaved suitable to his station, with the
utmost integrity, and to the satisfaction of all those with whom he
was concerned. In short, he is allowed to have lived an unblemished
life till he engaged in this iniquitous transaction, the occasion of
which, he accounted for in the following manner.

He said, he had been upwards of ten years in the employment of
Mr *Benson*, a gentleman of that country, of a very opulent fortune,
and well esteemed; that he had married a relation of Mr *Benson*'s, and
having been so long in his service, master of different vessels belonging
to the same owner, and experienced many instances of his friendship,
he could not but consider him as the master of his fortune, and rested
his whole dependence upon his favour.

After bringing home the ship *Nightingale* safe from a former voyage,
he had a fit of illness, which reduced him in his circumstances pretty
much. On his recovery, *Benson* sent for him, and proposed fitting out
the same vessel; and then, for the first time, communicated his design
of making a large insurance upon her, and having her destroyed.
Lancey said the proposal startled him, but recollecting himself, replied,
'Sir, I flatter myself you have never known me guilty of a bad action
since I have been in your service, and surely your mention of this
matter to me now, is only with a view of trying my integrity.'

Some time afterwards, *Benson* invited him with some other gentlemen to dine with him. *Lancey* went, and was very kindly received, and desired to stay till the rest of the company were gone: He did so, and as soon as they were by themselves, *Benson* walked with *Lancey*, to a pleasure-house in the garden, renewed his former proposal and urged him to a compliance with great earnestness; till at last *Lancey* plainly told him, that if such were the conditions of continuing in his service, he must seek out for business somewhere else, for he could not prevail with himself to come into such a scheme.

They had drank plentifully before, and *Benson* still plied him with more wine and more arguments; upon which he touched upon a tender string; his necessities, his wife, and two children. 'Why will you, says *Benson*, stand so much in your own light? Consider your circumstances, consider your family; you may now have an opportunity of making them and yourself happy.' His arguments unfortunately prevailed, and *Lancey* was undone. The prospect of such large advantages, joined to *Benson*'s strong and repeated assurance of protection, gilded the bait till *Lancey* swallowed it. The temptation was great; but what punishment can be bad enough for the tempter?

To these last motives, *Lancey* ascribed his embarking in this flagitious conspiracy; but having once engaged in it, he acknowledged he was particularly active in carrying it into execution, and equally tenacious of the credit of his seducer.

In what manner, and by whom this villainous scheme was put in execution, has already been related in the course of the trial, and therefore need not here be repeated, except some circumstances relating to the protest, *viz.* That on *Thursday* the 6th of *August*, *Lancey* with *Lloyd* the Chief-mate, *Anthony Metherall* Second-mate and *James Bather* the Boatswain, went by the express directions of Mr *Benson*, before Mr *Narcissus Hatherly*, of *Biddeford*, notary public, and there swore, among other falsities, that the ship *Nightingale*'s taking fire, was purely *accidental* and *casual*, and proceeded from some *unforeseen accident* or *cause*, which was *not* in their *power* to *hinder* or *prevent*, and not from *carelessness, wilfull neglect* or *mismanagement*, to their, or either of their *knowledge* or *belief*; and that the loss of their ship and cargo, and every thing on board, was a *total* and *unavoidable* loss by *accident* of fire.

Every thing having thus succeeded to his wish, Capt. *Lancey*, not in the least apprehensive of detection, went home to his family, where his first care was, to secure the wages of his evil-doings. To this purpose he wrote to his correspondent at *Exeter*, whom he had employed to procure him an insurance of 130*l.* upon this voyage, acquainting him with his pretended loss; which he followed in about a fortnight after, with another letter, accompanied by proper vouchers for the recovery of the money so insured. As this last letter may serve to illustrate the intention of this foul conspiracy, we shall insert it from a copy allowed by *Lancey* to be genuine.

Northam, August 23, 1752.

SIR,

I have sent you by this post, the police, my protest, and my *affidavit,* annexed to the invoices of my loss, besides 15 guineas advanced to the sailors, which I imagine I shall be able to come at, but rely on your superior judgment to make application for me, as I am so much a sufferer; besides sundry other *items,* I have omitted in my invoice, which really were on board, at the time when I sustained by loss.

I am, Sir, your most obedient servant,

John Lancey.

To Mr John Williams, *Merchant,* at *Exon.*

Mean while, *Lancey,* having no particular employment, spent his time at home, and about the neighbourhood, with all seeming unconcern; and when *Lloyd,* on the 26th of *August,* told him he heard that *Bather* was going or gone to *Exeter,* and upon what account, he seemed to give no credit to it, neither did he attempt to secrete himself on that occasion.

However, in a few days, he was fully and fatally convinced of the truth of *Lloyd*'s intelligence; for on the 29th, as he was returning from a walk he had been taking, he was accosted by the Constable of *Northam,* and a bailiff or the Sheriff of *Exeter,* who told him, that information having been made against him by *Bather*, for wilfully destroying the ship *Nightingale*, with intent to defraud the insurers, a warrant was granted against him, and the rest of the ship's crew, which they were come to execute.

Lancey very chearfully submitted, and being taken into custody, was carried to a public-house in the neighbourhood. No sooner was the Captain's detainer known abroad, but as many of the crew as were thereabout surrendered themselves to the same warrant; however, only *Lancey*, *Lloyd* and *John Sennet* were detained, and the rest immediately discharged. *Lancey* was permitted to go to his own house unattended, and *Lloyd* and *Sennet* to their respective lodgings on their bare parole, that they would appear the next morning at the same house; which they did, and proceeded from thence together to *Exeter*, and after examination, were put under a strong guard in an inn. After another examination, *Sept.* 14, *Lancey* and *Lloyd* were committed to the county gaol, and *Sennet* to *Bridewell*.

They continued in the gaol of *Devon* about three months; and in the beginning of *December* were removed by *habeas corpus* to *London*; where, on their arrival, they were examined before Sir *Thomas Salisbury*, Knt. Judge of the Admiralty; when they were both ordered to stand committed. In the course of this examination, a proposal was made to *Lancey*,[1] and some time given him to consider of it, which very probably would save both his life and liberty, had he embraced it; but he rejected it, chusing rather to fall a victim than make a sacrifice; and so on *Monday* the 18th, they were both sent to the *Marshalsea*.

During their confinement here, several applications were made to get them admitted to bail, but unsuccessfully, till *July* 3, 1753, when Dr *Haye*, and Dr *Smanbrooke* moved the Court of Admiralty in behalf of their clients, *John Lancey*, *Thomas Pow*, *John Lloyd* and *John Sennet*, that a session might be held, and their clients tried; or that they might be bailed or discharged. Upon which motion, the court resolved that *John Lancey* be admitted to bail in 1000*l.* and two sureties in

[1] Presumably to give evidence in return for a less severe punishment.

500*l.* each; *John Lloyd* in 500*l.* with two sureties in 250*l.* each; and *Thomas Pow* in 1000*l.* with two sureties in 250*l.* each.

This resolution of the court flattered their hopes for some time; but were soon convinced, that they were built on an unstable foundation. The grand seducer, who had prompted them to the commission of the crimes, and had involved them in all these difficulties, *Benson*; whose power they expected would protect them, and whose riches were to support them, was himself obliged, by a precipitate flight, to seek an *asylum* in a foreign country. Thus, being unable to comply with the terms of their being bailed, they were forced to submit to a continuance of imprisonment; and were remanded to *Newgate* to take their trial at the next sessions of Admiralty.

While *Lancey* was in the *Marshalsea* he had contracted an acquaintance with a celebrated young lady, who was very desirous of continuing her visits to him in his new apartment; this he absolutely refused, and desired to be excused with good manners, accompanied with some wholesome advice.

In the several conversations, says the Ordinary, that passed between the prisoner and me, I don't remember that he ever expressed any resentment, against either his prosecutors, or *Bather* who made the discovery, whose account he admitted, in general to be true. For two days and two nights, he would not suffer his prayers to be interrupted, even by sleep, and to his last hour behaved with a steadiness and composure, very seldom seen on the like solemn occasion.

He suffered at *Execution Dock, June* 7, 1754.

EDWARD TRELAWNY
From *The Adventures of a Younger Son* (1831)

Trelawny (b. 1792), as the title of his memoirs shows, was a younger son who left his comfortable home (and oppressive father) in search of adventure on the high seas. At 17, after a short time in the navy, he

*met the charismatic Dutch-American privateer De Ruyter under whom
he served. De Ruyter soon made Trelawny a captain and they sailed
the Asian seas side-by-side for four years; the following extract from
Trelawny's memoirs describes this period. After his beloved Arabian
wife Zula died, and De Ruyter went to Italy for Napoleon in 1813,
Trelawny returned to England. He became an intimate friend of Byron,
Percy Bysshe Shelley and Mary Shelley, and in fact found Shelley's
body after his death in 1822. The following year he and Byron went
to Greece together to fight for Greek independence. Trelawny died in
1881, and his ashes were buried, as he had arranged nearly sixty years
earlier, beside Shelley's in Rome. Although strictly speaking Trelawny
was a privateer, not a pirate, his description of taking a Chinese trader's
ship at the turn of the nineteenth century cannot differ much from the
description a real pirate would have given.*

Continually in chase of something, I fell in, among other coasting
and country craft, with a Chinese junk, drifted out of her course, on
her return from Borneo. She looked like a huge tea-chest afloat, and
sailed about as well. She was flat-bottomed and flat-sided; decorations
of green and yellow dragons were painted and gilded all over her; she
had four or five masts, bamboo yards, mat sails and coir rigging,
double galleries all round, with ornamented head and stern, high as
my main top, and was six hundred tons burden. Her interior was a
complete bazaar; swarms of people were on board, and every individual, having a portion of tonnage in measured space, had partitioned
off his own, and converted it into a shop or warehouse; they were
like the countless cells of a bee-hive, and must have amounted to
some hundreds. All sorts of handicraft trades were going on, as if on
shore, from iron forging to making paper of rice straw, and glass of
rice, chasing ivory fans, embroidering gold on muslins, barbacuing
fat pigs, and carrying them about on bamboos for sale. In one cabin
a voluptuous Tartar[1] and a tun-bellied Chinese had joined their
dainties together; a fat dog, roasted entire, stuffed with turmeric,

[1] A central Asian (as opposed to the saying on p. 65 and note 1).

rice, suet and garlic, and larded with hog's grease, the real, delectable and celebrated sea-slug, or sea-swallow's nest, shark's fins stewed to a jelly, salted eggs and yellow-dyed pilaff formed their repast. A mighty china bowl of hot arrack punch stood in the centre of the table, from which a boy was continually ladling out its contents. Such voracious feeders I never beheld; they wielded their chop-sticks with the rapidity and incessant motion of a juggler with his balls. The little, black, greedy twinkling eye of the Chinese, almost buried in mounds of fat, glistened like a fly flapping in a firkin of butter. The Tartar, with a mouth the size of the ship's hatchway, seemed to have a proportionate hold for stowage. Understanding these were the two principal merchants on board, I had come to speak to them; but like hogs, buried up to the eyes in a savoury waste of garbage, there was no moving them from the dainties they gloated on. A sailor, who had conducted me, whispered his Tartar owner who I was; he grunted out some reply, and with a greasy paw, placed several handfuls of boiled rice on a corner of the table, indented it with his fist, poured into the hollow some of the hog's lardings out of the platter containing the roast dog and then, adding five or six hard-boiled salt eggs, motioned me to sit down and eat.

Driven away by these unclean brutes, I went into the Tartar captain's cabin, built over the rudder. He was stretched on a mat, smoking opium through a small reed, watching the card of the compass, and chanting out, 'Kie! Hooé – Kie! Chee!' Finding I might as well ask questions of the rudder as of him, I hailed the schooner to send a strong party of men.

We then commenced a general search, forcing our way into every cabin, when such a scene of confusion, chattering, and noise followed, as I never had heard before. Added to this, there was the mowing and gibbering of monkeys, apes, parrots, parroquets, bories, mackaws, hundreds of ducks, fish-divers, pigs, and divers other beasts and birds, hundreds of which were in this Mackow[1] ark. The consternation and panic among the motley ship's crew, and merchant-passengers,

[1] Macao.

are neither to be imagined nor described. They never had dreamed that a ship, under the sacred flag of the emperor of the universe, the king of kings, the sun of God which enlightens the world, the father and mother of all mankind, could, and in his seas, be thus assailed and overhauled. They exclaimed, 'Who are you? – Whence did you come? – What do you here?' Scarcely deigning to look at the little schooner, whose low, black hull, as she lay athwart the junk's stern, looked like a boat or a water-snake, they wondered at so many armed and ferocious fellows, not believing that they could be stowed in so insignificant a vessel whose hull scarcely emerged from the water. A Hong silk merchant, while his bales were handed into one of our boats, offered us a handkerchief apiece, but protested against our taking his great bales, when we could not possibly have room for them.

A few grew refractory, and called out for aid to defend their property. Some Tartar soldiers got together with their arms; and the big-mouthed Tartar and his comrade, swollen out with their feed of roast dog and sea-slug, armed themselves, and came blowing and spluttering towards me. I caught the Tartar by his mustachios, which hung down to his knees; in return he snapped a musket in my face; it missed fire; his jaw was expanded, and I stopped it for ever with my pistol. The ball entered his mouth, (how could it miss it?) and he fell, not so gracefully as Caesar, but like a fat ox knocked on the head by a sledge-hammer. The Chinese have as much antipathy to villainous saltpetre, except in fire-works, as Hotspur's neat and trimly dressed lord,[1] and their emperor, the light of the universe, is as unforgiving and revengeful towards those who kill his subjects, as our landed proprietors are towards those who slaughter their birds. An English earl told me the other day he could see no difference between the crime of killing a hare on his property, and a man on his property, arguing that the punishment should be the same for both. However, I have killed many of the earl's hares, and a leash or two of Chinese in my time, instigated to commit these heinous crimes

---

[1] Reference to Shakespeare's *Henry IV*, *Part One*, I, 3, 32: Hotspur refers to the King Richard II, whom he betrayed to Henry.

by the same excitement – that of their being forbidden and guarded against by vindictive threats of pains and penalties.

But to return to the junk. We had a skirmish on the deck for a minute or two, a few shots were fired, and a life or two more lost in the fray. The schooner sent us more men, and no further opposition was made. Then, instead of gleaning a few of the most valuable articles, and permitting them to redeem the remainder of the cargo by paying a sum of money, as the rogues had resisted, I condemned her as lawful prize. We therefore began a regular pillage, and almost turned her inside out. Every nook, hole and corner were searched; every bale cut, and every chest broken open. The bulky part of her cargo, which consisted of camphor, woods for dyeing, drugs, spices and pigs of iron and tin, we left; but silks, copper, selected drugs, a considerable quantity of gold dust, a few diamonds and tiger-skins were ours; and, not forgetting Louis, who had entreated me to look out for sea-slug, I found some bags of it in the cabin of my late friend, the defunct merchant. Neither did I neglect the salted eggs, which with rice and jars of melted fat, victualled the ship. I took some thousands of these eggs, a new and excellent sort of provision for my ship's company. The Chinese preserve them by merely boiling them in salt and water till they are hard; the salt penetrates the shell, and thus they will keep for years.

The philosophic captain, whose business it was to attend to the navigation and pilotage of the junk, having nothing to do with the men or cargo, continued to inhale the narcotic drug. His heavy eye was still fixed on the compass, and his drowsy voice called out, 'Kie! Hooé! – Kie! Chee!' Though I repeatedly asked him whither he was bound, his invariable answer was 'Kie! Hooé! – Kie! Chee!' I pointed my cutlass to his breast, but his eyes remained fixed on the compass. I cut the bowl from the stem of his pipe, but he continued drawing at the reed, and repeating, 'Kie! Hooé – Kie! Chee!' On shoving off, as I passed under the stern, I cut the tiller ropes, and the junk broached up in the wind, but I still heard the fellow singing out, from time to time, 'Kie! Hooé! – Kie! Chee!'

We had altogether a glorious haul out of the Chinaman. Every part of our little vessel was crammed with merchandise. Our men exchanged their tarred rags for shirts and trowsers of various coloured silks, and looked more like horse-jockeys than sailors. Nay, a few days after I roused a lazy and luxurious old Chinese sow from the midst of a bale of purple silk, where she was reclining; perhaps she thought she had the best right to it, as it might have belonged to her master, or because she was one of the junk's crew, or probably she was the owner herself transmigrated into this shape, – there needed little alteration. I also got some curious arms, particularly the musket, or fowling-piece, which, had it obeyed its master's intention, would have finished my career. The barrel, lock and stock, are deeply chased all over with roses and figures of solid gold worked in. I preserve it now, and it has recalled the circumstance by which it came into my possession; otherwise, it might have been driven, like any others of greater moment, from my memory by the lapse of time, and by more recent events.

6

Sex Offenders

From Jonathan Wild's 'An Answer to a Late Insolent Libel,
Entitled a Discovery of the Conduct of Thieves and
Thief-Takers, &c.' (1718)

*Hitchin, Under-Marshal of Newgate Prison and thus in the pay of
the City of London, was the thief-taker whom Jonathan Wild (see 'A
Miscellany') gradually ousted – after learning his trade in Hitchin's
employ. In 1718, when Hitchin tried to reassert his authority, with
an anonymous pamphlet condemning Wild, supposedly by a prisoner in
Newgate, Wild hit back with this pamphlet, deriding Hitchin's methods
and motives and concluding with an exposé of Hitchin's homosexuality.
Nine years later, Hitchin was arrested for attempting to sodomize a
man who informed on him afterwards – but seems to have been fairly
acquiescent at the time of the supposed incident – convicted, fined £20,
sentenced to stand in the pillory in the Strand and given six months in
prison (an unusual punishment reserved for crimes the court found hard
to deal with or define; see also the case of Sally Salisbury). Hitchin,
well aware of the hostility displayed towards homosexuals in the stocks,
took the precaution of wearing a suit of armour to endure his punishment;
but this did not protect him from violent attacks on his person. He had
to be removed from the stocks by the authorities before his allotted
hour was up, because he was being so harassed, and he died of the
injuries he sustained at the hands of the mob less than six months later.*

One night the M——l invited his man, the buckle-maker,[1] to a house
near the end of the Old Bailey, telling him he would introduce him
to a company of he-whores. The man not apprehending rightly his
meaning asked if they were hermaphrodites. 'No, ye fool,' said the
M——l, 'they are sodomites, such as deal with their own sex instead
of females.'

---

[1] The Marshal, Charles Hitchin (actually an Under-Marshal), and Jonathan Wild,
who had trained as a buckle-maker.

This being a curiosity the M——l's man [Wild] had not hitherto met with he willingly accompanied his master to the house, which they had no sooner entered but the M——l was complimented by the company with the titles of 'Madam' and 'Ladyship'.

The man asking the occasion of these uncommon devoirs the M——l said that it was a familiar language peculiar to that house. The M——l's man was not long in the house before he was more surprised than at first. The men calling one another, 'My dear,' hugging and kissing, tickling and feeling each other as if they were a mixture of wanton males and females, and assuming effeminate voices, female airs, etc., some telling others that they ought to be whipped for not coming to school more frequently.

The M——l was very merry in this assembly and dallied with the young sparks with a great deal of pleasure until some persons came into the house that he little expected to meet with in that place; and then finding it out of his power to secure the lads to himself he started up of a sudden in a prodiguous rage, asking the frolicking youth if they were become so common as to use those obnoxious houses, and told them that he would spoil their diversion, upon which he made his exit with his man.

Going out of the house he said he supposed they would have the impudence to make a ball. An explanation whereof being desired by the man the M——l informed him that there was a noted house in Holborn[1] to which those sorts of persons used to repair and dress themselves in woman's apparel for the entertainment of others of the same inclinations in dancing and the like in imitation of the fair sex; telling him that if he were to come into the room where they were present upon such an occasion that he would take them for so many cats caterwauling.

When the M——l had told his man this story says he, 'I'll be revenged of these smock-faced young dogs. We'll secure them and send them to the Compter.'

In order to which the M——l, being acquainted with their customary

---

[1] Probably Mother Clap's house (see below).

walks, placed himself with a constable in Fleet Street and dispatched his man to the Old Bailey with some likewise to his assistance to apprehend them on their return home.

About the usual hour of their separation several of the sporting sodomites were seized by the M—l and his man and their assistants (in women's apparel) and conveyed in the same dresses to the Compter. The next morning they were carried before the Lord Mayor in the dresses and they were taken in, by His Lordship's order, some having gowns, petticoats, head cloths, fine laced shoes, furbelow scarves, masks and complete dresses for women; others had riding hoods, some were dressed like shepherdesses, others like milkmaids with fine green hats, waistcoats and petticoats, and others had their faces painted and patched and very extensive hoop petticoats, which were then very lately introduced.

Appearing in these dresses of ridicule before My Lord Mayor (after examination) His Lordship committed them to the work-house, there to continue at hard labour during pleasure, and as a part of their punishment ordered them to be publicly conveyed through the streets in their various female habits.

The young tribe of sodomites were, pursuant to My Lord Mayor's order, carried in pomp to the work-house . . .

From the several accounts before mentioned, which are incontestably true in every particular, the principles and character of the M—l sufficiently appear. I shall conclude my treatise with a petition to His Excellency, apprehending he may nevertheless by art and insinuation obtain the preferment he desires, though in my opinion the only place he is capable of executing thoroughly is the infamous post of Jack Ketch Esq.:[1]

The Humble Petition of J—n W—ld to C—s H—n, City M—l, upon his publishing a paper entitled The Thief-Taker's Proclamation. *Humbly Sheweth.*

That whereas you have by an insolent libel lately published,

---

[1] The slang name for the hangman at Tyburn, derived from a real executioner of the late seventeenth century named Jack Ketch.

dedicated to the Lord Mayor, aldermen and common council of this opulent city, strenuously asserted your undoubted right to and qualification for the laudable post of T—f-T—r General of Great Britain and other of His Majesty's dominions abroad and made so powerful an interest as to stand fair for the said employment (if such a post will be allowed) and you having also as ambassador of Beelzebub lately published (under another's name) your Royal proclamation setting forth the great encouragement you will give to the profession of thief-taking and the plundering of the public. I think it my interest by an early application to petition your Excellency (amongst great numbers of others equally qualified) for some post or employment under you, and I'll assure you I'll serve your Excellency with the same infidelity and perfidiousness as you have hitherto done the Magistracy of the City of London in your office of M—l.

Particularly I'll take care that no woman of the town shall walk the streets or bawdy house be kept without your Excellency's licence and trial of the ware; that no sodomitish assembly shall be held without your Excellency's presence and making choice for your own use, in order to which I'll engage to provide a female dress for your Excellency much finer than what your Excellency has been hitherto accustomed to wear; that those pickpockets which shall desist from their business, and not commit robberies upon the persons of everybody they meet, shall as you have desired be sent to Newgate for contempt and not continuing the same crimes as formerly, according to your example in the case of the bisket-baker; to return £100 exchequer bills to the right owners, but to share the money with your Excellency, to hang all thieves presuming to act without delivering their effects to your Excellency; to send honest clergymen to the Compter; to plunder women of the town and everybody else for money when my purse is exhausted with gaming; to take watches from persons buying them without your Excellency's leave; to give daily attendance on the pickpocket pupils in Moorfields for their encouragement; to exert my courage equal to your Excellency on the apprehension of the two burglar boys; and in short to imitate your Excellency in all illegal practices you have been guilty of since your suspension in the service of My Lord Mayor; the particulars whereof are at large inserted in the treatise to which this is annexed; to set for my merit to your favour and your great dessert and experience in the tracks of Tyburn.

All which being considered and a just regard being had to my faithful services when I had the honour of being your assistant and acquired that little knowledge I have in iniquity I humbly hope you'll be graciously pleased to bestow upon me some office or employment if it be only to take up and expose the worthy reformers of this city according to your pious inclinations and glorious examples.

And your petitioner will ever pray etc.

JONATHAN WILD

POSTSCRIPT

The City M—l, pretending in his scandalous treatise that he is the only person of resolution fit to apprehend malefactors and to work a reformation; I think it my duty to advertise the public that if the magistracy of this city think fit to direct any persons of reputation to apply themselves to me they will be let into such important discoveries, tending to the distribution of justice, as may not be expected, without any mercenary views or expectations, but merely for the good of mankind.

They will find a willingness to concert proper measures and courage to execute beyond what is to be met with in that cowardly lump of scandal, the M—l, who pretends to do good offices only for the sake of the reward; and I shall be glad to be tried whether I am not ready to enter upon such hazardous attempts as the dastardly C—s H—n dares to engage in.

WILLIAM ROBINS *Tried for rape of Mary Tabor, and acquitted in 1720*

From the 1734 *Select Trials*

Seven-year-old Tabor was clearly raped by Robins but he was acquitted because a doctor said that the 'lacerations' on her vagina could have been made by riding a horse – which she was not asked about – and because witnesses Robins himself called testified to his good character. A child's injuries were not considered proof against an adult man's word. Because the costs of bringing a case to trial were borne by the prosecutor, very few cases like this came to trial because the evidence was almost always seen as inconclusive. That most of the cases in this section are taken from the Select Trials *rather than any of the* Newgate Calendars *shows that sexual crimes like these did not have the popular appeal that lurid murders or clever confidence tricks had. The complete entry is given.*

William Robins, *for a* Rape, *Jan.* 1720

William Robins, of St *James's*, *Westminster*, was indicted for assaulting, ravishing and carnally knowing *Mary Tabor*, a girl of about 7 years of age, on the 24th of *Dec.* last.

Mary Tabor, the child's mother. My husband took the child out with him on *Christmas* Eve, and when she came home she seem'd to be very uneasy, and every now and then would be wriggling her backside about. *Where have you been, hussy*, says I? *Why*, says she, *I have been sitting upon our taylor's shop-board.* So she said no more to me then; but on *Monday* she complain'd, that she smarted sadly, and could not make water (and't please your Lordship) and so I wonder'd what a dickens was the matter, tho' little did I dream how the *poor thing* had been serv'd. But however she grew worse on *Tuesday*, and then I began to examine the case, and found her very much out of sorts. *Ye young baggage you*, says I, *how comes this about?*—*Why*, says she, William, *our taylor, put his finger into where I make water. And did he put nothing else there, hussy,* says I? *Yes,* says she, *the thing that he makes water with.*

Elizabeth Smith. The child's privy-parts were swell'd, and rent downwards, and there had been force used with her.

Joseph de Layer, Peter du Hamel and *John West,* surgeons, depos'd, that they found those parts very sore, and much bruis'd; that the girl had a running, which still continu'd; that there had been a penetration, and she had been forc'd by a man.

John Tabor. The prisoner confessed to me, that my girl had been with him on *Christmas* Eve, but deny'd, that he did any thing to her. Other witnesses depos'd, that the prisoner's stall is next the street, that but one man may work in it at a time, and that it has a flap to shut up; that the child was well before that *Saturday,* and that no marks were found on her linnen till afterwards.

The prisoner, in his defence, deny'd, that the child was with him that day, or that he ever offer'd to do any thing like what was alledg'd against him,—and then he call'd his witnesses.

John Brown. I view'd the child with 2 other surgeons. It did not appear that a penetration had been made by man, for the passage was not large enough. I try'd to pass my probe, but it would not go up. The girl was not lacerated, there was a running indeed; but I have known the like, occasion'd by a child's riding on a horse.—Another surgeon depos'd to the same effect.

Mary Tomlins. I live over-against the prisoner, and his shop, being next the street, is as publick as the highway, and somebody or other is always at it. He was hard at work that day for a tenant of mine to finish his coat for *Christmas-day,* and work'd till midnight, tho' I did not know so much till afterwards.—There is a window to shut up, when the prisoner goes out.

Then 5 or 6 witnesses appear'd to the prisoner's reputation, who gave him the character of an honest, civil man, tho' (as one of them said) he would run after the girls a little. The jury acquitted him.

GEORGE DUFFUS *Tried for sodomy, and acquitted; convicted of attempted sodomy in 1721*
From the 1734 *Select Trials*

Duffus fits the prejudiced eighteenth-century stereotype of the promiscuous homosexual, seeking to corrupt innocent heterosexual men and drag them down with him to the depths of iniquity and certain damnation. (The whole entry is given.)

George Duffus, *for* Sodomy, *December* 1721

George Duffus was indicted for assaulting and committing in and upon the body of *Nicholas Leader*, the unnatural sin of sodomy, on the 9th of *October* last.

Nicholas Leader. The first time of my seeing the prisoner was at a meeting-house in *Old Gravel-lane*. When service was ended, he came to me, and appearing very devout, began some discourse in commendation of the minister, by which means, for three or four *Sundays* successively, he endeavour'd to insinuate himself into my good opinion, and indeed I took him to be a religious young man. He invited me to drink with him at Mr *Powel*'s, in the *Minories*;[1] I comply'd; and at parting, he asked me where he might hear of me another time; I told him, at the *Three Merry Potters*, at the *Hermitage*. He promised to come and see me in a few days, and was as good as his word; we sat together drinking and talking 'till it was pretty late, when he told me that he lived a great way off, and therefore should be glad if I'd let him lie with me that night.[2] As I mistrusted nothing, I made no objection to it; but as soon as we were got into bed, he began to hug me and kiss me, and call me his dear. I asked him what he meant by it? He answer'd, *No harm, nothing but love*, and presently got upon me, and thrust his tongue into my mouth. I threw him off.

[1] In the East End near Moorfields.
[2] It was quite usual for two men to share a bed like this.

He got on again three or four times, and I as often served him as before, and told him if he would not lie still, I would kick him out of bed. With that he suddenly seized me by the throat, so that he had almost strangled me, turned me upon my face and forcibly enter'd my body about an inch, as near as I can guess; but in struggling, I threw him off once more, before he had made an emission, and having thus forced him to withdraw, he emitted in his own hand, and clapping it on the tail of my shirt, said, *Now you have it!* I had then turned him out of door, but for fear of disturbing my antient grandmother, who lay sick in the next room. Next morning he told me, that I need not be so concerned at what he had done to me, for he had done the same to several others, and named in particular, a cabbin-boy. In a few days after, I acquainted some of my friends with it, and they advised me to prosecute him. Upon which, I procured a warrant from Justice *Tiller*, and, taking a constable with me, went on *Sunday* morning to the same meeting as before, where we found the prisoner. The Constable whispering me, and then sitting down by him, he suspected, I suppose, that we had some design against him, and so took his hat and went out, and we followed him, and he perceiving it, began to run; but we pursued, and soon overtook him. He cry'd for mercy, and begg'd that we would not expose him to public shame; adding, that we were all sinners, and it was hard for a man to suffer for the first fault.

Mr *Powell.* The first time I saw the prisoner was at a lecture, he follow'd me out, and began to tell me what an excellent discourse we had had, how affecting it was, and what comfort and refreshment his soul had felt under the precious teachings of such a heavenly man. This occasioned a pretty deal of religious conference between us, at the end of which he said, he should be glad to drink with me at any other time; but it being the Lord's-Day, he did not care to go into a publick-house then. So we made an agreement to meet at my father's in the *Minories*, on the 12th of *October* last. We met accordingly, and spent the evening in religious discourse. When it grew late, he told me his wife was out of town, and he had a pretty way home, and therefore wished I would let him lie with me for one night. I readily consented, as I not at all suspecting his design; but we had not been long in bed, before he began to kiss me, and take hold of my privities. *How lean you be!* says he, *Do but feel how fat I am!* and so he endeavour'd to convey my hand to his privities. I turned from him, and lay upon my back; he got upon me, kept me down and thrust his yard betwixt my thighs, and emitted. He told me, that I need not be troubled, or wonder at what he had done, for it was what was very common, and he had often practised it with others. At the same time, he desired me to act the same with him; but I refused, and told him, I was a stranger to all such practices, and if I had known what a sort of a man he had been, I would never have lain in the same bed with him.

The spermatic injection not being prov'd, the court directed the jury to bring in their verdict *special*.

The judges meeting afterwards to consider of this verdict, they agreed in their opinion, that the prisoner had not compleated the felony of which he stood indicted. But that he might not escape the hands of justice entirely, a bill of indictment against him for attempting to commit sodomy with *Nicholas Leader*, was laid before the Grand Jury of *Middlesex*, who finding it *billa vera*,[1] he was brought upon his trial at the sessions in *March* following, when *Nicholas Leader* deposed, that, being in bed with the prisoner, the prisoner seized him by the throat, forcibly turned him on his face, and endeavour'd to commit sodomy with him.

The jury found him guilty, and he was sentenced to pay a fine of twenty marks,[2] to suffer two months imprisonment and to stand upon the pillory near *Old Gravel-Lane*.

[1] True bill.
[2] One mark was worth 13*s*. 4*d*.

ARTHUR GRAY *Convicted of breaking and entering with the intent to ravish in 1721; pardoned*
Ballad reproduced in the 1734 *Select Trials*

Arthur Gray was a footman who developed a passion for Griselda Murray, a relative of his master. Murray was a noted beauty, and former maid-in-waiting to Queen Caroline. One night she was staying at her father George Baillie's house in St James's, as she did when she was in London, when in the middle of the night Gray thrust open her bedroom door and entered, brandishing a sword and a pistol which he admitted he had brought with him to 'put her in fear, and force her to comply'. Murray testified that Gray cried, 'Madam, I mean to ravish ye, for I have entertained a violent love for you a long time, but as there is so great a difference betwixt your fortune and mine, I despair of enjoying my wishes by any means but force.' She spent three-quarters of an hour begging him not to hurt her, but he replied, 'No, I have ventured my life for your sake already, and therefore am resolutely bent to go through with my design, let the consequence be what it will – All the rest of the family are asleep, and if I lose this opportunity, I can never expect another. Your making a noise will signify nothing – I must and I will' – and tried to rip the bedclothes off her. In the scuffle she was able to alert her parents and the household, and was rescued.

Gray was convicted and sentenced to death, but Griselda Murray procured a pardon for him; this was the cause of much salacious society gossip, insinuating that Murray (who belonged to a racy set) had in some way encouraged Gray's affections. Friends like Lady Mary Wortley Montagu and Lord Hervey, respectively bitchy and sympathetic, wrote poems and ballads on the subject. Others speculated that Gray fabricated his passion for Murray to disguise his real motive, blackmail, saying that he had been hoping to catch her in bed with her purported lover, the progressive Bishop Burnet.

VIRTUE *in Danger: Or, a Lamentable Story how a virtuous* LADY *had like to have been ravish'd by her Sister's* Footman.

To the Tune of, *The Children in thee Wood.*

WRITTEN *by a* LADY.

Now ponder well, ye ladies fair,
    These words that I shall write:
I'll tell a tale shall make you stare,
    Of a poor lady's fright.

She laid her down all in her bed,
    And soon began to snore,
It never came into her head
    To lock her chamber-door.

A footman of her sister dear,
    A sturdy *Scot* was he,
Without a sense of godly fear,
    Bethought him wickedly.

Thought he this lady lies alone,
    I like her comely face;
It would most gallantly be done,
    Her body to embrace.

In order to this bold attempt,
    He ran up stairs apace;
While she, poor lady, nothing dreamt,
    Or, dreamt it was *his Grace*.[1]

The candle flaming in her eyes,
    Made her full soon awake:
He scorn'd to do it by surprize,
    Or her a-sleeping take.

[1] Bishop Burnet.

A sword he had, and hard by it,
  A thing appear'd withal,
Which we, for very modesty,
  A pistol chuse to call.

This pistol in one hand he took,
  And thus began to woo her.
Oh! how this tender creature shook,
  When he presented to her.

Lady, quoth he, I must obtain,
  For I have lov'd thee long:
Would you know how my heart you gain'd,
  You had it for a song.

Resolve to quench my present flame,
  Or you shall murder'd be;
It was those pretty eyes, fair dame,
  That first have murder'd me.

The lady look'd with fear, around,
  As in her bed she lay;
And tho' half dying in a swoon,
  Thus to herself did say:

'Who rashly judge,' (it is a rule)
  'Do often judge amiss:
I thought this fellow was a fool;
  But there's some sense in this.'

She then recover'd heart of grace,
  And did to him reply,
'Sure *Arthur*, you've forgot your place,
  Or know not that 'tis I.

'Do you consider who it is,
    That you thus rudely treat?
'Tis not for scoundrel scrubs to wish
    To taste their master's meat.'

Tut, tut, quoth he, I do not care;
    And so pull'd down the cloaths:
Uncover'd lay this lady fair,
    From bubbies down to toes.

'Oh! *Arthur*, cover me' (she said)
    'Or sure I shall get cold':
Which presently the rogue obey'd;
    He could not hear her scold.

He laid his sword close by her side;
    Her heart went pit-apat:
'You've but one weapon left,' (she cry'd)
    'Sure I can deal with that.'

She saw the looby¹ frighted stand,
    Out of the bed jump'd she,
Catch'd hold of his so furious hand;
    A sight it was to see!

His pistol-hand she held fast clos'd,
    As she remembers well;
But how the other was dispos'd
    There's none alive can tell.

The sword full to his heart she laid,
    But yet did not him slay;
For when he saw the shining blade,
    God wot, he ran away.

When she was sure the knave was gone,
    Out of her father's hall,

¹ lout.

This virtuous lady straight began
    Most grievously to bawl.

In came Pawpaw, and Mawmaw dear,
    Who wonder'd to behold:
'Oot★ *Grisee*, what a noise is here,
    Why stond you in the cold?'

'Mawmaw,' she said, (and then she wept)
    'I have a battle won;
But if that I had soundly slept,
    My honour had been gone.'

'A footman of my sister, he –'
    'A footman!' cried Mawmaw,
'Dear Daughter this must never be,
    And we not go to Law.'

This lady's fame shall ever last,
    And live in British song;
For she was, like Lucretia[1] chaste
    And eke was much more strong.

★ *The lady's name was* Grissel.

MARGARET CLAP *Tried for keeping a 'sodomitical house',
convicted and sentenced to stand in the stocks, to pay a fine, and to
two years' imprisonment in 1726*
Trial record

*The aptly named 'Mother Clap' kept what was called a sodomitical
house – not exactly a brothel without women, but more a meeting place
for homosexual men – for over a decade, in Holborn which in the eighteenth
century was a mish-mash of tiny streets and alleyways. Cross-dressing*

---

[1] Legendary chaste Roman matron.

was a popular pursuit at Mother Clap's, and there were rooms where couples could adjourn to have sex; it sounds very like the place Jonathan Wild described being taken to by Charles Hitchin (see above). When Mother Clap was put into the pillory at Smithfield, she was so badly assaulted by the crowds that, like Hitchin, she died later of her injuries.

Margaret 'Mother' Clap's trial July 1726

Margaret Clap was indicted for keeping a disorderly house, in which she procured and encouraged persons to commit sodomy, December 10 1725, and before and after.

Samuel Stephens. On Sunday night, the 14th of November last, I went to the prisoner's house in Field Lane, in Holborn, where I found between 40 and 50 men making love to one another, as they called it. Sometimes they would sit in one another's laps, kissing in a lewd manner and using their hand indecently. Then they would get up, dance and make curtsies, and mimic the voices of women. 'O, Fie, Sir! – Pray, Sir – Dear, Sir, – Lord, how can you serve me so? – I swear I'll cry out. – You're a wicked devil, – and you've a bold face. – Eh, ye little dear toad! Come, buss!' – Then they'd hug, and play, and toy, and go out by couples into another room on the same floor, to be married, as they called it. The door of that room was kept by — Eccleston, who used to stand pimp for 'em, to prevent anybody from disturbing them in their diversions. When they came out, they used to brag, in plain terms, of what they had been doing. As for the prisoner, she was present all the time, except when she went out to fetch liquors. There was among them William Griffin, who has since been hanged for sodomy; and — Derwin, who had been carried before Sir George Mertins, for sodomitical practises with a link-boy.[1] Derwin bragged how he had baffled the link-boy's evidence; and the prisoner at the same time boasted, that what she had sworn before Sir George in Derwin's behalf, was a great means of bringing him off. I went to

---

[1] See Cant Glossary.

the same house on two or three Sunday nights following, and found much the same practises as before. The company talked all manner of gross and vile obscenity in the prisoner's hearing, and she appeared to be wonderfully pleased with it.

Joseph Sellers deposed to the same effect, adding, that he believed there were above 40 sodomites taken from that house and committed to prison in one night.

Prisoner. As for Derwin's being carried before Sir George Mertin's, it was only for a quarrel. I hope it will be considered that I am a woman, and therefore it cannot be thought that I would ever be concerned in such practises.

The evidence being full and positive, and no body appearing to her character, the jury found her guilty. Her sentence was, to stand in the pillory in Smithfield, to pay a fine of twenty marks and suffer two years imprisonment.

FRANCIS CHARTERIS *Tried and convicted of rape in 1730, and pardoned in 1731*
From 'The History of Colonel Francis Charteris' (1732), Dr Arbuthnot's epitaph of Charteris (1732) and an anonymous satire written in 1732 on Charteris's death

Colonel Charteris (b. 1675), a portrait of whom can be seen hovering greedily in the background of the first plate of Hogarth's Harlot's Progress, *was a notorious figure in early eighteenth-century London: an inveterate gambler (and confirmed cheat), he preferred to take his winnings in land than in cash; a hardened whoremonger, he debauched and deserted women (including the famous courtesan Sally Salisbury) from all sections of society. One woman who turned him down was Anne Bond, a naive servant-girl he hired in 1729 with the express purpose of seducing. She refused all his advances, and his money, until one day he grew frustrated enough to whip her and rape her at gunpoint, afterwards accusing her of theft and turning her out of his house. She retaliated by accusing him formally of rape. Charteris was convicted — for the second time — but pardoned by the King; and died of a venereal disease within the year. His fate shows the degree to which the law favoured the rich and well-connected, as the bitter anonymous satire, written after his death, illustrates. Dr Arbuthnot (1667–1735), society doctor, was the friend of Alexander Pope, who included Charteris as an example of vice in Epistles II and II of his* Moral Essays.

Whilst these things were in agitation, the Colonel that he might not lye idle, sent out his emissaries to provide him some fresh game; amongst which, one of them, very unfortunately for Mr *Ch-rtr-s,* falling into company with one *Anne Bond,* a good likely young woman, ask'd her if she wanted a good service? To which she replying in the affirmative; then says the good woman, go along with me, I know a very honest gentleman, one Colonel *Harvey,* and I don't doubt but I have interest enough to get you the place. The girl very readily accepting the offer, and thanking her for her kindness, went with her to the Colonel's House in *George-Street* near *Hanover-Square,* where she sending up word to the Colonel, that she had brought him an industrious girl, that would make him a good servant; he, after asking a few trifling questions, hired her for five pounds a year; which done, he order'd a servant to fetch her clothes from the inn, and buy some holland[1] for shifting. On her return the Colonel offer'd her the holland, telling her, she should have a clean shift every day; but she modestly refus'd it, and answer'd, that she had already a sufficient number for any one in her station.

She had not continued long with him before he made his addresses to her; and in order to bring him to his bow, presented her with a fine snuff-box, which she refus'd to accept, whereupon he told her, he only gave it her to keep for him, and that if she lost it, she must

---

[1] cotton cloth.

pay for it. Some time after she was inform'd by the housekeeper that she must lye in her master's room, because he was very much indispos'd, wherefore she must lye with her in the truckle-bed. To this, after some hesitation, she consented, on being assured that the curtains were so close drawn about the bed, that the Colonel could not see her undress. In the night the Colonel order'd the housekeeper to come to bed to him, which she accordingly did, after which he call'd the girl, but she would not comply, which very much incensed him, and made him swear execrably.

After this, finding no arguments, not even gold, would prevail on her, he resolved to have recourse to force; and accordingly on the Tenth of *November*, in the morning, sending for her up into his chamber, he fastened the door, and throwing her suddenly upon a couch, cramm'd his night cap into her mouth to prevent her crying out, and enjoy'd her *nolens volens*;[1] after which, she being inconsolable, and not to be pacify'd by any arguments he cou'd use, took up a horsewhip, and lash'd her very severely; then charging her with a robbery, order'd her to be turn'd out of doors.

'Here continueth to rot the body of
COLONEL DON FRANCISCO;
Who with an inflexible constancy,
And inimitable uniformity of life,
Persisted in spite of age and infirmity
In the practice of every human vice,
Excepting prodigality and hypocrisy;
His insatiable avarice
Exempting him from the first,
And his matchless impudence
From the second.
Nor was he more singular
In that undeviating viciousness of life

---

[1] Although she was unwilling.

Than successful in accumulating wealth;
Having
Without trust of public money, bribe,
Work, service, trade or profession,
Acquired or rather created
A ministerial estate.
Among the singularities of his life and fortune
Be it likewise commemorated
That he was the only person in his time
Who would cheat without the mask of honesty;
Who would retain his primeval meanness
After being possessed of 10,000 pounds a year:
And who having done, every day of his life,
Something worthy of a gibbet,
Was once condemned to one
For what he could not do.[1]
Think not, indignant reader,
His life useless to mankind;
PROVIDENCE
Favoured or rather connived at
His execrable designs,
That he might remain
To this and future ages
A conspicuous proof and example
Of how small estimation
Exorbitant wealth is held in the sight
Of the ALMIGHTY,
By his bestowing it on
The most unworthy
Of all the descendants
Of Adam.'

---

[1] This accusation of Charteris's impotence is the only one I have seen.

Blood! Must a Colonel, with a lord's estate
Be thus obnoxious to a scoundrel's fate?
Brought to the bar, and sentenced from the bench
For only ravishing a country wench?
Shall gentlemen receive no more respect?
Shall their diversion thus by laws be checked?
Shall they b'accountable to saucy juries, –
For this or t'other pleasure? H–ll and Furies!
What man thro' villanies would run a course
And ruin families without remorse
To heap up riches – if when all is done
An ignominious death he cannot shun?

JOHN DEACON AND THOMAS BLAIR *Convicted of
sodomitical practices in 1743*
From the 1764 *Select Trials*

*The case of Deacon and Blair illustrates the homophobia of eighteenth-
century society, which excused the rape of a seven-year-old girl but
fell upon these two men, practising consensual sex in a dark corner of
a courtyard, and brought them before the court. (The entry is given
in full.)*

Deacon *and* Blair, *for sodomitical Practices,* January 1743

John Deacon and *Thomas Blair* were indicted; *John Deacon* for unlawfully
and wickedly laying hands on *Thomas Blair*, with an intent to commit
the detestable crime of sodomy; and *Thomas Blair*, for unlawfully,
voluntarily and wickedly permitting and suffering the said *John
Deacon*, to lay hands on him the said *Thomas*, with an intent to commit
the said detestable crime of sodomy, *October* 18.

Robert Pert. I am one of the constables of *Farringdon Without*; there
is a court behind the chapter-house in St *Paul's Church-yard*, which is

suspected as a place which people of this sort frequent. On the 18th of *October*, between 12 and 1 in the morning, I was going my rounds with my partner; when I came to this court, I heard a whispering; I went softly into the court, imagining something of this kind was transacting; to appearance, at first, I only saw the youngest, whose name is *Deacon*, for he was full against the other, and seemed to hug round him; his breeches were down, and his shirt appeared: I then thought it was a man and a woman, for the youngest was in the same motion as a man is when he is embracing a woman; they were so close, that if I had had the presence of mind to put my hand between them, I could not have done it. I called out, and said, *In the name of God, what are you doing? Who or what are you?* They seemed to jostle before they could get from one another; they had both their breeches down. Upon which I called to my partner, and told him they were a couple of *sodomites*, and he laid hold of them: Then I called the watchmen, and carried them to the watch-house; I asked them what they did there? *Blair* said, he went to ease nature. *I think*, said I, *it is in a very odd way. D—n you, Sir*, said he, *if I must tell you, I was at sh—te.* As he said he went to ease nature, I ordered a watchman to take a lanthorn to see, and I went myself, and there was no such thing. I asked him what he had to say for himself? He said he was a gentleman, and a Master of Languages, and I used him ill. He sent for some people to come to his character, but nobody came; and the other had but an indifferent character. I carried them before Alderman *Calvert*, and he examined them separate: I was present, and they did not agree in their accounts; *Deacon* said he went to piss, and *Blair* said he went to sh—te. *Blair* said, he never saw *Deacon*, but *Deacon* said he saw *Blair*, and that he went to piss, and said he would piss there; and that *Blair* said to *Deacon*, he might if he would. *Blair* begged of me, as he was going before the Alderman, that he might speak to me in private: says he, *It is in your power to ruin me for ever, or to save me.* Said I, I will say nothing but what I saw, and that I will upon oath.

    Blair. What posture was I in? Was I not easing nature?

    Pert. He did make a motion of squatting two or three times when I first saw him. – He was not sitting down, he was standing up, shuffling to put up his breeches. – I could see them perfectly by the lamp, tho' they got to the darkest corner of the court.

Blair. I will speak as modestly as I can. Ask him whether he saw the flesh standing to this abomination.

Pert. I cannot say any thing to that. – I had no light of my own, there was a sufficient light of the lamp.—I was within a quarter of a yard of them when I called out, and then I drew back.

Blair. This one question will be found material: I do not know whether that honourable gentleman is upon the bench that I was before; I told him the same story, that I was easing nature, and this gentleman made the same objection then as he does now, that he could not see it: I said, Mr Alderman, what I am going to propose is not cleanly or decent, but if you will please to order any servant to go along with me into a back place, I will convince them that I put that into my breeches, by his pulling me away in a hurry, that I should have left behind me: Ask him whether I did not say so?

Pert. He did propose that; but he might easily have done that in the night-time; I should have smelt him in the watch-house, if any such thing as that had been done, for he set close to me a great while. As he was going from the *Compter* to *Guildhall*, he said he hoped the young man had not confessed any thing; I told him, I should not trouble myself with any thing he had said, he would hear that when he came there.

Peter Line, the other Constable, confirmed the evidence of his partner, in every particular, and so did *Wright*, a watchman.

Blair, in his defence, spoke thus; my Lord, that *Sunday* in the afternoon, I went to the other end of the town, to wait on some gentlemen, and was in company with several of them from between three or four till nigh eight at night, and after that had been in two or three companies; between eight and nine I was thinking of coming home it was a pretty heavy rain then, which obliged me to stay longer than I designed, and I went to the *Moor-cock* to drink a tankard of beer; and by drinking beer and other liquors, it gave me a looseness, which occasioned all this trouble and ignominy. And if there is a God above, I speak sincerely, and it is in the presence of my great God, who sees me, I declare I had no more thought of committing that accursed abomination, than I have of blowing up this house; and as to that man, I did not speak to him, as I hope for mercy from God, I do not know whether he is a man or not; I was obliged to squat down in that place, and had done it twice by the way before. Besides, I was too much in liquor, I could not possibly commit that abomination, had I been ever so much inclined to it.

Mr *Pert*. He was in high spirits, but not drunk, he talked very well.

Deacon. Coming home, I stopt in that place to make water, and a person came close to me, and said, by your leave I must sh–te by you; and while he was there, somebody cried out, *What are you doing here?* I said, no ill. Said he, *What, you are two buggerers, I suppose*. Said I, *There is no such thing*, and presently they laid hold of me, and took me to the watch-house.

Mary Appleby gave him the character of a very honest young fellow. Both guilty.

7

Highwaymen

JAMES HIND *Convicted of high treason in 1652, and hanged, drawn and quartered*

From chapbook tale of Hind's life and 'To the Memory of Captain Hind', a ballad in Johnson's *A General History of the Lives of the . . . Highwaymen*

On his first expedition as a highwayman, Captain Hind took £15 from his victims, and then returned £1 to them for their travel expenses, 'with so much grace and pleasantry that the gentleman vowed he would not injure a hair of his head, though it were in his power'. Hind was a staunch royalist, who fought with the Scots against Cromwell at Worcester, and accosted regicides whenever he could, in one case crying:

I neither fear you nor any king-killing villain alive. I have now as much power over you as you lately had over the king, and I should do God and my country good service, if I made the same use of it; but live, villain, to suffer the pangs of thine own conscience, till justice shall lay her iron hand upon thee, and require an answer for thy crimes, in a way more proper for such a monster, who art unworthy to die by any other hands but those of the common highwayman, or at any other place than Tyburn. Nevertheless, though I spare thy life as a regicide, be assured, that unless thou deliverest up thy money immediately, thou shalt die for thy obstinacy.

Celebrated as much for his generosity to the poor as for his courtesy to ladies, Hind was the original 'gentleman of the road'. In 1652 he was betrayed to Cromwell's administration by a friend, and arrested. He was brought to the bar in London, but there was not enough evidence to convict him of any crime; then he was convicted of manslaughter in Reading, an old crime; and then in Worcester of high treason. Before he died he proclaimed that he regretted nothing but not living to see his royal master restored.

No Jest like a true jest.

CHAPTER I
Containing Hind's birth, and how he first came to be
a high-way-man

Captain James Hind (the subject of our ensuing discourse) was born
at Chiping-Norton in Oxfordshire: his father having no more children
but he, put him to school, intending to make him a scholar, but he
minded his wagish pastimes more than his book, which his father
perceiving, bound him prentice to a butcher, but he having a running
pate,[1] soon grew weary of that also, and in conclusion ran away from
his master, comes up to London, there grows acquainted with a
company of roaring deboys[2] blades, who by their evil examples made
him as bad as themselves. To be short, as they seldom abounded
with money, so they scorned to be long in want. When their stock
grew short, they rode a cutting[3] for more. At last the knot[4] was
discovered, the chief of them hanged, and Hind (only) escaped, with
the loss of his horse; and now he sets up for himself . . .

CHAPTER III
How Hind was betrayed by two whores, who sent two
high-way-men to take his money, and how he rob'd them

Hind having gotten a good purchase of gold, past away the day very
merrily, and then towards night he rides to an inn which stood in
the private rode, where it seems some high-way-men did use: after
he had seen his horse carefully drest and fed he came into the house,
where were two handsome ladies by the fire, he bespoke a good
supper, and invited them unto it, when supper was ready he called

---

[1] roving disposition.   [2] debauched.   [2] robbing.   [3] gang.

for wine, and made them merry. They seemed very coy to him, but he knowing their humours, pulled out of his pocket a handful of gold: singing, *Maids, where are your hearts become, look you what here is.* And after much mirth, to bed he went, and presently after came in the two men which kept these two whores, to whom they related all the courtesie of Hind, and that he had abundance of gold about him: they resolve to watch his going and to follow him in the morn: but Hind being wakeful, was up and mounted before the 2 ladies were stirring: when they[1] heard his horse prance they look out of the window, and seeing he had so good a horse, were ready to fall out who should have him. I will have the horse, says one, and you shall have his money, nay, I'le have his horse says the other: in conclusion they quickly made themselves ready, and rode after Hind, when they had overtook him, they askt him which way he rode, he answers them towards Cambridge; they tell him they would be glad of his company: now riding in a place where no people were nigh, one of the thieves sings, *Maids where are your hearts become? look you what here is*: Hind seeing their intent, and knowing he was betrayed, answered them in the same tune. *Now you rogues you are both undone, look you what here is,* and drawing forth his pistol, and firing at one of them, by chance shot his horse in the head, who presently fell down with his master's leg under him, the other seeing this, betook himself to flight, but Hind quickly overtook him, and made him deliver such money as he had, and cutting his girts and his bridle, made him work enough to catch his horse again: Hind now rides to the other thief, who lay but in little ease, he alights and pulls the horse from his leg, and then helps him up, and takes away his money also, saying is there but one master thief in England, and would you venture to rob him? verily, were you not of my profession, neither of you should have lived, but seeing you ventured hard for it, thou deservest something. So Hind gave him his money back again to buy him another horse, saying unto him, disgrace not your selves with small sums but aim high, and for

[1] the pimps.

189

great ones: for the least will bring you to the gallows. So Hind shaking the poor thief by the hand, left him to his partner to catch the horse, and bid him farewel . . .

CHAPTER XV

How Hind went into Scotland to the Scotch King at Sterling, and how he was apprehended in London

Hind being ever weary of staying long in a place, shipt himself for Scotland, when he was landed he went and presented his service to the King[1] at Sterlin, the King being informed who it was, had some discourse with him, and commended him to the Duke of Buckingham, then present to ride in his troop because his life-guard was full, he came into England with the same troop, was in the ingagement[2] at Warington, came into the fight at Worcester, and staid till the K[ing] was fled. Hind being in the city, seeing the gates full of dying persons, leapt over the wall on foot by himself, travelled the country and lay three days under bushes and hedges because of the souldiery, afterwards he came to Sir Io. Pickington's wood where he lay 5 days, from thence he come to London and lodged five weeks very securely: but on Nov. 9. 1651. a discovery was made of Captain Hind's frequenting one Denzies a barber over-against St Dunstans Church in Fleet-Street, who went by the name of Brown, this information was communicated to certain gentlemen belonging to the Right Honourable Mr Speaker, who with great care so ordered the business that there was no suspition at all: to his chamber door they went, forc'd it open, and immediately with their pistols cockt, seized on his person, carried him to Mr Speaker's house in Chancery-Lane, and so secured him for that night. The next day being munday, by order from the Right Honourable the Counsel of State, the said Captain Hind was brought to Whitehall, who was examined before a Committee, and

[1] Charles II.   [2] battle.

divers questions put to him concerning his late ingagement with Charles Stuart, and whether he accompanied the Scotch King, to the furtherance of his escape, to which he answered, That he never saw the King since the fight at Woster,[1] neither knew he of his getting the field, but was glad that he had made so happy an escape. After some time spent about his examination, 'twas ordered he should be sent prisoner to the gate house till the next day. So the next day by special order from the Counsel of State, he was brought from thence in a coach, with iron bolts on his legs, Cap. Compton, and two other messengers belonging to the state, guarding him, and about two of the clock in the afternoon he was put into Newgate, where he lay till the next sessions . . .

CHAPTER XVI
Containing the conclusion of the story, and Captain Hinds last farewel to Worcester.

On Munday the 1. of March 1651 he was arraigned before the Right Honourable Judge Warberton for killing one Pool his companion at Knowl, a little village in that country; after evidence given in against him, he was found guilty of manslaughter, and condemned to dye, but on the next morning the Act of Oblivion being sent acquitted all former offences, only the indictment of high-treason against the state, and for that fact he was carried [to] Worcester, and there hang'd and quartered on Friday, Sep. 24 1652.

> Thus Fate the great derider did deride,
> Who liv'd by robberry, yet for treason dy'd.

[1] Worcester.

TO THE MEMORY OF CAPTAIN HIND

By a Poet of his own Time

Whenever Death attacks a throne,
Nature through all her parts must groan
The mighty monarch to bemoan.

He must be wise, and just, and good,
Though nor the state he understood,
Nor ever spared a subject's blood.

And shall no friendly poet find
A monumental verse for Hind? –
In fortune less, as great in mind

Hind made our wealth one common store,
He robb'd the rich to feed the poor: –
What did immortal Caesar more?

Nay, 't were not difficult to prove,
That meaner views did Caesar move:
His was ambition, Hind's was love.

Our English hero sought no crown,
Nor that more pleasing bait, renown;
But just to keep off fortune's frown.

Yet when his country's cause invites,
See him assert a nation's rights!
A robber for a monarch fights!

If in due light his deeds we scan,
As nature point's us out the plan,
Hind was an honourable man.

Honour, the virtue of the brave,
To Hind that turn of genius gave,
Which made him scorn to be a slave.

Thus, had his stars conspired to raise
His natal hour, this virtue's praise
Had shone with an uncommon blaze.

Some new epocha had begun
From every action he had done –
A city built, a battle won.

If one's a subject, one at helm,
'Tis the same vi'lence, says Anselm,[1]
To rob a house, or waste a realm.

Be henceforth then, for ever join'd,
The names of Caesar and of Hind –
In fortune different, one in mind.

CLAUDE DU VALL *Convicted of highway robbery, and
hanged in 1670*
From Johnson's *A General History of the Lives of the . . .
Highwaymen* and Du Vall's final speech from Smith's *General
History of the Lives of the Most Notorious Highwaymen*

*Du Vall was trained as a footman and came to England in a noble
retinue when Charles II was restored to the throne. Footmen often
became highwaymen: they were trained as outriders, hired to protect
an equipage from robbery, so they had the requisite skills of hard riding
and sure shooting; used to living well, they were noted for their insolent,
often insubordinate, attitude (indeed this might be encouraged as some
rakish peers felt it reflected well on them for their footmen to cultivate
a sense of hauteur) that was easily translated into the desire to live
free of the shackles of service, by their own rules. Du Vall's flair,
independence and taste for the high life mimicked the values of the*

---

[1] (1033–1109), medieval philosopher.

dissolute Restoration aristocracy he had once worked for. Johnson's account is given in full.

CLAUDE DU VALL

Du Vall was born at Dumfort in Normandy. His father was a miller, and his mother was descended of an honourable race of tailors. He was educated in the Catholic faith, and received an education suited to a footman. But though the father was careful to train up his son in the religion of his ancestors, he was without religion himself. He talked more of good cheer than of the church; of sumptuous feasts than of ardent faith; of good wine, than of good works. One time old Du Vall was seized with a severe illness, and there were strong hopes that he would die a natural death. In this extreme illness a ghostly father visited him with his *Corpus Domini*,[1] informing him that, having heard of his dangerous situation, he had brought his Saviour to confirm him in his last moments. Upon this old Du Vall, drawing aside the curtains, beheld a goodly fat friar, with the host in his hand. 'I know,' said he, 'that it is our Saviour, because he comes to me in the same manner as he went to Jerusalem: it is *an ass* that carries him.'

Du Vall's parents were freed of the trouble and expense of rearing their son, at the age of thirteen. We first find him at Rouen, the principal city of Normandy, in the character of a stable-boy. Here he fortunately found retour horses[2] going to Paris: upon one of these he was permitted to ride, upon condition of assisting to dress them at night. His expenses were likewise defrayed by some English travellers that he met upon the road.

Arrived at Paris, he continued at the same inn where the Englishmen put up, and, by running messages, or performing the meanest offices, he subsisted for a while. He continued in this humble station until the Restoration of Charles II, when multitudes from the Continent resorted to England. In the character of a footman to a person of

---

[1] Body of our Lord, the sacrament.

[2] returning horses, i.e. hired by post and going back to their original stable.

quality, Du Vall also repaired to that country. The universal joy which seized the nation upon that happy event, contaminated the morals of all: – riot, dissipation, and every species of profligacy abounded. The young and sprightly French footman entered keenly into these amusements. His funds, however, being soon exhausted, he deemed it no great crime for a Frenchman to exact contributions from the English. In a short time he became so dexterous in his new employment, that he had the honour of being first named in an advertisement issued for the apprehending of some notorious robbers.

One day, Du Vall and some others espied a knight and his lady travelling along in their coach: seeing themselves in danger of being attacked, the lady took up a flageolet, and commenced playing, which she did very dexterously. Du Vall taking the hint, pulled one out of his pocket, commenced playing and, in this posture, approached the coach. 'Sir,' said he to the knight, 'your lady plays excellently, and I make no doubt but she dances well. Will you step out of the coach, and let us have the honour to dance a bourant with her upon the heath?' 'I dare not deny any thing, sir,' the knight readily replied, 'to a gentleman of your quality and good behaviour; you seem a man of generosity, and your request is perfectly reasonable.' Immediately the footman opens the door, and the knight comes out. Du Vall leaps lightly off his horse, and hands the lady down. It was surprising to see how gracefully he moved upon the grass; scarcely a dancing-master in London, but would have been proud to have shown such agility in a pair of pumps, as Du Vall showed in a pair of French riding-boots. As soon as the dance was over, he handed the lady to the coach, but just as the knight was stepping in, 'Sir,' says he, 'you forget to pay the music.' His worship replied, that he never forgot such things, and instantly put his hand under the seat of the coach, pulled out an hundred pounds in a bag, which he delivered to Du Vall, who received it with a very good grace, and courteously answered, 'Sir, you are liberal, and shall have no cause to regret your generosity; this hundred pounds, given so generously, is better than ten times the sum taken by force. Your noble behaviour has excused you the other three hundred pounds which you have in the coach with you.' After this he gave him his word that he might pass undisturbed, if he met any other of his crew, and then wished them a good journey.

At another time, Du Vall and some of his associates met a coach upon Blackheath, full of ladies, and a child with them. One of the gang rode up to the coach, and, in a rude manner, robbed the ladies of their watches, rings, and even seized a silver sucking-bottle of the child's. The infant cried bitterly for its bottle, and the ladies earnestly entreated he would only return that article to the child, which he barbarously refused. Du Vall went forward to discover what detained his accomplice; and the ladies renewing their entreaties to him, he instantly threatened to shoot his companion, unless he returned that article, saying, 'Sirrah, can't you behave like a gentleman, and raise a contribution without stripping people; but, perhaps, you had some occasion for the sucking-bottle, for, by your actions, one would imagine you were hardly weaned.' This smart reproof had the desired effect, and Du Vall, in a courteous manner, took his leave of the ladies.

One day Du Vall met Hooper, master of the hounds to Charles II, who was hunting in Windsor Forest; and, taking the advantage of a thicket, he demanded his money, or he would instantly take away his life. Hooper, without hesitation, gave him his purse, containing at least fifty guineas; in return for which, Du Vall bound him neck and heel, tied his horse to a tree beside him and rode across the country.

It was a considerable time before the huntsmen discovered their master. The squire being at length released, made all possible haste to Windsor, unwilling to venture himself into any more thickets for that day, whatever might be the fortune of the hunt. Entering the town, he was accosted by Sir Stephen Fox, who inquired if he had had any sport. 'Sport!' replied Hooper, in a great passion, 'yes, sir, I have had sport enough from a villain who made me pay full dear for it; he bound me neck and heel, contrary to my desire, and then took fifty guineas from me, to pay him for his labour, which I had much rather he had omitted.'

England now became too contracted a sphere for the talents of our adventurer, and in consequence of a proclamation issued for his detection, and his notoriety in the country, Du Vall retired to his native country. At Paris he lived in a very extravagant style, and carried on war with rich travellers and fair ladies, and proudly boasted that he was equally successful with both; but his warfare with the latter was infinitely more agreeable, though much less profitable, than with the former. In the true language of a warrior, he avowed that his fortune was as good as that of Marlborough, who never laid siege to a city that he did not take. The adventures of his gallantry are, however, of such a nature, that decorum forbids their recital; and certainly, it is no great compliment to the delicacy or taste of him who first recorded them. It is sufficient to mention, that his gallantries emptied his coffers, and excited him to renewed depredations to feed his licentious desires, until he became confirmed in every species of vice.

There is one adventure of Du Vall, at Paris, which we shall lay before our readers. There was in that city a learned Jesuit, confessor to the French king, who had rendered himself eminent, both by his politics and his avarice. His thirst for money was insatiable, and increased with his riches. Du Vall devised the following plan to obtain a share of the immense wealth of this pious father.

To facilitate his admittance into the Jesuit's company, he dressed himself as a scholar, and, waiting a favourable opportunity, went up to him very confidently, and addressed him as follows: 'May it please your reverence, I am a poor scholar, who have been several years travelling over strange countries, to learn experience in the sciences, principally to serve mine own country, for whose advantage I am determined to apply my knowledge, if I may be favoured with the patronage of a man so eminent as yourself.' 'And what may this knowledge of yours be?' replied the father, very much pleased. 'If you will communicate any thing to me that may be beneficial to France, I assure you no proper encouragement shall be wanting on my side.' Du Vall, upon this, growing bolder, proceeded: 'Sir, I have spent most of my time in the study of alchymy, or the transmutation of metals, and have profited so much at Rome and Venice, from great men learned in that science, that I can change several metals into gold, by the help of a philosophical powder, which I can prepare very speedily.'

The father confessor was more elated with this communication, than all the discoveries he obtained in the way of his profession: his knowledge, even, of his royal penitent's most private secrets gave him less delight than the prospect of immense riches which now burst upon his avaricious mind. 'Friend,' said he, 'such a thing as this will be serviceable to the whole state, and particularly grateful to the king, who, as his affairs go at present, stands in great need of such a curious invention. But you must let me see some proof of your skill, before I credit what you say, so far as to communicate it to his majesty, who will sufficiently reward you, if what you promise be demonstrated. Upon this the confessor conducted Du Vall to his house, and furnished him with money to erect a laboratory, and to purchase such other materials as were requisite, in order to proceed in this invaluable operation; charging him to keep the secret from every living soul. Utensils being fixed, and every thing in readiness, the Jesuit came to witness the wonderful operation. Du Vall took several metals and minerals of the basest sort, and put them in a crucible, his reverence viewing every one as he put them in. Our alchymist had prepared a hollow stick, into which he conveyed several sprigs of real gold; with this stick he stirred the operation, which, with its heat, melted the gold and the stick at the same time, so that it sunk, imperceptibly, into the vessel. When the excessive fire had consumed all the different materials which he had put in, the gold remained pure, to the quantity of an ounce and a half. This the Jesuit ordered to be examined, and, ascertaining that it was actually pure gold, he became devoted to Du Vall; and, blinded with the prospect of future advantage, he credited every thing our impostor said, furnishing him with whatever he demanded, in hopes to be made master of this extraordinary secret. Thus were our alchymist and Jesuit, according to the old saying, as 'great as two pickpockets'. Du Vall was a professed robber; and what is a court-favourite, but a picker of the people's pockets? So that it was two sharpers endeavouring to outsharp one another. The confessor was as candid as Du Vall could wish. He showed him all his treasures, and several rich jewels which he had received from the king; hoping, by these obligations, to incline him to discover his wonderful secrets with more alacrity. In short, he became so importunate, that Du Vall was apprehensive of too minute an inquiry, if he denied the request any longer; he therefore appointed a day when the whole was to be disclosed. In the meantime, he took an opportunity of stealing into the chamber where the riches were deposited, and where his reverence generally slept after dinner: finding him in deep repose, he gently bound him, then took his keys, and unhoarded as much of his wealth as he could carry off unsuspected, after which he quickly took leave of him and France.

It is uncertain how long Du Vall continued his depredations after his return to England; but we are informed that, in a fit of intoxication, he was detected in the whole at Chandos-street, committed to Newgate, convicted, condemned and executed at Tyburn, in the twenty-seventh year of his age; and so much had his gallantries and handsome figure rendered him the favourite of the fair sex, that many a bright eye was dimmed at his funeral, his lifeless corpse was bedewed with the tears of beauty, and his actions and death were celebrated by the immortal author of the inimitable 'Hudibras'.[1]

I should be very ungrateful (which, amongst persons of honour, is a greater crime than that for which I die,) should I not acknowledge my obligation to you, fair English ladies. I could not have hoped that a person of my nation, birth, education and condition, would have had so many powerful charms to captivate you all, and to tie you so firmly to my interest that you have not abandoned me in distress, or in prison, that you have accompanied me to this place of death, of ignominious death. How mightily, and how generously have you rewarded my little services. Shall I ever forget that universal consternation amongst you when I was taken, your frequent, your chargeable visits to me at Newgate, your shrieks, your swoonings

[1] Samuel Butler (1613–80).

when I was condemned, your zealous intercession and importunity for my pardon? You could not have erected fairer pillars of honour and respect to me, had I been an Hercules. It has been the misfortune of several English gentlemen, in the times of the late usurpation, to die at this place upon the honourablest occasion that ever presented itself, the endeavouring to restore their exiled sovereign; gentlemen, indeed, who had ventured their lives, and lost their estates, in the service of their prince; but they all died unlamented and uninterceded for, because they were English. How much greater, therefore, is my obligation, whom you love better than your own countrymen? Nevertheless, ladies, it does not grieve me that your intercession for my life proved ineffectual; for now I shall die with little pain, an healthful body and I hope a prepared mind. For my confessor has showed me the evil of my way, and wrought in me a true repentance; witness these tears, these unfeigned tears.

BENJAMIN CHILD *Convicted of highway robbery, and hanged in 1721*
From *The Whole Life History of Benjamin Child, Lately Executed for Robbing the Bristol Mail* (1722), his introduction to crime and his dying speech

The young Benjamin Child 'was comely, and of a towardly disposition, (though being brought into the world when Mercury the god of thieves and Venus the goddess of lovers, had the joint ascendancy, somewhat addicted to pilfering and stealing kisses from the girls in a corner)'. He studied arithmetic, 'it being necessary that he should be a good accountant before he took upon him to tell other folk's money for them', and became a clerk, but was dismissed for insubordination. He turned to teaching after this, but he debauched the two daughters of the old clergyman who owned the school, and came back to London, 'now being hardened into a more confirmed state of wickedness'. The capital was 'the most proper and most spacious sanctuary for the reception and concealment that are abandoned to the most profligate courses. And where should he take up his abode at his arrival, but in the parish of Covent Garden, that receptacle of sharpers, pickpockets and strumpets?' In London Child fell into a world of gambling and womanizing, and turned to robbery to finance his new habits, as the first part of the excerpt describing his descent into crime shows. But, in the tradition of Hind, he used his profits to help others, on one occasion paying the debts for, and thus freeing, every inhabitant of the Debtor's Prison in Salisbury. He was reported to have left £10,000 at his death, divided in his will between various mistresses.

From hence it was, that he acquired the knowledge of taking to those courses, which he was, to the end of his life, very dextrous in the pursuit of: for gaming houses are allowed to be the fittest places of resort for men of extravagance and loose principles: and there is not one of these, wherein associates are not to be picked up; who, from their own experience, can construct others, of desperate fortunes, how to remedy their disasters, by the same means which have retrieved their own.

At one of these frequented haunts it was, that this our Benjamin, who instead of having the silver cup put into his sack by others, as in the case of his name-sake in sacred writ, took the liberty of doing it with his own, grew acquainted with Spicket and Lindley, two notorious highwaymen (the first some time since executed, and the last transported to Guinea) who first entered him at the robbery of a waggon from Bishops-Stortford in Hertfordshire, from whence they took £200 in money, belonging to a baker, living at the further end of Goswell Street, in the road to Islington, besides goods and bills directed to other tradesmen in London; the latter of which, if signed at the bank, never failed of a current exchange at the houses abovementioned.

Being thus initiated in the art of surveying his Majesty's roads, and made a priest, as it were, to officiate at the altar erected to the nimble god Mercury, he made such daily improvements therein, as what with his acquirements in company with the persons just mentioned, and what with the purchases that he made in looking out for booty by himself, he found himself in a condition to keep three fine geldings at a livery stable in Finsbury, and as many mistresses in other parts of the town, to whom he reported at pleasure after the fatigues of the day spent, either in pursuit of the hare with the common hunt's dogs, or in laying wagers at horse races, or bidding travellers stand, who had scarce any chance to save what he asked them for.

The first of these was Mrs Anne W–kins, who was his favourite, and by whom he had three children, two girls and a boy; which, if you will believe the mother (who says, she had never to do with any one man breathing besides Child) are as like the father, as if they were spit out of his mouth. The second, Mrs Elizabeth St–ly, who is now with child by him, after her ground had been tilled by half the sparks in the town, without bearing any fruit before. And the third, Mrs Mary Ch—, as errant a jilt as ever stood upon two legs, and could no more be true to one man than to twenty.

Thus, from being kept by others, he came to be a keeper himself, which put him up to many shifts and tricks, besides excursions on the highway; for more sins than a few must be committed for the support of three extravagant lewd women, besides himself, who had a servant in a livery, and such change of clothes, even made up of velvets of all colours, as made him come up to the port and appearance, in his own person, as any nobleman.

A True Copy of the Paper delivered by Mr Benjamin Child to his Friend at the Place of Execution

It being customary for men, under my unhappy circumstances, to declare what religion they die of, or whether they suffer wrongfully or justly, at the place of execution, I am to assure the world, in the first place, that though the prejudice of education has misled me, for the greatest part of the time I have been at man's estate, against the principles of the Church of England, yet I die in that communion; being perfectly persuaded by the Divines, who have taken great pains with me for that end, that the doctrines, which are taught by that church, are pure and holy, and entirely conducive to eternal salvation.

I think myself likewise obliged in conscience, in this my last hour, to declare, not only my guiltiness as to the crime I am now brought hither to suffer for, but many others of the same ill tendency, and heartily ask pardon of all that have been injured by my means, either by open assaults on the road, or collusory practises in private, to defraud and cheat them; and particularly of a gentlewoman of this county, whom I drew aside, and borrowed a large sum of money of, under promises of marriage. And as I, in my own person, forgive all the people whatsoever, without distinction or reserve, even my prosecutors; among whom my thanks are due to Captain B——[1] for undeserved favours: and hold myself bound to him, whose evidence has taken away my life, and that Mr Wade may repent, and not associate himself, for the time to come, with such as may take away his after the same manner.

To conclude; I am thankful both to judge and jury, for the righteousness of his judgement, and their verdicts; and though I could have wished the sentence, which is now going to be pronounced, might have been mitigated so far, as to have permitted me Christian burial, according to the rites of that church; yet it may deter others from giving into the same wicked courses, and bring them to a true sense of their duty to God and man. To him to whom all honour is due, be ascribed all honour and glory, for making me, the vilest of his whole creation, the instrument of so great good.

And now, having made this my last declaration, I commend my soul into the hands of a gracious Redeemer, who, by his sufferings upon earth has made satisfaction for the sins of the whole world; in full confidence that, through his wounds, mine shall be healed; and that though the fowls of the air shall 'destroy this body, yet in my flesh shall I see God'.

---

[1] Prosecutor in Child's last trial.

RICHARD TURPIN *Convicted of sheep-stealing, and hanged in 1739*
From Jackson's *Newgate Calendar*

Turpin (b. 1706) was not the hero he has been made out to be since his death, most notably by the nineteenth-century novelist William Harrison Ainsworth who also mythologized the housebreaker Jack Sheppard. He was trained as a butcher, which helped him when he became a cattle-thief – he knew which cuts of meat were most valuable and how to carve up an animal; then he progressed to highway robbery, working in a notorious gang of cut-throats based in Epping Forest, Essex. When Turpin killed a man, he became the most wanted man in England, with a reward of £100 on his head; a few weeks later, he shot and killed his partner, Tom King, by mistake while trying to elude a captor. At this point he left Essex and headed north, reaching York not in a single night, as Ainsworth erroneously wrote, but over a period of months. There he soon fell into crime again, and was arrested in 1739 for stealing horses. After his death, his name became legendary, especially among gypsies who frequently named their children Dick in his honour.

Going first to Long Sutton, in Lincolnshire, he stole some horses, for which he was taken into custody, but he escaped from the constable as he was conducting him before a magistrate, and hastened to Welton, in Yorkshire, where he went by the name of John Palmer, and assumed the character of a gentleman.

He now frequently went into Lincolnshire, where he stole horses, which he brought into Yorkshire, and either sold or exchanged them.

He often accompanied the neighbouring gentlemen on their parties of hunting and shooting; and one evening on a return from an expedition of the latter kind, he wantonly shot a cock belonging to his landlord. On this, Mr Hall, a neighbour said You have done wrong in shooting your landlord's cock; to which Turpin replied, that if he would stay till he reloaded his gun, he would shoot him also.

Irritated by this insult, Mr Hall informed the landlord of what had passed; and application being made to some magistrates, a warrant was granted for the apprehension of the offender, who being taken into custody, and carried before a bench of justices, then assembled at the quarter-sessions, at Beverley, they demanded security for his good behaviour, which he being unable or unwilling to give, he was committed to Bridewell.

On enquiry, it appeared that he made frequent journeys into Lincolnshire, and on his return always abounded in money, and was likewise in possession of several horses; so that it was conjectured that he was a horse-stealer and highway-man.

On this the magistrates went to him on the following day, and demanded who he was, where he had lived and what was his employment? He replied in substance that about two years ago he had lived at Long Sutton, in Lincolnshire, and was by trade a butcher, but that having contracted several debts for sheep that proved rotten, he was obliged to abscond, and come to live in Yorkshire.

The magistrates not being satisfied with this tale, commissioned the clerk of the peace to write into Lincolnshire, to make the necessary inquiries respecting this supposed John Palmer. The letter was carried by a special messenger who brought an answer from a magistrate in the neighbourhood, importing that John Palmer was well known, though he had never carried on trade there: that he had been accused of sheep-stealing, for which he had been in custody, but had made his escape from the peace officers, and that there were several informations lodged against him for horse-stealing.

Hereupon the magistrates thought it prudent to remove him to York Castle, where he had not been more than a month, when two persons from Lincolnshire came and claimed a mare and foal, and likewise a horse, which he had stolen in that county.

After he had been about four months in prison, he wrote the following letter to his brother in Essex: —

York, Feb. 6, 1739

'Dear Brother,

I am sorry to acquaint you that I am now under confinement in York Castle, for horse-stealing. If I could procure an evidence from London to give me a character, that would go a great way towards my being acquitted. I had not been long in this country before my being apprehended, so that it would pass off the readier. For Heaven's sake, dear brother, do not neglect me; you will know what I mean, when I say,

I am yours,

JOHN PALMER.'

This letter being returned, unopened, to the Post office in Essex, because the brother would not pay the postage of it, was accidentally seen by Mr Smith, a schoolmaster, who having taught Turpin to write, immediately knew his hand, on which he carried the letter to a magistrate, who broke it open; by which it was discovered that the supposed John Palmer was the real Richard Turpin.

Hereupon the magistrates of Essex dispatched Mr Smith to York, who immediately selected him from all the other prisoners in the castle. This Mr Smith, and another gentleman, afterwards proved his identity on his trial.

On a rumour that the noted Turpin was a prisoner in York castle, persons flocked from all parts of the country to take a view of him, and debates ran very high whether he was the real person or not. Amongst others who visited him was a young fellow who pretended to know the famous Turpin, and having regarded him a considerable time with looks of great attention, he told the keeper he would bet him half a guinea that he was not Turpin, on which the prisoner, whispering to the keeper, said, Lay him the wager, I'll go you halves.

When this notorious malefactor was brought to trial, he was convicted on two indictments, and received sentence of death.

After conviction he wrote to his father, imploring him to intercede with a gentleman and lady of rank to make interest that his sentence might be remitted; and that he might be transported. The father did what was in his power; but the notoriety of his character was such, that no person would exert themselves in his favour.

This man lived in the most gay and thoughtless manner after conviction, regardless of all considerations of futurity, and affecting to make a jest of the dreadful fate that awaited him.

Not many days before his execution, he purchased a new fustian frock and a pair of pumps, in order to wear them at the time of his death: and, on the day before he hired five poor men, at ten shillings each, to follow the cart as mourners; and he gave hatbands and gloves to several other persons; he also left a ring, and some other articles to a married woman in Lincolnshire, with whom he had been acquainted.

On the morning of his death he was put into a cart, and being followed by his mourners, as above-mentioned, he was drawn along to the place of execution, in his way he bowed to the spectators with an air of the most astonishing indifference and intrepidity.

When he came to the fatal tree, he ascended the ladder; when, his right leg trembling, he stamped it down with an air of unassumed courage, as if he was ashamed to be observed to discover any signs of fear. Having conversed with the executioner about half an hour, he threw himself off the ladder and expired in a few minutes.

The spectators of the execution seemed to be much affected at the fate of this man, who was distinguished by the comeliness of his appearance. The corpse was brought to the Blue Boar, in Castle gate, York, when it was interred in the church yard of St George's parish, with an inscription on the coffin, with the initials of his name, and his age. The grave was remarkably deep, and the people who acted as mourners took such measures as they thought would secure the body; yet about three o'clock on the following morning, some people were observed in the church yard, who carried it off; and the populace having an intimation whither it was conveyed, found it in a garden belonging to one of the surgeons of the city.[1]

Hereupon they took the body, laid it on a board, and having carried it through the streets, in a kind of triumphal manner, they then filled the coffin with unslacked lime, and buried it in the grave where it had been before deposited.

[1] The corpses of criminals were thought to have healing qualities. See Introduction.

JAMES MACLEANE *Convicted of highway robbery, and hanged in 1750*
From 1764 *Select Trials*

Macleane, the 'Gentleman Highwayman', lived in style in St James's for two years, frequenting London's best society, and supporting several mistresses; when asked, he explained that he lived off the revenues of his non-existent family estates in Ireland. Macleane's veneer of gentility never slipped, even when, masked, he held up coaches demanding, 'Your money or your life!' Once he stopped Horace Walpole, and by accident his pistol discharged and a bullet skimmed Walpole's cheek; horrified by this act of inadvertent violence, Macleane apologized before relieving him of his purse. In prison he repented of his crimes, and went to his death neither in fear nor pride: 'He was not arrogant enough to brave death, nor so much wedded to life as to dread it as a coward.'

[After a middle-class upbringing as the son of a well-to-do Scottish parson, and several years drifting from one job to another, Macleane set himself up as a shopkeeper and found some stability with his bride.]

With this sum [her dowry] he set up a grocer and chandler's shop, in *Wellbeck-street*, near *Cavendish-square*. While his wife lived he kept even with the world, and maintained his family in decency, tho' with much difficulty; for he was more the man of pleasure than business. Those who knew him at that time, generally say he was a harmless inoffensive man; but being surprized at his way of life, were apt to suggest strange things of him, but no one could lay any thing wicked or notorious to his charge while he lived in that neighbourhood. His wife died about three years after their marriage, leaving him two daughters, of whom her mother, on her death-bed, took the charge, as she afterwards did of that one who survived him.

Deprived of his wife, who had managed all the affairs of the shop and business, he was too much addicted to idleness and pleasure, to confine himself to the occupation of a grocer; he sold off his goods, and with the remains of his effects, which he had not augmented, but greatly diminished by trade, he commenced gentleman fortune-hunter.

He was scarce six months embarked in this fallacious project, before he had, in folly and extravagance, exhausted all he had left of his late wife's fortune, and was at a loss how to raise any more to supply present necessities, much less to support the figure he made. It went to his soul to descend again from the fine gentleman to the menial servant, and he soon grew melancholy on the (to him) dreadful prospect of being obliged to dispose of his cloaths and equipage for mere bread. He was in this gloomy disposition, when he was visited by a countryman of his, one *Plunket*, an apothecary. His friend in a familiar way, asked the cause of his melancholy; on which the other opened his real circumstances, to which he was not before a stranger. *Honey*, says *Plunket*, *I thought Macleane had spirit, and resolution, with some knowledge of the world. A brave man cannot want; he has a right to live, and need not want the conveniencies of life, while the dull, plodding, busy knaves carry cash in their pockets. We must draw upon them to supply our wants; there need only impudence, and getting the better of a few idle scruples; there is scarce courage necessary; all we have to deal with are such mere poltroons.* This discourse was soon understood by the unhappy *Macleane*, who though at first shock'd at the bare mention of it, yet the necessity of his pride and indolence suggested so strongly, that he yielded to the temptation; and from that time, which might be about eight months after his wife's death, enter'd into a particular intimacy with *Plunket*, agreed to run all risques together, and, present or absent at any enterprize, to share all profits; of which, till the fatal discovery, they kept a fair and regular account.

Though *Macleane* believed himself possessed of as much courage as any man, yet on his first attempt, (nor could even long practice harden him) he felt every symptom of fear and cowardice, aggravated by the stings of conscience, which vice could not harden. However, the success of the first enterprize (on a grazier coming from *Smithfield* market, from whom, on *Hounslow Heath*, they took above 60 *l.*)

encouraged him to stifle the checks of conscience, and to persevere in a way, which though it appeared to him wicked, yet was found so lucrative. In this transaction he was no more than passive, stood by without speaking a word, or so much as drawing his pistols, but inwardly in greater agony than the man that was robbed; so that if any resistance had been made, he had certainly taken the first hint of trusting to his heels. However, the man parted peaceably with his money, and they had time to divide it, and squander it without suspicion or molestation.

The next robbery they committed was on a coach in the road from St *Albans*. By agreement he was to stop the coachman, and present his pistol on one side, while *Plunket* did the same on the other. But though he rode frequently up with intention to give the word, yet his heart failed him; and *Plunket*, lest they should miss the booty, did it himself; and it was with some faultering *Macleane* demanded their money after the coach was stopt, and no danger seemed near. However, he grew more resolute, and, to redeem his credit with *Plunket*, who began to rally him on his pusillanimity, he once, by himself, robbed a gentleman in *Hyde-park* on horseback, of his watch and money, and was the acting man in the robbery of *Horatio Walpole*, which indeed he owned, and declared the firing of the pistol was accidental.

He reigned long and successfully, and was never but once afraid of a discovery; to avoid which he went over to *Holland*, till the storm was blown over; pretending a friendly visit to his brother, to whom he gave some sham account of the manner of his living; and was by him introduced to some very polite assemblies of dancing, and where it was said some purses and gold watches were lost; and since *Macleane*'s confinement, the suspicion seemed to be fixed on him, though at that time no such thing was thought of. After he had staid some time in *Holland*, he returned to his old trade.

With these collections from the public he lived in splendor; but to avoid impertinent questions often shifted his lodgings, tho' in all public places he made the gayest appearance, and kept company not only with the most noted ladies of the town, but some women of fortune and reputation were unguarded enough to admit him into their company, without any other recommendation than his appearing in all places of public resort, with great impudence, and a variety of rich cloaths. He had the good fortune even to make some progress in the affections of a young lady, who really deserved a better fate, but his character was blown by a gentleman, who knew him too well to think himself obliged to accept of a challenge sent him on that account by *Macleane*, and the lady was saved from total ruin.

By this means he supplied all the extravagance of his disposition, yet he never once thought of his daughter, and seldom visited his mother-in-law, who took care of her; and lest he should be plagued with her importunities, or that she might take the liberty of a person so nearly concerned in him, to ask about the means of his gay appearance, he made his visits short and seldom, and always concealed from her his abode.

Justice at length laid her iron hands upon him, and made even himself chiefly instrumental in bringing him to condign punishment; for it is observable, and he often made the remark himself, that if a particular fate had not directed him to dispose of the goods in the manner he did it, and to strengthen the suspicion by a judicial confession, there was, as yet, no man, but *Plunket*, his accomplice, that could hurt him. For, after he had, on the 26th of *June*, robbed the *Salisbury* stage-coach of their money, and two portmanteaus; and the same morning, by an artifice, robbed Lord *Eglington*, who was so good-natured as not to appear against him, they divided the spoil at *Macleane*'s lodgings, who was so infatuated, that tho' the cloaths were advertised and described in the public papers, to offer the lace, stripped off Mr *Higden*'s waistcoat, to the very laceman of whom it had been bought, and to desire a salesman to come to his lodgings to purchase the cloaths, who bought them, and by whose means Mr *Higden* was brought to view them, knew his property and had Mr *Macleane* immediately taken up by a warrant, and carried before Justice *Lediard*; what passed at his examination there, we have before given an account of.

He was so much in favour with the fair sex, that some presented him with money, which, with other compassionate contributions from the same weak quarter, he lived at the *Gatehouse* with as much ease as a tortured conscience, and the dread of death could permit him. The notice taken of him by some persons of distinction, perhaps, gave him some hopes of his life, which never left him till he left *Newgate*, and in a great measure disturbed his preparation for eternity.

JOHN RANN *Convicted of highway robbery, and hanged in 1774* From *An Account of John Rann Commonly Called Sixteen String Jack* (1774)

Jack Rann was born in the parish of St George's, around Hanover Square in London's West End. After a scanty education, he became a hackney coachman; but he soon found that this profession could not support his taste for extravagant clothes and living, and turned to highway robbery. He was known as 'Sixteen String Jack' because he wore eight ribbons at each knee to fasten his breeches; at his first trial he appeared with his handcuffs tied with pale blue ribbons. Rann was arrested and tried seven times, but it was not until his seventh trial that any crime could be pinned to him, and he was convicted at last. In the year Rann was executed, Horace Walpole – who twenty years before had been the victim of James Macleane – complained that the roads of London were 'so infected by highwaymen that it is dangerous stirring out almost by day' (letter to Horace Mann). But as it became more difficult for highwaymen to make a living – with the invention of the steam train, roads contained fewer rich pickings; and the Bow Street Runners, while not a modern police force, were increasingly efficient – Rann's career was the final flourish of his breed: insouciant, flamboyant and unrepentant.

Rann has, in his general behaviour and especially previous to his trial, and at his examinations before the magistrates, assumed an air of gaiety and affectation, ill becoming his situation, and at the same time betraying a low turn of mind; the common effect of ignorance and its natural and almost inseperable companion, impudence.

One of the most extraordinary circumstances is, that he has very frequently boasted of his enormities in public company; made no scruple to recite the particulars of his robberies, and even mentioned the time when he thought his career of iniquity would be at an end. He has been often heard to say, 'I have so much money, I shall spend that, and then I shant last long.' It has been frequent in his mouth that he should be hanged about November; and it is not long since he betted a crown's worth of punch that he should suffer before Christmas.

Two or three days after his acquittal, he engaged to sup with Miss — at her lodgings in Bow Street, but not being punctual to his appointment, the lady went to bed; and about midnight arrived, but not being able to get admittance at the door, he attempted to get in at the one pair of stairs window, and very nearly accomplished his purpose, when he was perceived by the watchman, who immediately secured him.

Upon his being brought before Sir John Fielding, Miss appeared in his behalf, and assured the bench that he could have no felonious intention, as he only attempted to get into her apartment, where he knew himself to be a welcome guest, and would have gained a ready admission, had she not unluckily fell asleep. No other charge being brought against him, he was dismissed, after being exhorted in a very pathetic manner by the magistrate, to leave his vicious courses, and apply himself to some honest means of obtaining a livelihood.

The Sunday following our hero appeared at Bagnigge-Wells, elegantly dressed in a scarlet coat, a tambour[1] waistcoat, white silk stockings, laced hat, etc. and publickly declared himself to be a highwayman. Having drank very freely, he became extremely quarrelsome and abusive, and several scuffles ensued, in one of which having lost a ring from his finger, he appeared quite indifferent, saying in a careless manner, 'It was but an hundred guineas gone, which one

---

[1] embroidered.

evenings work would replace.' He became at length so extremely turbulent, that some of the company proposed turning him out of the house; but they met with so obstinate a resistance, that they were obliged to give up their design. However a number of young fellows, possessed of more spirit than discretion, attacked this magnanimous hero, and forced him through the window into the road. This so derogatory to his honour, ruffled him so much that he uttered the most horrid execrations against the frequenters of Bagnigge-Wells, for the indignity they had shewn to a gentleman of his figure.

Some time after Rann had been tried for the robbery of Mr Devall on the highway, (as already mentioned) he was arrested for twenty pounds, and not being able to pay the debt or give bail to the action, he was confined in the Fleet. While he was in this situation, he was visited by a great number of ladies of easy virtue, as well as young fellows, of very suspicious characters, by whom his debt was soon paid and he was released.

At another time Rann, and two of his companions, being at a public house near Tottenham-Court Road Turnpike, two sheriffs officers, who had a writ against Rann, entered the room and arrested him. As he had not cash sufficient to pay the debt he deposited his watch, and his companions advanced him three guineas, which, together with his watch, made more than the amount of the debt, as a balance when the watch was redeemed, being to be returned to Rann, he told the bailiffs if they would lend him five shillings, he would treat them with a bowl of punch. This being complied with the liquor was called for; during the time of drinking, Rann complained that they had not treated him like a gentleman. When Sir John Fielding's people come after me (said he) they use me genteelly; they only hold up their finger, becon, and I follow them as quiet as a lamb.

The officers being gone, Rann and his companions mounted their horses and rode off; but our hero returned in an hour or two, stopped at the turnpike and asked the Toll-Man if he had been wanted. 'No,' said the man. 'What do not you know me.' 'No.' 'Why, I am Sixteen String Jack, the famous highwayman; have any of Sir John Fielding's men been this way.' 'Oh! yes,' cried the Toll Man, 'they have. Some of them are but just gone through.' Rann replied, 'if you see them again, tell them I am gone towards London'; and rode off at his leisure. It is reported that a nobleman was robbed near the spot that afternoon; but it does not appear with any certainty, nor pretend to assert that Rann was one of the highwaymen.

At the last races at Barnet, Rann appeared on the course dressed like a sporting peer of the first rank. He was distinguished by the elegance of his appearance, in a blue sattin waistcoat laced with silver, and was followed by hundreds from one side of the course to the other, whose curiosity was excited to behold a genius, whose exploits were so notorious to the world.

Rann attended at Tyburn on the execution before the last, he alighted from the coach in which he came, and going within the ring made by the constables, he desired permission to take his station in that place, that he might have a good view of what passed, 'for' said he, 'perhaps it is very proper that I should be a spectator on this melancholy occasion.'

On Wednesday the 28th of September 1774, John Rann, and William Collier were examined at the public office in Bow street, on a suspicion of their having robbed Dr William Bell, Chaplain to her Royal Highness the Princess Amelia, of his watch and eighteen pence in money, on the highway, near Ealing in Middlesex.

Dr Bell, in a circumstantial narrative acquainted the bench, that between three and four o'clock in the afternoon on Monday the 26th of September, as he was riding near Ealing, two men, rather of a mean appearance, passed him; and that he observed they had suspicious looks; though at that time, had he any [he had no] idea of their attacking him: however, at about half an hour after three, one of them, which he believed (but would not swear) to be Rann, crossed the head of his horse, and demanded his money, saying, 'give it me, and take no notice, or I'll blow your brains out.' The Doctor then offered him eighteen pence, which was all the silver he had, but in searching for more, the highwayman found, and took his watch.

The evening of the day this robbery was committed, between eight and nine o'clock, Eleanor Roache (who was kept by Rann,) and her maid offered a watch to pledge with Mr Cordy a pawnbroker in Oxford Road, who suspecting it was not honestly come by, stopped it, and applied to the maker, Mr Grignion of Ruffel Street, Covent Garden, who informed him that it belonged to Dr Bell.

Mr Clarke a peace officer, informed the magistrates, that on going to Miss Roache's lodgings on the Monday night, in consequence of the hints obtained by Mr Cordy's stopping the watch, he found there two pairs of boots, very wet and dirty, which had evidently been worn that day. And Mr Halliburton, another peace officer, waited at Roache's lodgings till Rann and Collier came thither, when they were both apprehended.

It likewise appeared on his examination, that on the following morning (Tuesday) two horses were brought to Miss Roache's lodgings, on which the prisoners were again to have taken a ride; but they were then, happily in custody; there could be no doubt but the horses were intended for the use of Rann and Collier, as, that the latter had paid for the hire of them; though they both denied knowing any thing about them.

Hereupon the prisoners were committed to Tothil Field's Bridewell for further examination on the Wednesday following; and Miss Roache was sent to New Prison as the supposed receiver of Dr Bell's stolen watch. The curiosity of the people was so great to see Rann, that above a thousand people had assembled in Bow Street.

On Wednesday October the 5th, John Rann, William Collier and Eleanor Roache, (together with Christian Stewart, Roache's servant girl) were again brought to Sir John Fielding's office, when Dr Bell deposed, in substance, as he had done the preceeding week, and positively swore that the stolen watch was his property. Hannah Craggs swore to the being present at Miss Roache's lodgings when the prisoners went away on horseback, on the day of the robbery. Mr Cordy also proved the stopping the Doctor's watch, when it was offered him in pledge the same evening, by Miss Roache; but the most strong and corroborating circumstance of their guilt appeared in the next evidence.

William Hills (a servant of the Princess Amelia) who swore to his having seen Rann (whom he had long known) with a companion, ascending the hill at Acton, about twenty minutes before Dr Bell was robbed; and this answered extremely well to the distance from Acton to the place where the robbery was committed.

Christian Stewart on being examined, behaved with great duplicity; pretend at first that she knew nothing of the prisoners, though she afterwards acknowledged that she knew Collier; and from hence arose a very just suspicion that she was well acquainted with the parties, and the nature of their occupation.

As the charge was now sufficiently supported by the evidence which was collected together on the examination, John Rann and William Collier were committed to Newgate to take their trials for the highway robbery; Eleanor Roache to Clerkenwell Bridewell, and Christian Stewart to that of Tothil Fields.

On Wednesday October the 20th 1774, John Rann, alias Sixteen String Jack, was conducted from Newgate to the New Sessions House in the Old Bailey, together with his accomplice William Collier, to take their trials for robbing Dr William Bell, on the highway, near Gunnersbury Lane of his watch and eighteen pence in money.

The evidence given on their trial was in substance the same with that given at Bow Street, as already recited, and the jury after consultation found them both guilty death;[1] some favourable circumstances appeared on the trial in favour of Collier, which induced the jury to recommend him to the court, for his Majesty's mercy.

When Rann was brought down to take his trial, he appeared very careless and indifferent, having by no means a proper sense of the unfortunate and truly wretched situation in which all the spectators viewed him. He was dressed in a new coat and waistcoat of pea green cloth, with new buckskin breeches, ruffled shirt and a hat bound round with silver strings. The trial lasted two hours, and the auditors were more affected (if we may judge from appearance) than the culprit.

He was so confident of being acquitted, that he had ordered a

[1] That is, they were found guilty, and sentenced to death.

genteel supper to be provided for the entertainment of a number of his particular friends and associates on the joyful occasion; alas! how great the disappointment of the company, when they heard the fate of the unhappy wretch.

On Tuesday the 26th of October 1774, John Rann, William Collier and Eleanor Roache received sentence, the two first to be executed at Tyburn, and the last to be transported for fourteen years. When Rann had received his sentence, he attempted to force a smile; but it was evidently the smile of a man whose heart was tortured with grief and vexation . . .

Since conviction, his behaviour is not the least amended: on Sunday the 23rd of October not less than seven girls dined with him; the company was very cheerful, and the wicked culprit appeared quite insensible to the dreadful situation his crimes have brought him into.

8

Confidence Tricksters

MARY CARLETON *Convicted of returning from
transportation, and hanged in 1663*
From Johnson's *A General History of the Lives of the . . .
Highwaymen*

*'Princess' Mary Carleton was born in Canterbury in about 1625 and at
first seemed destined to lead a normal, humble life, marrying a shoemaker
and bearing him two children. But both children died in infancy, and she
grew dissatisfied with her lot and left Canterbury and the poor cobbler
for Dover where she married a rich surgeon. 'A woman of her figure,
beauty and address was not long before she procured another husband,'
relates Johnson. Tried for bigamy, she was acquitted by some sleight of
fortune, and went to Europe. In Germany she acquired a rich, doting
older lover whom she left at the altar – taking the money and jewels he
had given her. In 1663 she returned to England (where the excerpt
below begins), assuming the identity of a German princess, and continued
successfully to part fools from their money. For some time she worked as
an actress, gaining fame. Eventually, she was convicted of stealing a silver
tankard, and transported to Jamaica, but she returned to England after
serving only two years of her sentence. A thief-catcher recognized her,
and she was brought before the Old Bailey once again. Although she
tried to plead her belly (a woman with child was always transported
instead of being hanged; but Carleton was forty-eight-years old) she was
found to be not pregnant and hanged at Tyburn. On the scaffold she
addressed the crowd, owning 'that she had been a very vain woman and
hoped that her fate would deter others from the same evil ways'.*

She landed at Billingsgate one morning very early in the end of March
1663, and found no house open until she came to the Exchange
Tavern, where, in the following manner, she attained the rank of a
German princess. In that tavern she got into the company of some
gentlemen whom she perceived were full of money, and these addressing her in a rude manner, she began crying most bitterly, exclaiming
that it was extremely hard for her to be reduced to this extreme

distress who was once a princess. Here she repeated the story of her extraction and education, and much about her pretended father, the Lord Henry Vandwolway, a Prince of the Empire, and independent of every man but His Imperial Majesty. 'Certainly,' said she, 'any gentleman here present may conceive what a painful situation this must be to me, brought up under the care of an indulgent father, and in all the luxuries of a Court, to be reduced thus low. But alas! what do I say? Indulgent father! Alas! was it not his cruelty which banished me, his only daughter, from his dominions, merely for marrying without his knowledge a nobleman of the Court whom I loved to excess? Was it not my father who occasioned my dear lord and husband to be cut off in the bloom of his age by falsely accusing him of a design against his person – a deed which his virtuous soul abhorred.' Here she pretended that the poignancy of her feelings would allow her to relate no more of her unfortunate history.

The whole company was touched with compassion at the melancholy tale, which she related with so much unaffected simplicity that they had not a doubt of its authenticity. Compassionating her unfortunate situation, they requested her acceptance of all the money they had about them, promising to return again with more. They were as good as their promise, and she ever after went by the name of the unfortunate German Princess.

The man who kept the inn, knowing that she was come from the Continent, and seeing that she had great riches about her, he was disposed, more than ever, to believe the truth of her story. Nor was madam backward to inform him that she had collected all that she possessed from the benevolent contributions of neighbouring princes, who knew and pitied her misfortunes. 'Nor durst any one of them,' continued she, 'let my father know what they have done, or where I was, for he was so much more powerful than any of them, that if he understood that any one favoured me, he would instantly make war upon them.'

King, the innkeeper, being convinced of her rank and fortune, John Carleton, his brother-in-law, no doubt receiving proper information from King, became enamoured of the Princess, and presumed to pay his addresses to her. She was highly displeased at first, but from his importunity she was, at last, prevailed upon to descend from her station and receive the hand of a common man. Poor Carleton thought himself the happiest of mortals, in being then so highly honoured by a union with such an accomplished and amiable princess, possessed of an ample fortune, though far inferior to what she had a right to expect from her noble birth.

But, during this dream of pleasure, Mr King received a letter informing him that the woman who resided at his house, and was married to his brother-in-law, was an impostor; that she had already been married to two husbands, and had eloped with all the money she could lay her hands on: that he said nothing but what could be proved by the most unquestionable evidence in a court of justice. The consequence was that a prosecution was instituted against her for the crime of polygamy; but from insufficient evidence she was acquitted.

She was then introduced as an actress among the players, and by them supported for some time. Upon her account the house was often crowded, and the public curiosity was excited by a woman who had made such a figure in the world, and received great applause in her dramatic capacity. She generally appeared in characters suited to her habits of life and those scenes which were rendered familiar to her by former deceptions and intrigues. But which tended chiefly to promote her fame was a play called *The German Princess*, written principally upon her account, in which she spoke the following prologue in such a manner as gained universal applause.

> I've past one trial, but it is my fear
> I shall receive a rigid sentence here:
> You think me a bold cheat, but 'case 'twere so,
> Which of you are not? Now you'd swear I know,
> But do not, lest that you deserve to be
> Censured worse than you can censure me;
> The world's a cheat, and we that move in it,
> In our degrees, do exercise our wit;
> And better 'tis to get a glorious name,
> However got, than live by common fame.

The Princess had too much mercury in her constitution to remain long within the bounds of the theatre, when London itself was too limited for her volatile disposition. She did not, however, leave the theatre until she had procured many admirers. Her history was well known, as well as her accomplishments and her gallantry, and introduced her into company. She was easy of access, but in company she carried herself with an affected air of indifference.

There were two young beaux in particular who had more money in their pockets than wit in their heads; and from the scarcity of that commodity in themselves, they the more admired her wit and humour. She encouraged their addresses until she had extracted about three hundred pounds from each of them, and then, observing their funds were nearly exhausted, she discarded them both, saying she was astonished at their impudence in making love to a princess!

Her next lover was an old gentleman about fifty, who saw her, and though he was acquainted with her history, yet he resolved to be at the expense of some hundreds a year, provided she would consent to live with him. To gain his purpose he made her several rich presents, which, with seeming reluctance, she accepted. When they lived together as man and wife, she so accommodated herself to his temper and dispositions that he was constantly making her rich presents, which were always accepted with apparent reluctance, as laying her under so many obligations. In this manner they continued, until her doting lover one evening coming home intoxicated, she thought it a proper opportunity to decamp. So soon as he was asleep she rifled his pockets, found his pocket-book containing a bill for a hundred pounds and some money. She also stripped him of his watch, and taking his keys opened his coffers, and carried off everything that suited her purpose. She next went and presented the bill, and as the acceptor knew her she received the money without hesitation.

Having thus fleeced her old lover, she took up lodgings in a convenient place under the character of a young lady with a thousand pounds, and whose father was able to give her twice as much, but disliking a person whom he had provided as a husband for her, she had left her father's house and did not wish to be discovered by any of her friends. Madam continued, at the same time, to have different letters sent her from time to time, containing an account of all the news concerning her father and lover. These were left carelessly about the room, and her landlady reading them, she became confirmed in the belief of her story.

That woman had a rich nephew, a young man whom she introduced to her acquaintance, who became enamoured of her, and to gain her favour presented her with a gold watch. She was hardly prevailed upon to accept of that present. Her lover already thought the door of paradise was open to him, and their amour proceeded with all that felicity that young lovers could wish. But in this season of bliss, a porter knocked at the door with a letter. Her maid, as previously directed, brought it in to her, which she had no sooner read than she exclaimed, 'I am undone! I am ruined!' and pretended to swoon away. The scent bottle was employed, and her enraptured lover was all kindness and attention. When she was a little recovered she presented the letter, saying, 'Sir, since you are at last acquainted with most of my concerns, I shall not make a secret of this; therefore, if you please, read this letter, and know the occasion of my affliction.' The young gentleman received it, and read as follows: –

'DEAR MADAM, – I have several times taken my pen in hand on purpose to write you, and as often laid it aside again for fear of giving you more trouble than you already labour under. However, as the affair so immediately concerns you, I cannot in justice hide what I tremble to disclose, but must in duty tell you the worst of news, whatever may be the consequence of my so doing.

'Know, then, that your affectionate and tender brother is dead. I am sensible how dear he was to you, and you to him, yet let me entreat you, for your own sake, to acquiesce in the will of Providence as much as possible, since our lives are all at his disposal who gave us being. I could use another argument to comfort you, that with a sister less loving than you would be of more weight than that I have urged; but I know your soul is above all mercenary views. I cannot, however, forbear to inform you that he has left you all he had; and further, that your father's estate of £200 per annum can now devolve upon no other person than yourself, who are now his only child.

'What I am next to acquaint you with, may perhaps be almost as bad as the former particular. Your hated lover has been so importunate with your father, especially since your brother's decease, that the old gentleman resolves if ever he should hear of you any more, to marry you to him, and he makes this the condition of your being again received into his favour, and having your former disobedience, as he calls it, forgiven. While your brother lived he was every day endeavouring to soften the heart of your father, and we were but last week in hopes he would have consented to let you follow your inclinations, if you would come home to him again; but now there is no advocate in your cause who can work upon the man's peevish temper; for, he says, as you are now his sole heir, he ought to be more resolute in the disposal of you in marriage.

'While I am now writing I am surprised with an account that your father and lover are preparing to come to London, where they say they can find you out. Whether or not this be only a device I cannot tell, nor can I conceive where they could receive their information, if it be true. However, to prevent the worst, consider whether or not you can cast off your old aversion and submit to your father's commands; for, if you cannot, it will be most advisable, in my opinion, to change your residence. I have no more to say in the affair, being unwilling to direct you in such a very nice circumstance. The temper of your own mind will be the best instructor you can apply to; for your future happiness or misery during life depends on your choice. I hope that everything will turn for the best. From your sincere friend,

'S. E.'

Her lover saw that she had good reason to be afflicted, and while he seemed to feel for her he was no less concerned about his own interest. He advised her immediately to leave her lodgings, and added that he had very elegant apartments which were at her service. She accepted of his offer, and she and her maid, who was informed of her intentions and prepared to assist her, immediately set out for the residence of her lover. When introduced to their new apartment they did not go to bed, as they resolved to depart next morning, but lay down to rest themselves with their clothes on. When the house was all quiet they broke open his desk, took out a bag with a hundred pounds, two suits of clothes, and everything valuable that they could carry along with them.

Her numerous and varied adventures would far exceed the limits appropriated to one life in this volume. It is sufficient to observe that rather than her hands should be unemployed or her avaricious disposition unpractised, that she would carry off the most trifling article; that according to the proverb, 'All was fish that came into her net,' and that when a watch, a diamond or piece of plate could not be found, a napkin, a pair of sheets or any article of wearing apparel would suffice.

She one day, along with her pretended maid, went into a mercer's shop in Cheapside, and purchased a piece of silk to the value of six pounds. She pulled out her purse to pay the merchant, but to her surprise found that she had no money except some large pieces of gold for which she had so high an esteem that she could not think of parting with them. The polite merchant could not think of hurting the feelings of a lady so elegantly dressed, and accordingly dispatched one of his shopkeepers along with her to receive his money. They went all three into a coach which was ready to receive them. Arrived at the Royal Exchange, Madam ordered the coachman to stop, when upon the pretence of purchasing some ribbons that would suit the silks, her maid carried out the parcel and went along with her, leaving the shopman in the coach to wait their return. The young man waited in the coach until he was impatient and ashamed, and then returned home to relate his misfortunes and the loss of his master.

The transfer of invention and of villainy was easy to the next adventure. Madam waited upon a French weaver in Spitalfields, and purchased goods to the amount of forty pounds. He went home with her to carry the goods and to receive his money. She desired him to make out a bill for the whole goods, as the one half belonged to a lady in the next room. With all the ceremony natural to a Frenchman he sat down to write his account, while she took the silk into the adjacent room to show it to her niece, to whom the one half belonged.

By means of a bottle of wine that Madam had placed before the French weaver, one half hour passed over without much uneasiness. At length his patience was exhausted, and having called up the people in the house, he inquired for the lady who came in with him, and who told him she was only gone to the next room. To the utter confusion and disappointment of poor Monsieur, he was informed that his lady was gone, and would, they believed, return no more to that dwelling. The Frenchman was instantly in a violent passion, and quarrelled with the people in the house. To calm his rage and to convince him that they were not confederates in her villainy, they conveyed him to the next room, and showed him that the proper entry to her room was by a back stair, adding that she had only taken their room for a month, for which she had paid them, and that her time being expired, they knew not where she had gone.

Determined to collect her contributions from householders instead of travellers, she next took lodgings from a tailor. As it was natural for a generous, good-hearted lady to promote the prosperity of the family where she resided, Madam employed the tailor to make the goods she had procured from the mercer and the weaver. Convinced that he had got an excellent job as well as a rich lodger, the tailor with mirth and song sat down to make Madam's dresses. As she acquainted him that upon a specified day she was to have a large party, the tailor called in several journeymen to his aid and had them all finished by that time. Meanwhile she gave her landlady one pound to purchase what things she deemed necessary, promising to pay her the remainder the following day. The day arrived, the guests appeared, an elegant entertainment was served up and plenty of wine drank. None were without their due portion. The tailor had his glass served so plentifully that his wife had to lend him her assistance to his bedchamber. This answered the designs of our Princess. She and all her company departed one by one, carrying away a silver tankard, or salt, or knife, or fork, while the maid carried off all the clothes that were not upon their backs. The moment they reached the street the maid was placed in a coach with the booty, and the rest of the company took different directions, and none of them were discovered.

Thus a merry night brought a sorrowful morning to the poor industrious tailor.

MARY TOFT *Not tried for any crime but almost pulled off an elaborate hoax in 1726, after which she was put into Bridewell* From *The Anatomist Dissected, Or the Man-Midwife finely brought to Bed* by 'Lemuel Gulliver' (1726)

In November 1726 Mary Toft, a young woman from Godalming in Surrey, began 'giving birth' to parts of animals – a rabbit's liver, the legs of a cat – and then to entire baby rabbits. She claimed to have chased two rabbits in a field one day and from then on only to have thought about rabbits until she began producing them. Ever more distinguished mid-wives and doctors were sent to examine her, including Nathanael St Andre, Swiss anatomist to the Royal Household sent by King George I, who wrote a forty-page treatise on the phenomenon; none could find anything amiss. William Hogarth made an engraving called 'The Cunicularii, Or the Wise Men of Godliman in Consultation'; the 'Rabbit Lady', as she was known, was talked about in all of London's salons and written about by every gossip from Jonathan Swift to Lord Hervey. But by the seventeenth 'birth' of what sometimes looked like fully-grown dead rabbits, suspicions had begun to be aroused. Finally, the physician Sir Richard Manningham exposed her fraud, and Toft confessed that she had staged the whole thing hoping to profit from her celebrity. The 'Rabbit Lady' was sent to Bridewell, but soon fell into obscurity – and poverty, judging from the fact that she faced charges for handling stolen goods in 1740 – and died in 1763. These extracts are from an anonymous satirical pamphlet attacking St Andre's credulity in the affair; he was forced to apologize publicly for his credulity after Toft's confession.

For, to begin with his narative; a true surgeon, one, I mean, orderly and properly educated in that worthy profession, would never have

suffer'd his curiosity to be at all alarm'd by seeing a letter from
Guildford, which mention'd *a woman's being deliver'd of five rabbits*:
suppose one were to see a letter from *Battersea*, importing that a
woman there had been deliver'd of five cucumbers, or indeed a
hundred letters, would that lead a man of sense to believe any thing,
but, either that the people who wrote those letters had been grossly
impos'd upon themselves, or intended to impose upon him. Either
of these two things may, and do happen every day; but it was never
known, that ever any creature brought forth any one creature of a
species in all respects different from it self, much less five or seventeen
such creatures; for which therefore, a man of common sense, much
more a penetrating and quicksighted anatomist, should look upon all
such letters with the utmost contempt.

Yet it was the sight of two or three such letters (and those flagrant
with most conspicuous tokens of imposture) which induc'd Mr
St André, at this time of the year, to take two journeys to *Guildford*,
in order to enquire into the truth of what, in nature, it was impossible
should be true. However, to *Guildford* he came for the first time;
where I shall attend him a while, and watch his motions, perhaps to
a better purpose than he did those of the rabbit-bearing woman: for
tho', with all his skill he was not able to detect her fraud, I hope
with very little of mine to display his ignorance.

In the first place, how stupid must he have been, not to suspect
a trick, when *Howard*, upon being sent for, came and acquainted him,
that the woman was actually in labour of the fifteenth rabbit. This puts me
in mind of what, above six and forty years ago, I learn'd at school;
where the sagacity of old *Simo*[1] in the *Andria* of *Terence* appears, to
the utter shame of our modern *St Andrians*: the old gentleman had
reason to suspect fraud from the known character of a crafty knave
he had to deal with; and whose business it was to make him believe,
that a certain lady was just then in labour: accordingly as they
approach her house, she contrives to be in one of her labour pains,

[1] Simo tries various ploys to get his son Pamphilus and his beloved Glycerium
together.

and cries out so loud that the old man must needs hear it; upon which, I remember, he says, with much humour and judgment, *Hui tam cito? ridiculum, postquam ante ostium me audivit stare, approperat. Non sat commode divisa sunt temporibus tibi, Dave, haec.* For thus, had he been credulous enough to go to *Guildford* to inquire into this cheat, he would have said, in plain *English*, upon the like occasion, *What a pox, is she so quick? this is the damn'dest joke that ever was: the moment she hears I am arrived, she falls into one of her labour pains: ah*, Howard! *this was not well tim'd of you by any means.*

But, to return from this digression, if the woman was *actually in labour of the fifteenth rabbit*, why should Mr *Howard* leave her, and stay with Mr *St André* till they call'd him again, when she was said to be in one of her labour pains? Here a wise man would have smelt a rat instead of a rabbit: and much more, when this woman in labour pains, and who had been in labour some time then, nay fourteen times before, was *found dress'd in her stays, and sitting on the bed-side*; and that not for want [of] help to put her to bed; for there were *several women near her*. A man must have a spritely genius for swallowing imposture that was not stagger'd at such an appearance. This sure it was that prompted Mr *St André* to wave all such reflections, and proceed *immediately to examine her*; when, tho' by his own confession, he *did not find the parts prepar'd for her labour*, (which was another plain indication of the roguery) yet he was weak enough to *wait for the coming on of fresh pains*, and *in three or four minutes after to think he deliver'd her of the intire trunk, strip'd of its skin, of a rabbit about four months growth* (he meant to have said, of an animal of the size and figure of a rabbit of four months growth) *in which the heart and lungs were contain'd, with the diaphragm intire.* Well, what does my gentleman then? He *instantly cut of a piece of them, and tried them in water*; in which they swam, and when they were *press'd to the bottom, rose again.* Now, it being notoriously the property of the lungs of a *foetus* to sink, and of a creature which has been some time brought forth alive to swim, in water; what but an absolute prepossession in favour of this filthy miracle, or a consummate ignorance in these matters could have hinder'd any sober inquirer from being determin'd in relation to this cheat, by the foregoing trial. Yet Mr *St André* never boggles at this, nor at the impossibility of the trunk of such a creature's (suppos'd but just before to be alive) being stript of its skin, by the contractive faculty of the womb; nor at the woman's being *chearful and easy, and walking by her self from the bed-side to the fire the moment she was deliver'd*: but goes on *conjecturing* in a yet more absurd manner, that these creatures, (as big as rabbits of four months growth, which must be within a trifle as big as full-grown ones,) were bred in the *fallopian tubes*; and came into the *uterus* one after another, where they lay and kick'd; till they were press'd to death, and flead, and that all their bones broken, in such manner, that they were sensibly heard to snap, by the violent convulsive motions of it.

DR WILLIAM DODD *Convicted of forgery, and hanged in 1777*

From Dodd's defence in court, and the public support for him, from Jackson's *Newgate Calendar*, and Dodd's execution, from 'A Relation of Dr. Dodd's behaviour in Newgate' by the Reverend Villette, Ordinary of Newgate (1777)

Dr Dodd was a respected and successful cleric who was for some time chaplain to King George III. Burdened by debts, he attempted to forge a note of hand for £4,000 (by the most conservative estimate, about £500,000 today) in the signature of his pupil and patron, Lord Chesterfield, but was discovered, tried and convicted. Although he was sentenced to death (the usual penalty for forgery), there was enormous public sympathy for his cause; but even the efforts of influential friends like Dr Johnson were unable to procure for him a pardon or reduction of his sentence and he died on the scaffold, proclaiming his guilt in a moving speech that left the crowd in tears.

I now stand before you a dreadful example of human infirmity. I entered upon public life with the expectations common to young men whose education has been liberal, and whose abilities have been flattered; and when I became a clergyman, I considered myself as not impairing the dignity of the order. I was not an idle, nor I hope, an useless minister; I taught the truths of Christianity with the zeal of conviction, and the authority of innocence. My labours were approved – my pulpit became popular: and I have reason to believe, that of those who heard me, some have been preserved from sin, and some have been reclaimed – Condescend, my lord, to think, if these considerations aggravate my crime, how much they must embitter my punishment! Being distinguished and elevated by the confidence of mankind, I had too much confidence in myself, and thinking my integrity, what others thought it, established in sincerity, and fortified by religion, I did not consider the danger of vanity, nor suspect the deceitfulness of my own heart. The day of conflict came, in which temptation seized and overwhelmed me! I committed the crime which I entreat your lordships to believe that my conscience hourly represents to me in its full bulk of mischief and malignity. Many have been overpowered by temptation, who are now among the penitent in heaven!

To an act now waiting the decision of vindictive justice, I will now presume to oppose the counter balance of almost thirty years (a great part of the life of man) passed in exciting and exercising charity in relieving such distresses as I now feel – in administering those consolations which I now want. I would not otherwise extenuate my offence, than by declaring, what I hope will appear to many, and what many circumstances make probable, that I did not intend finally to defraud; nor will it become me to apportion my own punishment by alleging that my sufferings have not been much less than my guilt. I have fallen from reputation which ought to have made me cautious, and from fortune, which ought to have given me content. I am sunk at once into poverty and scorn; my name and my crime fill the ballads in the streets; the sport of the thoughtless, and the triumph of the wicked! It may seem strange my lord, that, remembering what I have lately been, I should still wish to continue what I am! but contempt of death, how speciously soever it may mingle together with heathen virtues, has nothing in it suitable to Christian penitence. Many motives impel me to beg earnestly for life. I feel the natural horrors of a violent death, the universal dread of untimely dissolution. I am desirous to recompense the injury I have done to the clergy, to the world, and to religion, and to efface the scandal of my crime, by the example of my repentance; but, above all, I wish to die with thoughts more composed and calmer preparation. The gloom and confusion of a prison, the anxiety of a trial, the horrors of suspense, and inevitable vicissitudes of passion, leave not the mind in a due disposition for the holy exercises of prayer and self-examination. Let not a little life be denied me, in which I may, by meditation and contrition, prepare myself to stand at the tribunal of Omnipotence, and support the presence of that Judge who shall distribute to all according to their works – who will receive and pardon the repenting sinner, and from whom the merciful shall obtain mercy! For these reasons, my lords, amidst shame and misery I yet wish to live; and most humbly implore, that I may be recommended by your lordships to the clemency of his Majesty.

Here he sunk down overcome with mental agony; and some time elapsed before he was sufficiently recovered to hear the dreadful sentence of the law, which the Recorder pronounced upon him in the following words.

Dr William Dodd,

You have been convicted of the offence of publishing a forged and counterfeit bond, knowing it to be forged and counterfeited; and you have had the advantage which the laws of this country afford to every man in that situation, a fair, an impartial, and an attentive trial. The jury to whose justice you appealed, have found you guilty; their verdict has undergone the consideration of the learned judges, and they have found no ground to impeach the justice of that verdict; you yourself have admitted the justice of it; and now the very painful duty that the necessity of the law imposes upon the court, to pronounce the sentence of that law against you, remains only to be performed. You appear to entertain a very proper sense of the enormity of the offence you have committed; you appear to be in a state of contrition of mind, and I doubt not have duly reflected how far the dangerous tendency of the offence you have been guilty of, is increased in the influence of example, in being committed by a person of your character, and of the sacred functions of which you are a member. These sentiments seem to be yours; I would wish to cultivate such sentiments; but I would not wish to add to the anguish of a person in your situation by dwelling upon it. Your application for mercy must be made else where – it would be cruel in the court to flatter you; there is a power of dispensing mercy where you may apply. Your own good sense, and the contrition you express will induce you to lessen the influence of the example, by publishing, your hearty and sincere detestation of the offence of which you are convicted: and that you will not attempt to palliate or extenuate, which would indeed add to the degree of the influence of a crime of this kind being committed by a person of your character and known abilities; I would therefore warn you against any thing of that kind. Now, having said this, I am obliged to pronounce the sentence of the law, which is – That you Dr Wm Dodd, be carried from hence to the place from whence you came; that from thence you are to be carried to the place of execution, when you are to be hanged by the neck until you are dead.

To this Dr Dodd replied, Lord Jesus receive my soul.

Great exertions were now made to save Dr Dodd. The newspapers were filled with letters and paragraphs in his favour. Individuals of all ranks exerted themselves in his behalf: parish officers went, in mourning, from house to house, to procure subscriptions to a petition to the king: and this petition, which, with the names, filled twenty-three sheets of parchment, was actually presented. Even the Lord Mayor and Common Council went in a body to St James's to solicit mercy for the convict.

On the morning of his execution he appeared composed, and being asked how he had been supported, he said he had had some comfortable sleep, whereby he should be the better enabled to perform his duty. In the vestry, adjoining to the chapel, he exhorted his fellow-sufferer [Harris], who had attempted to destroy himself, but had been prevented by the vigilance of the Keeper. He spoke to him with great tenderness and emotion of heart, entreating him to consider that he had but a short time to live, and that it was highly necessary that he, as well as himself, made good use of their time, implored pardon of God under a deep sense of sin, and looked to that Lord by whose merits alone sinners could be saved. He lifted up his hands, and cried out, 'O Lord Jesus, have mercy upon us, and give, O give unto him, my fellow sinner, that as we suffer together, we may go together to Heaven.' His conversation to this poor youth was so moving, that tears flowed from the eyes of all present.

In the chapel at prayer, and the holy communion, true contrition and warmth of devotion appeared evident in him throughout the whole service. After it was ended, he again addressed himself to Harris in the most moving and persuasive manner, and not without effect; for he declared that he was glad he had not made away with himself, and said he was easier, and hoped he should now go to Heaven. The Doctor told him how Christ had suffered for them; and that he himself was a greater sinner than he, as he had sinned more against light and conviction, and therefore his guilt was greater; and that as he was CONFIDENT that mercy was shewn to his soul, so he should look to Christ, and trust in his merits.

He prayed God to bless his friends, who were present with him, and to give his blessing to all his brethren, the clergy; that he would pour out his spirit upon them, and make them true ministers of Jesus Christ, and that they might follow the divine precepts of their heavenly Master. Turning to one who stood near him, he stretched out his hand, and said, 'Now, my dear friend, speculation is at an end: all must be real! What poor ignorant beings we are!' He prayed for the Magdalenes, and wished they were there to sing for him the 23d Psalm.

After he had waited some time for the officers, he said, 'I wish they were ready, for I long to be gone.' He requested of his friends, who were in tears about him, to pray for him; to which he was answered by two of them, 'We pray more than language can utter.' He replied, 'I believe it.'

On his seeing two prisoners looking out of the windows in the yard, he went to them, and exhorted them so pathetically, that they both wept abundantly. He said once, 'I am now a spectacle to men, and shall soon be a spectacle to angels.'

Just before the Sheriff's Officer came with the halters, one who was walking with him, told him that there was yet a little solemnity he must pass through before he went out. He asked, 'What is that?' 'You will be bound.' He looked up, and said, 'Yet I am free, my freedom is there,' pointing upwards. He bore it with Christian patience, and beyond what might have been expected; and when the men offered to excuse tying his hands, he desired them to do their duty, and thanked them for their kindness. After he was bound, the Ordinary offered to assist him with his arm; but he replied with seeming pleasure, 'No! I am as firm as a rock.' As he passed along the yard, the spectators and prisoners wept and bemoaned him; and he, in return, prayed God to bless them.

On the way to execution he consoled himself in reflecting and speaking on what Christ had suffered for him; lamented the depravity of human nature, which made sanguinary laws necessary; and said he could gladly have died in the prison-yard, as being led out to public execution tended greatly to distress him. He desired the 51st Psalm to be read to him, and also pointed out an admirable penitential prayer from Rossell's Prisoner's Director.[1] He prayed again for the King, and likewise for the people.

When he came near the street where he formerly dwelt, he was much affected, and wept. He said, probably his tears would seem to be the effect of cowardice, but it was a weakness he could not well help; and added, he hoped he was going to a better home.

When he arrived at the gallows, he ascended the cart, and spoke to his fellow-sufferer. He then prayed, not only for himself, but also for his wife, and the unfortunate youth that suffered with him; and declaring that he died in the true love of the gospel of Christ, in perfect love and charity with all mankind, and with thankfulness to his friends, he was launched into eternity, imploring mercy for his soul, for the sake of his blessed redeemer.

[1] Book of advice for condemned prisoners (1742).

‖ JOHN DYER *Tried and convicted of forgery, and hanged 1790*
‖ From Knapp and Baldwin's *Newgate Calendar*

*This pitiful apprentice was executed, aged nineteen, for forging a note
of hand to buy candles. (The complete entry is given.)*

JOHN DYER,
EXECUTED FOR FORGERY

The case of this thoughtless malefactor adds another instance of the
fatal consequences attending young men who give loose to what they
. . . call pleasures.

John Dyer brought great trouble and disgrace on most respectable
parents and connexions. He received his education at Westminster
school; from thence he was placed in a merchant's counting-house,
and had not seen quite nineteen years when he atoned for his crime
by his life.

The melancholy transaction was the forgery of the insignificant
sum of ten pounds ten shillings; and if we were charitable enough to
give credit to his defence, and taking into view his youth and
inexperience, we may be almost led to believe that he did not know
the fatal consequences of committing forgery.

On the 7th of May 1789, Dyer called at the shop of Mr Scott,
wax-chandler, in New Bond Street, and ordered 36lb. of candles,
which he pretended were for Sir William Hamilton; and in payment
tendered a bill of exchange for ten pounds ten shillings, dated Richmond, Surrey, April 22d, 1790, at fourteen days after date, drawn by
Charles Thomas, on Messrs Hankey, bankers, London; and accepted.

Dyer received the balance; and the candles, when sent as he
directed, being refused, Mr Scott instantly suspected that he had
been imposed upon by a forgery. The unfortunate youth was soon
found, and committed to Newgate.

When put on his trial every spectator's heart was filled with pity;
and, being called on for his defence, he said that he received the bill

from Mr Kelsy, his employer, who ordered him to put the name of Mr Miller on the back; and that he was ignorant of the consequence of so doing; and that he acted merely as a servant; but, bringing no proof, he was found guilty, and, though interest was made to save his life, he died ignominiously on the gallows, at Newgate, August 5th, 1790.

JOHN HATFIELD *Tried and convicted of assuming a false identity, and hanged in 1803*
From the police notice for Hatfield's arrest, 5 November 1802, reprinted in Knapp and Baldwin's *Newgate Calendar* and Mary Robinson's discovery of Hatfield's deception, from *The Life of Mary Robinson* (1803)

In 1792, Captain Budworth described in A Fortnight's Ramble in the Lakes *the beautiful fourteen-year-old Mary Robinson, daughter of a local innkeeper, whom he encountered on his walking tour of the Lake District. 'Her hair was thick and long, of a dark brown . . . her face was a fine oval with full eyes and lips as red as vermilion . . . She looked an angel.' The Beauty of Buttermere, as Mary came to be known, was, eight years later, just as beautiful and, according to the poet William Wordsworth, unspoiled by the attention lavished on her since the publication of Budworth's book. For the Romantics — including Thomas de Quincey and Samuel Coleridge as well as William and Dorothy Wordsworth — she came to represent Nature, Beauty and Innocence.*

It was his connection with the Beauty of Buttermere that catapulted the forty-three-year-old John Hatfield into the public eye in 1802. He had enjoyed a long career of opportunism, petty swindling and avoiding unpaid bills. Posing as Colonel Alexander Hope, brother of the Earl of Hopetoun, and an MP, Hatfield was in the Lake District trying to marry an heiress (her wedding clothes had been bought but no date was set), when he met and befriended Mary Robinson. He seems genuinely to have fallen in love with her, and at length persuaded her to elope with him to Scotland. When his deception was discovered, Hatfield ran away, deserting his bride to avoid arrest. Eventually caught and tried, his misfortune almost destroyed Mary. She bore Hatfield a son in June 1803, just before his trial, and was so anxious about her husband that her milk dried up and she could not suckle the newborn, who died of pneumonia aged only three weeks old. Hatfield protested to the end that he had never meant to harm anyone, and died proudly, calm, pale and collected, showing no signs of either levity or insensibility.

Fifty Pounds Reward

NOTORIOUS IMPOSTOR, SWINDLER AND FELON JOHN HATFIELD

Who lately married a young woman, commonly called THE BEAUTY OF BUTTERMERE

under an assumed name.

Height about 5' 10", age about 44, full face, bright eyes, thick eyebrows, strong but light beard, good complexion with some colour, thick but not very prominent nose, smiling countenance, fine teeth, a scar on one of his cheeks near the chin, very long, thick, light hair, with a great deal of it grey, done up in a club, stout, square-shouldered, full breast and chest, rather corpulent and stout-limbed but very active, and has rather a spring in his gait, with apparently a little hitch in bringing up one leg; the two middle fingers of his left hand are stiff from an old wound and he frequently has the custom of pulling them straight with his right; has something of the Irish brogue in his speech, fluent and elegant in his language, great command of words, frequently puts his hand to his heart, very fond of compliments and generally addressing himself to persons most distinguished by rank or situation, attentive in the extreme to females, and likely to insinuate himself where there are young ladies; he was in America during the War, is fond of talking of his wounds and exploits there and on military subjects, as well as of Hatfield Hall, and his estates in Derbyshire and Chester, of the antiquity of his family, which he pretends to trace to the Plantagenets; all which are shameful falsehoods, thrown out to deceive. He makes a boast of having often been engaged in duels; he has been a great traveller also (by his own account) and talks of Egypt, Turkey, Italy, and in short has a general knowledge of subjects which, together with his engaging manner, is well calculated to impose on the credulous.

He was seven years confined in Scarborough gaol, from when he married, and removed into Devonshire, where he has basely deserted an amiable wife and a young family.

He had art enough to connect himself with some very respectable merchants in Devonshire as a partner in business, but having swindled them out of large sums of money he was made a separate bankrupt in June last, and has never surrendered to his commission, by which means he is guilty of a felony.

He cloaks his deceptions under the mask of religion, appears fond of religious conversation, and makes a point of attending divine service and popular preachers.

To consummate his villainies, he has lately, under the very respectable name of the Honourable Colonel Hope, betrayed an innocent but unfortunate young woman near the Lake of Buttermere.

He was on the 25th October last, at Ravenglass, in Cumberland, wrapped in a sailor's greatcoat and disguised, and is supposed to be now secreted in Liverpool, or some adjacent port, with a view to leave the country.

Whoever will apprehend him, and give information to MR TAUNTON, no 4, PUMP COURT, TEMPLE, so that he may be safely lodged in one of his Majesty's gaols, shall receive Fifty pounds reward.
November 5th, 1802

———

The *pretended* Colonel's second arrival at Buttermere was some time in the last ten days of August 1802. He attempted without delay, and by every artifice of looks and language, to conciliate the affections of the young woman; and in the beginning of September, if not before, he offered to make her his wife, if she would go off with him and be married in Scotland. She gave a positive refusal, assigning as her reason the short period of his acquaintance with her, which rendered it impossible that his attachment for her should have been founded on any rational esteem for her; and the utter disproportion of the match. Her natural good sense informed her, that strange events are seldom happy events.

About this time he contrived to commence an acquaintance with an Irish gentleman, a member of the late Irish Parliament, who had been resident for some months at Keswick, with his wife and part of his family. With this gentleman, and under his immediate protection, there was likewise a young lady of family and fortune, and of great personal attraction. This gentleman, in an excursion with his party to Buttermere, had, at the request of the landlord of the Queen's Head Inn, permitted his servant to convey a small package of wine to the gentleman staying at the Char public house. In a cottage, where there is only one small sitting room, persons of pleasant manners, who happen to come at the same time, as naturally form a slight acquaintance as in the cabin of a packet[-ship]. One of the means which the adventurer used to introduce himself to this respectable family was the following: – Understanding that the gentleman had been a military man, he took an army list from his pocket and pointed to his assumed name, the Honourable Alexander Augustus Hope, Lieutenant Colonel of the 14th regiment of foot. I have thought it no waste of time to mention these minute circumstances, they may possibly be useful in the detection of some other rogue. This new acquaintance daily gained strength, and he shortly paid his addresses to the daughter of the above gentleman, and obtained her consent. The wedding clothes were bought; but, previously to the wedding-day being fixed, she insisted that the pretended Colonel Hope should introduce the subject formally to her friends. He was hourly expected to do so; and the gentleman was prepared to have required, that 'Colonel Hope's enthusiasm should not seduce him into an impropriety. They were strangers to each other. He must beg that Col. Hope would write to certain noblemen and gentlemen both in England and Ireland, whose names and addresses he would furnish him with, and obtain from them every necessary information respecting himself and the young lady under his protection. As some days would elapse before the answer could be received, he proposed to employ that time in a trip to Lord Hopetoun's seat,' etc. It was this circumstance which expedited his marriage with Mary of Buttermere; and, feigning a pretence for his absence, he married the *Beauty of Buttermere*.

From this time he played a double game: it seems to have been a maxim with him to leave as few *white* interspaces as possible in the *crouded map of his villanies*. His visits to Keswick became frequent, and his suit to the young lady assiduous and fervent. Still however, both at Keswick and Buttermere, he was somewhat shy of appearing in public. He was sure to be engaged in a fishing expedition on the day on which any company was expected at the public house at Buttermere; and he never attended the church at Keswick but once. The former circumstance could not excite any reasonable suspicion; it is assuredly not necessary to be an impostor, in order to avoid as carefully as possible a crowd of strange faces in a small public house: the latter circumstance appeared more extraordinary, as great and continued pretensions to religion, and to religious exercises, formed an outstanding part of his character. He himself once assigned a frivolous and foolish excuse for his continued absence from the church, but the people of Keswick, those few at least who had noticed the circumstance, candidly attributed this neglect to his being of a Scottish family and education.

A week or two after poor Mary's refusal to go off with him to Scotland, he renewed his entreaties, and gave her a written promise of marriage, which she returned to him, persevering in her former opinion, and determined at all events not to do any thing which she could not do openly, and in the face of all among whom she was born and had lived. This in a woman of her situation, must surely be considered as a great proof of virtue and uncommon good sense, if we reflect that she had no doubt of his being the man he pretended to be. Nor can there be a doubt that when the whole particulars of this unfortunate connexion are made known, her former character for modesty, virtue and good sense, will be fully established in the eyes of the world. How could she suspect him, knowing him to be received into the intimacy of persons of undoubted rank, respectability and consequent knowledge of the world? It is probable he would have desisted from this pursuit, if he could have induced the young lady beforementioned to have consented to a private marriage.

Our adventurer finding his schemes baffled to obtain this young lady and her fortune, applied himself wholly to gain possession of Mary Robinson. He made the most minute enquiries among the neighbours into every circumstance relating to her and her family, and declared his resolution to marry her publickly at her parish church by a license. Mary told him, that she was not ignorant that he had paid his addresses to Miss —, a match every way more proportionate. This he treated as a mere venial artifice to excite her jealousy, in part perhaps an effect of despair, in consequence of Mary's repeated refusal. The conclusion is already well known. The pretended Colonel Hope, in company with the clergyman, procured a license on the 1st of October, and they were publickly married in the church of Lorton, on Saturday, October the 2d. Is there on earth that prude or that bigot who can blame poor Mary? She had given her lover the best reason to esteem her, and had earned a rational love by innocent and wise conduct. Nor can it be doubted that the man had really and deeply engaged her affections. He seems to have fascinated every one, in all ranks of society; and if Mary had remained an exception, it would have detracted more from her sensibility than it would have added to her prudence.

On the day previous to his marriage, our adventurer wrote to Mr —, informing him, that he was under the necessity of being absent for ten days on a journey into Scotland, and sent him a draft for thirty pounds, drawn on Mr Crump, of Liverpool, desiring him to cash it and pay some small debts in Keswick with it, and send him over the balance, as he feared he might be short of cash on the road, this Mr —, immediately did, and sent him ten guineas in addition to the balance. On the Saturday, Wood, the landlord of the Queen's Head, returned from Lorton with the public intelligence, that Colonel Hope had married the *Beauty of Buttermere*. As it was clear, whoever he was, that he had acted unworthily and dishonourably, Mr —'s suspicions were of course awakened. He instantly remitted the draft to Mr Crump, who immediately accepted it; and at last ninety-nine in a hundred of the people at Keswick were fully persuaded that he was a true man, and no cheat. Mr M—, the friend of the young lady whom he first paid his addresses to, immediately on this, wrote to the Earl of Hopetoun. Before the answer arrived, the pretended Honourable returned with his wife to Buttermere. He went only as far as Longtown. He had bought Mary no clothes, pretending that on his arrival at the first large town they might be all procured in a few hours. A pair of gloves was the only present he made her.

At Longtown he received two letters, seemed much troubled that some friends whom he expected had not arrived there, stayed three days and then told his wife that he would again go back to Buttermere. From this time she was seized with fears and suspicions. They returned however, and their return was made known at Keswick. A Mr Harding, a Welsh judge, and a very singular man, passing through Keswick heard of this adventurer, and sent his servant over to Buttermere with a note to the supposed Colonel Hope, who observed, 'that it was a mistake, and that the note was for a brother of his'. However, he sent for four horses, and came over to Keswick, drew another draft on Mr Crump for 20*l*. which the landlord at the Queen's Head had the courage to cash. Of this sum he immediately sent the ten guineas to Mr —, who came and introduced him to the judge, as his old friend Colonel Hope. Our adventurer made a blank denial that he had ever assumed the name. He had said his name was Hope, but not that he was the honourable member for Linlithgow, etc. etc. and one who had been his frequent companion, his intimate at Buttermere gave evidence to the same purpose.

On the pretender's return to Buttermere he found poor Mary in tears; she had received a letter from a gentleman at Keswick, informing her that her husband was an impostor; she gave it to him and he chid her for believing such false suggestions, threatening to call the writer to account, with whom he afterwards had an interview, and insisted on receiving satisfaction for this injury of his character. The next morning was appointed for a meeting, but the pretended Colonel took his leave before the appointed hour.

In spite however of his impudent assertions, and those of his associate, the evidence against him was decisive. – A warrant was given by Sir Frederick Vane, on the clear proof of his having forged and received several franks as the member for Linlithgow, and he was committed to the care of the constable. The constable, as may be well supposed, was little used to business of this kind. Our adventurer affected to make light of the affair, laughed and threatened by turns, and ordered a dinner at the Queen's Head at three o'clock. In the mean time he should amuse himself on the lake, which the constable unsuspiciously permitted. He went out in a boat, accompanied by his old friend the fishing tackler; and a little before three o'clock, a considerable number of the inhabitants assembled at the foot of the lake, waiting anxiously for his return, and by far the greater part disposed to lead him back in triumph. 'If he was not this great man, they were sure that he would prove to be some other great man'; but the dusk came on; neither the great man nor his guide appeared. Burkitt had led him through the Gorge of Borrowdale, up through Rosthwait and so across the Stake, the fearful Alpine Pass, which leads over Glaramara into Langdale, and left him at Langdale Chapel – a tremendous journey in the dusk! but his neck was probably predestined to a less romantic fate.

It will hardly be believed, how obstinately almost all classes at Keswick were infatuated in his favour, and how indignantly they spoke of the gentleman who had taken such prudent and prompt measures to bring the impostor to detection. The truth is, the good people of the vales had as little heard, and possessed as little notion of the existence of this sort of wickedness, as of the abominations of Tiberius[1] at Capua. – 'What motive could he have to marry poor Mary? Would a sharper marry a poor girl without fortune or connexion? If he had married the Irish young lady, there would be something to say for it, etc.' It was no doubt delightful to the people of the vales, that so great a man, that a man so generous, so condescending, so

---

[1] Tyrannical Roman Emperor (AD 14–37), whose reign was marked by treason trials and executions.

affable, *so very* good, should have married one of their own class, and that to a young woman who had been so long their pride, and so much and deservedly beloved by them. Their reasonings in the impostor's favour were, to be sure, very insufficient to counteract the evidence against him; yet of themselves they were not unplausible. It is a common blunder with those who know more of the world than the inhabitants of the secluded vales among the mountains can be supposed to know, to admit of no other passion, as the motive of crimes, except the love of money or of power.

Our adventurer in his rapid flight from Keswick, left behind him his carriage, which was taken possession of by the landlord, as a pledge for his 20*l*.; and in it were found all his plate and linen, as well as a very costly dressing box, which in a few days was opened by virtue of an order from a neighbouring magistrate. It contained a very elegant pair of pistols, and complete assortment of toilet trinkets, all silver. The whole value of the box could not be less than 80*l*. There were discovered only one letter, a cash book, a list of several cities in Italy and a couple of names attached to each. From the cash book, nothing could be learned but that he had vested divers considerable sums (some stated to be on his own account) in the house of Baron Dimsdale and Co. of London; but on examining the box more narrowly, poor Mary found that it had a double bottom, and in the interspace were a number of letters addressed to him from his wife and children, under the name of Hatfield. For some days nothing else was discovered but a bill for 100*l*. drawn on a Devonshire bank, which he had left behind him with Mary's father and mother; and with which they were to have paid off a mortgage on this little property, but this proved to be an old bill that had been long paid, and on his own bank.

Among the other villanous schemes of this hardened wretch, it is said that he had attempted to persuade the old people to sell their little estate, to place the money in his own hands, and to go with him into Scotland: it is not improbable that if he had not been so soon detected, he might have prevailed upon the good old people to listen to his advice, and thus would they have been completely ruined.

9

A Miscellany

THE HAWKINS GANG *Convicted of highway robbery,
and hanged, 1722*
From Ralph Wilson's *A Full and Impartial Account of
all the Robberies committed by* JOHN HAWKINS,
GEORGE SYMPSON, *and their companions* (1722)

*The gang of highwaymen led by Jack Hawkins terrorized London in
the early 1720s, until it was broken up by the self-styled Thief-taker
General, Jonathan Wild, using techniques of interviewing and intimid-
ating suspects still used by police forces today. Wilson, who confessed
and acted as witness against his comrades in return for his own life,
wrote this account of his introduction to Hawkins and crime, and the
methods and tactics the gang used.*

John Hawkins, who by his many robberies has made himself as famous
in *England* as *Cartouche* was in *France*, at his death was 30 years old: he
was born of very honest parents, but poor; his father was a farmer, and
lived at *Staines* in *Middlesex*. His education had been but very slender,
for at 14 he waited on a gentleman; but leaving him, he became tapster's
boy at the *Red-Lyon* at *Brentford*, where he continued till he got another
gentleman's service: but being of an unsettled temper, he seldom tarried
long in a place. The last family he was in, was Sir *Dennis Dutry*'s, whom
he served as butler: he has often told me, if he had continued in that
station, he might soon have been master of very happy circumstances;
for being an handsome creditable servant, he was well liked and
approved of both by his master and lady. But as he was conscious of
those his personal perfections, like all the gentry of the blue-cloth,[1] he
soon became very assuming, so that he thought it but a small fault to
be out two or three nights in a week at the gaming-tables, which were
his destruction, as they are of all others who frequent them. These are
the nurseries of all our highway-men: here it is that young fellows
being stript of all their money, are prepared for the most desperate of

---

[1] Reference to the gentle airs liveried servants were thought to assume.

enterprizes. So it was with *Hawkins*, who by the repeated neglects of his master's business, having incensed the family against him, was turned off, not without a just suspicion of having first been a confederate in robbing his master's house of a considerable value in plate. This he never owned to me, but acknowledged he had pawned an old-fashioned piece of *Dutch* plate of Sir *Dennis*'s which he valued very much.

Having spoiled his character, he looked no more after a place; attending the gaming-tables was all his business, till he was reduced to such necessity that he wanted bread. In this melancholy condition, the Devil, who is ever ready upon such occasions, put it into his head that he must relieve himself by plundering his fellow-subjects. This he resolved to do, and, in order thereto, musters all his interest to procure an horse and a case of pistols.

He was now 24. His first expedition was to *Hounslow*-Heath, where he stopp'd a coach, and eased the passengers of about 11*l*. With this booty he returned safe to *London*. Now every body wou'd imagine that he, who so lately had tasted of the bitter cup of affliction, wou'd have applied this money to a proper use: instead of that, he repaired immediately to the *King's-Head* by *Temple-Bar*, and threw it all off.

Thus he went on a pretty while by himself, losing at play what he got upon the highway . . .

I [Ralph Wilson] shall now say something of myself. I am now 22, and was brought up at *Kirkleatham* in *Cleveland*, *Yorkshire*, at the school built there by Sir *William Turner*, formerly Lord-Mayor of *London*. At 17 I left the school, and was put clerk to Mr *Dixon* of *Lincoln's-Inn*, a very eminent and honest practitioner in chancery, whose advice, if I had observed, no doubt I had at this day been very happy. But his business being very great, and my industry at that time very little, we could not agree: in short, Mr *Dixon* returned the money he received at our articling, and so we parted.

Amongst the rest of my acquaintance at the gaming-tables, I was singled out by this *John Hawkins*; we became great cronies, and were very seldom asunder, till he was taken upon suspicion of robbing a coach in *Monmouth-street*, of which he was acquitted, tho guilty. My mother at this time being reconciled to me, sent for me home to

Whitby, where she lives. With her I tarried a twelvemonth; but being very desirous of coming to *London* again, I persuaded her to send me up, to try the law once more. She, who always encouraged any thing that looked like business in me, agreed to my request, and gave 100*l.* with me to Mr *Sandys* of *Grange-Court.* I had not been long with him before my old infection broke out, which swept away every thing I had, both money and clothes. By this extravagance making myself unfit for a clerk, I left Mr *Sandys.* Then it was I again met with my old friend *John Hawkins:* as yet I did not know directly what courses he followed, tho knowing he had no support from any relations, I suspected him very much; for which reason I began to withdraw myself from his company, for even at that time no man had a greater abhorrence of villany than myself.

Hawkins had now engaged with a fresh gang which was pretty numerous, one of which, *Pocock*, being apprehended, (according to custom) impeach'd all the rest. This impeachment dispersed the whole company, some to *Ireland*, others to *Wales*; and one *Ralphson*, to whose charge, as a trusty person, all the moveables were committed, thought it his best play to move off with the company's stock into *Holland.* By this fraud, and the impeachment, *Hawkins* was left destitute both of money and companions, for every body had got out of town, except his brother *Will. Hawkins* and *James Wright*; the first was taken upon *Pocock*'s information, and the last was in a salivation.[1] *Hawkins* himself skulk'd about the town, not daring to appear where he was known, except at such houses as he could confide in; one of which I used, and there it was I was first in his company after this matter broke out; for he having a great opinion that I would not prejudice him for the sake of reward, was not afraid to see me. In a few days *Hawkins* and I were together as often as ever, from whom I learnt every thing I have related. Some things I have omitted, as that he was present when Colonel *Floyer* shot *Wooldridge*; he told me also that it was he that shot General *Evans*'s servant: he has often lamented

---

[1] This word is not in slang dictionaries: it may be a misspelling of 'salvation', or a medical treatment (to do with saliva), or outdated thieves' slang.

his misfortune, that he should be guilty of that murder. He would, when he got into company with a clergyman, or any other learned person, be always asking some casuistical questions upon cases parallel to his own, which was this: *Hawkins* stopt the General and another gentleman in a coach, with this footman behind; the General fired at him, and so did the gentleman: upon this, *Hawkins* shot directly into the coach at them, but killed the footman behind. Now *Hawkins* fancy'd this was no murder, because he had no design against the deceased. But he was always told his design against the master made him as culpable as if he had intended it against the man, whom he killed peradventure. I was very fond of *Hawkins*'s company, because I took much pleasure in hearing him speak of his merry pranks and many robberies. *Wright* being now recover'd, he and *Hawkins* fell to their old game, and when they came home at night, I used to drink with them. The first robbery they committed after this re-union, was upon the Earl of *Burlington* and Lord *Bruce* in *Richmond-Lane*; they took from them 20*l.* two gold watches, and a saphire ring, which my Lord bid 100*l.* for to [Jonathan] *Wild*. This ring *Hawkins* pretended he could sell only for six pound; this seemed to the poor fellow to be a very good price, so that he gladly accepted of 3*l.* for his snack, tho *Hawkins* afterwards sold the same ring in *Holland* for 40*l.*

This *Wright* was born of very honest parents, and bred a barber; he was a man of the best temper and greatest fidelity to his companions I ever knew in an highwayman: how he became acquainted with *Hawkins*, I cannot say, but they two went on together after his salivation for about a month very prosperously before I engaged with them. It happen'd about this time, that meeting with a good-natur'd countryman, I borrowed 20*l.* of him; this was a great novelty to me, who had been starving for some weeks past, notwithstanding that I made all the haste I could to the tables, and lost it every farthing. This ill luck made me rage like a madman, and was the first thing that made me capable of any impression from bad company. From the gaming-tables, I went to *Hawkins* and *Wright*. We had drunk ourselves to a good pitch, when *Hawkins* began a discourse about robbing in the streets, but said it could not be done without a third man, and ask'd me if I durst take a pistol, and mount a horse: I told him, Yes, as well as any man, and that the want of money had made me ready for any thing. Upon this, he who was always glad of new companions, and, I am satisfy'd, with a very bad intent, offered very kindly to get me a horse against the next night; I consented, and so we went to bed. The next morning I remember'd what pass'd the night before, but resolved nothing less than to put what I had promised in execution: however, *Hawkins* was as good as his word.

When the night came, we fell to drinking again, and at a proper time of the night *Hawkins* told us all was ready; I being now as hot as the last night, and so in the same humour, objected nothing, but went away with them to the horses: we mounted about ten a-clock, and a little while after robbed Sir *David Dalrymple* by *Winstanley*'s water-works. It was put upon me to stop the coach by way of tryal, whether I was capable of being made a man of business; to my great misfortune, I performed my part so well, that *Hawkins* never cared to part with me afterwards.

We had but a very small booty from Sir *David*, I think about 3*l.* in money, a snuff-box and pocket-book, which Sir *David* offered 60*l.* for to *Wild*; but we returned it by a porter *gratis*, for we never dealt with *Wild*, neither did he know any of us.

The next morning after this robbery, it is impossible for me to express under what anxieties I labour'd, on a consideration that I had engaged in such base actions which I then apprehended, as I have found since, bring nothing but poverty and shame to him that follows them: besides, there is no life so gloomy as the life of an highwayman; he is a stranger to peace of mind and quiet sleep; he is made a property of, by every villain that knows or guesses at his circumstances: such a life is a hell to any man that has ever had any relish of a more generous way of living. But I was entred, and must go thorough; for *Jack Hawkins*, who before was all good humour and complaisance, was now become my tyrant: he gave himself a great deal of trouble to let me know, that I was as liable to be hang'd as he, and in all his actions express'd a satisfaction that he had me under a hank.[1] I have great

---

[1] in a restraining hold.

reason to believe that this pleasure of his did arise from his having one more added to his number, to make use of when his occasions required. The world may think I speak this to justify what I have lately done, but when they shall be apprized how vilely his brother has acted that part, and that such a method of saving their lives was always concerted beforehand between the two brothers, they will be of another opinion. In short, after this robbery I led a dog's life, and was much against my will obliged to take every thing in good part, for fear, by quarrelling, of bringing us all into trouble . . .

These robberies had put me into a good condition, if the pernicious itch of gaming had not been so prevalent upon me; whatever movables we got, I sold my part to *J. Hawkins* and *Wright*, and play'd away the money. They two having made up a sufficient cargo, were determin'd for *Holland*: accordingly *Hawkins* had every thing that belonged to them in his hands, ready to go off with, except a watch which *Wright* was gone by himself to fetch out of pawn; we were to meet him at the *Queen's-Head* upon *Tower-Hill*: but a messenger whom we sent beforehand to see how the land lay, brought us word that *Wright* was apprehended by *Jonathan Wild*, to whom he had been betray'd by one of his own acquaintance. This was a great alarm to us, for we were under a most violent apprehension that *Wright* would impeach us, but he proved himself to be quite another man.

Now *Will. Hawkins* and *Wright* were in prison together: the first being impeach'd, could not impeach; but the latter, if he had been inclined, might have taken that advantage to have saved his life: but he told *Hawkins*'s wife, that he would hurt nobody, much less her husband, because of his children. I shall have an opportunity presently to show how well this generosity was retaliated. In the mean time, *Jack Hawkins* and I were consulting where to conceal ourselves; at last we pitch'd upon *Oxford*, whither we walk'd a foot, and tarried there a month: in which time nothing remarkable happen'd, except that *Hawkins* defaced some pictures in the gallery above the *Bodleian* Library, for the discovery whereof the University bid 100*l*. A poor taylor, who had above measure distinguish'd himself for a Whig, was taken up and imprison'd for this fact, and very narrowly escaped a whipping.

By that time we had been a month at *Oxford*, the sessions at the *Old-Bailey* were ended; *Will. Hawkins* was discharged, and his friend *Pocock* hanged, but *Wright* was reserved till *Kingston*-Assizes. *Jack Hawkins* being very desirous to see his brother *Will.* told me he design'd for *London* the next day, and that he was sorry he could not lend me money to go along with him, but that he would in two or three days send me 2 *l.* and so he left me full of poverty and a bad conscience, two dismal companions. A little while after I received ten shillings from him, six whereof I ow'd at my quarters, which I paid, and with the rest set forwards to *London* a foot; when I arrived at *London*, I found that *Jack* and *Will. Hawkins* were gone for *Holland* with all *Wright's* goods to the value of 50 *l.* which they never gave him any account of, tho he was then starving in prison.

About the latter end of *October*, both the brothers returned from *Holland* to *London*, where we all joined; the most fatal joining I ever made in my life, for if I had not joined that heedless villain *Will. Hawkins*, in all probability I should not have been in this condition: but this cannot be recalled . . .

All this time we play'd least in sight our most convenient house was by *London-Wall*: this man knew all our circumstances, and in that knowledge found his account, for we seldom committed a robbery, but he had his snack by way of reckoning. We did not mind that, for as he kept a livery-stable, we had an opportunity of getting out at all times in the night; so that we harrass'd almost all the morning stage-coaches in *England*. One morning we robb'd the *Cirencester*, the *Worcester*, the *Glocester*, the *Oxford* and *Bristol* Stage-Coaches, all together; the next morning the *Ipswich* and *Colchester*, and a third morning perhaps the *Portsmouth* Coach. The *Bury* coach has been our constant customer; I think we have touch'd that coach ten times: for any of these, we never went further than the *Stones-End*; if we brought away their portmanteaus, we carried them to our old Cock *C—*, where we ransack'd them. I cannot help saying, that as this man participated of our prosperity, it is a pity he should not have his snack of our adversity; it would be of infinite service to the nation, if such a man could be sent abroad for better education. He has undone several young fellows, by spurring them to such actions as bring them to the gallows.

Our evening exercises were generally between *Hampstead*, *Hackney*, *Bow*, *Richmond* and *London*, and behind *Buckingham* wall, *etc*. We three committed numberless robberies, for *Sympson* was a stout brisk man, so that we carried every thing on with great success, and might have lived in that unhappy way several years, if we had not meddled with the mails, which are certain destruction to any body that rob them. Not one has escaped yet, that ever meddled with them . . .

Notwithstanding that my crimes have been great enough, yet those crimes have received great aggravations from flying reports; which I should not have taken notice of, but that I am willing to set the truth in a clear light. The first thing which surprizes me most, is, that it has been confidently reported by several news-writers, that my companions and self were guilty of that horrid fact of cutting the woman's tongue out, because she happen'd to stand by when we robb'd the *Bury*-coach, and knew us; and that I have acknowledged the same. In the first place, I never acknowledged any such thing; and in the next place, I can prove by things taken away from that coach in *Whitechapel* the same morning this fact is said to be done, that we were not the men; for doubtless the people to whom these things are restored, would not have been silent, if any such thing had been done by us: besides, this barbarity was given out to be committed beyond *Epping*, which is ten miles beyond the place where we committed the robbery.

Another thing is related of me, which I have no occasion to take notice of, any further than that 'tis false, that is, that I have impeach'd 22 men; for if I had, it had been the greatest justice in me to impeach all as well as the two I have impeach'd, if any more had been concern'd with me . . .

It has also been laid to my charge, That I made it my frequent practice to ravish the ladies whom we robb'd: I cannot think what wise person trump'd up this story, it appears to me the most nonsensical one

I ever heard; for as we always robb'd the coaches within four miles of the town, and very early in the evening or morning, when we had all our hands full in dismounting the horsemen who were upon the road, I cannot see any room for such an action. Besides, I defy any person to show that there has been any such thing done by any body within these five years, which is the longest time I have been in this town.

The next great charge is, That I used cruelties to any gentleman we robb'd: how false this is, I appeal to several gentlemen who have been robb'd by us; some in particular, who have been to see me, remember me for the great civility I showed above my companions.

The last and most heavy charge, is, That I am an atheist, a blasphemer and an irreligious fellow: The two first characters I utterly disclaim, and challenge any of my acquaintance to say I ever made use of any atheistical or blasphemous expressions. As to the last, indeed I cannot say much; for how is it possible that a man in such a course of wickedness could frequent divine service, or perform other duties of religion? Would it not be the greatest mockery for a man to pretend any such thing, when in his own conscience he design'd to commit robberies immediately after? I think no man can be truly religious, till he purposes to lead a new life; *which I am resolutely bent upon, by the assistance of Almighty God.*

JONATHAN WILD *Convicted of receiving stolen goods,
and hanged in 1725*
From 'Warrant of Detainder' issued at Wild's arrest, from
Knapp and Baldwin's *Newgate Calendar*; Wild's letter to King
George I begging for clemency (1725); and Anon., *Jonathan
Wild's Advice to his Successor* (1725)

*Wild (b. c. 1683) came to London from Wolverhampton as a young
man, was introduced to London's criminal underworld during his
four-year stay at a debtors' prison, then served his apprenticeship as a
thief-taker, or fence, under Charles Hitchin (see 'Sexual Offenders').
Wild's genius soon enabled him to outstrip Hitchin, and from 1714,
when he first set up his own office in Little Old Bailey, until 1724, he
controlled London's criminals, playing them off against one another
and the authorities in a Machiavellian web of intrigue and influence.
In 1724, the fall of Jack Sheppard (which he engineered to make an
example of Sheppard, who refused to work with him) heralded the
beginning of Wild's demise. He was thirty-nine, and no longer fuelled
by the ceaseless ambition and desire for power that had once driven
him; and he had made many enemies. Even the government, which had
been so naive as to consult him about the rising incidence of crime in
1720 − Wild had advised them to set the rewards for capturing
criminals (one of his own main sources of profit) higher − were becoming
aware that the advantages of having Wild − one's stolen property
could usually be recovered; the criminals were largely controlled − did
not justify his existence. A long list of his crimes was prepared after
his arrest ('Warrant of Detainder'), but he was finally convicted
merely for receiving stolen goods. It was an ignominious but fitting
end, since the law he had broken was informally known as 'Jonathan
Wild's Act'. In his defence he claimed that he had brought over
sixty-seven people to justice − to the gallows. Wild himself went there
amid a huge, hostile crowd which pelted him with rotten fruit and
eggs and howled for his blood when the executioner seemed to take a
long time hanging him. His corruption was used by contemporary*

political commentators like John Gay (with Peachum and Lockit in
The Beggars Opera*) and Henry Fielding (in* Jonathan Wild the
Great*) using Wild as a metaphor for the Prime Minister, Sir Robert*
Walpole.

I. That for many years past he had been a confederate with great numbers of highwaymen, pick-pockets, house-breakers, shop lifters and other thieves.

II. That he had formed a kind of corporation of thieves, of which he was the head or director, and that notwithstanding his pretended services, in detecting and prosecuting offenders, he procured such only to be hanged as concealed their booty, or refused to share it with him.

III. That he had divided the town and country into so many districts, and appointed distinct gangs for each, who regularly accounted with him for their robberies. That he had also a particular set to steal at churches in time of divine service: and likewise other moving detachments to attend at court, on birth days, balls, etc. and at both houses of parliament, circuits and country fairs.

IV. That the persons employed by him were for the most part felons convict, who had returned from transportation before the time for which they were transported was expired; and that he made choice of them to be his agents, because they could not be legal evidences against him, and because he had it in his power to take from them what part of the stolen goods he thought fit, and otherwise use them ill, or hang them, as he pleased.

V. That he had from time to time supplied such convicted felons with money and clothes, and lodged them in his own house, the better to conceal them: particularly some, against whom there are now informations for counterfeiting and diminishing broad pieces and guineas.

VI. That he had not only been a receiver of stolen goods, as well as of writings of all kinds, for near fifteen years past, but had frequently been a confederate, and robbed along with the above-mentioned convicted felons.

VII. That in order to carry on these vile practices, and to gain some credit with the ignorant multitude, he usually carried a short silver staff, as a badge of authority from the government, which he used to produce, when he himself was concerned in robbing.

VIII. That he had, under his care and direction, several warehouses for receiving and concealing stolen goods; and also a ship for carrying off jewels, watches and other valuable goods, to Holland, where he had a superannuated thief for his factor.

IX. That he kept in pay several artists to make alterations, and transform watches, seals, snuff-boxes, rings and other valuable things, that they might not be known, several of which he used to present to such persons as he thought might be of service to him.

X. That he seldom or never helped the owners to the notes and papers they had lost, unless he found them able exactly to specify and describe them, and then often, insisted on more than half the value.

XI. And lastly, it appears, that he has often sold human blood, by procuring false evidence to swear persons into facts they were not guilty of; sometimes to prevent them from being evidences against himself, and at other times for the sake of the great reward given by the government.

Wild's letter to George I:

'Tis nothing but your Majesty's wonted goodness and clemency that could encourage me to sue for your royal favour and pardon . . .

For since your Majesty has many times been graciously pleased to spare the lives even of traitors themselves, I cannot but hope for a reprieve from so good a prince, whom I can esteem no less than an inexhaustible fountain of mercy; wherefore, most dread and august sovereign, humbly prostrating myself at your royal feet, I presume to set forth my wicked and melancholy circumstances and from your bounty to seek that favour which is nowhere else to be found.

I have indeed been a most wicked and notorious offender, but was never guilty or inclined to treasonable practises, or murder, both of which I hold in the utmost detestation and abhorrence which affords me great comfort in the midst of my calamity and affliction.

I have a sickly wife loaded and oppressed with grief, who must inevitably go to the grave with me, if I suffer; or lead a most miserable life, she being already *non compos mentis*.[1]

If I receive your Majesty's royal favour of a reprieve, I do firmly resolve to relinquish my wicked ways and to detect (as far as in me lays) all such who shall persevere therein, as a testimony of which, I have a list ready to show to such whom your Majesty shall appoint to see it, which is all that can be offered by your Majesty's most dutiful, loyal and obedient petitioner.

Jonathan Wild's advice to his successor

Since the dead warrant is come down and our *Ordinary* has entreated me to prepare for execution I think it a duty incumbent on me to give my advice to any person who shall hereafter tread in the same path which I have for so many years past trod with impunity.

Though now, alas, old Father Greybeard, the Law, has overtaken me and I have no other prospect left than the unpleasant view of St Tyburn: as I find there is no shuffling from the point, nor no hopes of a reprieve, I shall lay down a plan whereby any future successor may pursue my occupation without the dreadful apprehension of a Paddington fate or the fear of incurring the displeasure of a national or legislative power.

Misfortune brings cunning to the unfortunate and we often improve by calamity. For what a life of ease and indolence conceals from the mind very often a little accident reveals and sets before us in a conspicuous light. So has my present misfortune afforded several new hints which, though too late for my purpose, may be of great service

---

[1] In fact she married Wild's assistant Quilt Arnold with unseemly haste after Wild's death.

for the future to anyone who may hereafter rise up with a genius similar to mine and teach him whereby he may evade the situation I am now in. And I do not in the least doubt that someone or other may think it worth his while to revive my occupation, especially when he is assured of the means to render himself obscure, it being a function of no small profit, requiring little industry, honour, honesty or conscience, though the appearance of these virtues are as necessary as the non-possession of them. The mask is the *summum bonum* of our sanction, a mask that may be put on at any time without incurring the displeasure of the Black Act or any other in the trammels of the law.

In order therefore to arrive at a proficiency in the various arts essential to form a complete thief-taker a proper connection should be framed with all the villains of the town; you are not to be ashamed of shaking a fist with a known scoundrel, nor sitting front to front with a perjurer, a highwayman or a murderer. Their haunts, their beats, their whores (the last especially because they are the most liable to betray them) should be well known. But of all this set of useful beings, the *rapper*, I think (as the *cant* phrase has it), is the most necessary man for your purpose. With him a strong connection will be of infinite advantage to you, yet it must be managed with very great caution, for should the world suspect an intimacy, conjectures may be formed which it is of the utmost importance to you to prevent.

The advantages arising to your profession from the use you can make of these fellows are so many and so obvious that it would be but loss of time to enumerate them.

But if any over-busy officer of justice should happen to detect them, give them up to the Law; nay, join loudly in the cry against them; but set your emissaries at work to counteract the mischiefs your clamour might occasion.

Make it a point, however, if any of them should be doomed to perpetual imprisonment, to allow them a small support by which means you may keep their hopes alive and prevent their turning the tables on you. Great prudence and caution is required in your dealings with these sort of people, and as their indolence and extravagance render them often in need of ready money to carry on their villainous schemes you must take care to let them run in your debt. You can never lose by them who pay cent. per cent. interest for their money; by this means they are always in your power, nor must you show them the least lenity without you have a further view of some extraordinary premium and that upon the surest grounds.

In my long connections with the villainous part of mankind I find no creatures in the world so artless as thieves. They are, in fact, the most stupid and infatuated gulls upon the earth, though by their dress and outward behaviour they all affect what is called the knowing taste; yet they are as simple and as easy to be hooked as the creatures they prey upon, for what they do is not so much by art or subtility as by force. Timidity in those who are injured by them is another help to their advantage, and as the vilest of vermin that teases the noblest beast have their attendant animalcula to prey upon them so are thieves constantly preyed upon by another species by whom they are perpetually irritated to some villainy or other either through fear, the hopes of a favour or infatuation.

A woman of the town is by much an over-match for the knowingest thief. She can always feign wants and necessities powerful enough to make a man undertake an action that he is sure to be hanged for if taken; and if not taken they can as easily gull him out of circumstances sufficient to hang him so that he lies in their power whenever he refuses to supply them with what they please to demand. Their pretended jealousies and suspicions, their artful tears, their affected love, soon operate in their favour. The return of lust in the *cully* lessens his apprehensions and he opens his mind to the very sphinx that betrays him.

For this reason a thief-taker should be well acquainted with the women of the town as the major part of a thief's retirement from his labours is in a bawdy-house with his favourite whore. You shall seldom hear of a man's robbing to support a family, but too commonly the extravagance of his whore, that excites him to actions of the vilest kind; therefore the only path to trace him by is the tract of lewdness. For this he very seldom fails to carouse in some infernal mansion where lust and vice conspire to drive away the reflections of crimes that are too terrible to stand the test of the serene hour in a more peaceful situation.

The gaming table is another retreat where thieves very often lose or lavish what they have hazarded their lives for on the road and become the prey of others more subtle than themselves. Consequently a connection with the most noted gamblers and sharpers is requisite; and a list of those houses where tables are kept you should always have by you, as gaming houses are the resort of those whom broken fortunes and extravagance have reduced to no other hopes of reinstating themselves in the world, but by a run of luck, which very often by their covetousness they pursue so far, that they are brought down to a worse situation than they were before they entered the room. But if by any misfortune you should be deprived of the blessings of sight be careful in the choice of a good physiognomist who shall attentively trace and faithfully relate the different workings of the mind which horror strongly paints in the face of a murder-working villain. A skilful observer may also easily discern the different kind of villainy the mind is working on. These having set down in the pocket-book of your memory, when you hear of any such crimes committed you may fire a shrewd guess at the person circumstances render most liable to be guilty.

Whoever therefore should think it worth his while to pursue the noble calling of thief-taker and seat himself at the head of affairs as I have done, after he has acquired a sufficient stock of knowledge of the most villainous part of human nature let him take care to secure himself and not, as I have, leave himself open to the displeasure of punishment of the powers above him. Let him, if possible, rather endeavour at their favour and under the mask of justice and public spirit gain their sanction for his villainy and by schemes of general utility work privately for his own interest. Let him be always seemingly arduous to support the government he lives under in the propagation of any grand undertaking whereby he may be of service to his country, and likewise not forget himself. All of which may be done without the least spark of real virtue, for this may serve to varnish over his other vices, which, though ever notorious, will not be looked into, much more punished upon this consideration that you have struck out some useful scheme which have saved the government the trouble of thinking and that it is a pity to cut off a man who, though a villain in himself, can be of service to his country. Thus rendered secure in the favour and esteem of your superiors you may perhaps be rewarded with some profitable and eminent employ. But among all the places and pensions that they can bestow that of a Marshal will answer your purpose better than any other office whatever because you will then have an opportunity of exercising your natural faculties with more power. For who shall dare control you in what you please to do or say? When you have secured the interest of those above you let those below you censure as they choose; you will then have a good sanction for your villainy; go on and prosper!

Thus fixed, strike out for some scheme for the more speedy apprehension of robbers and other villains, and let this be done under colour of the public safety and in regard to the properties of others. Have your emissaries always about you, such as have had art enough to keep out of the hands of the Law, and by interest and happy connections have made shift to escape hanging twice or thrice. Bailiffs or bailiffs' followers would do well for your purpose, but I pray you my good successor, whoever you may be, don't let the useful beings be stigmatized with the odious name of thief-takers, for a man who is of service to the honest part of mankind and is constantly endeavouring to rid his country of thieves and robbers to be rewarded with an appellation so vile and detestable as that of a thief-taker is enough to deter him from pursuit of his good intentions. Indeed, I am of opinion that he who rids his country of a villain cannot be styled with a juster epithet than that of a brave fellow.

With this character send for your emissaries for the public service. Let them be men picked and chosen for their resolution, men that will do or swear anything, who, not having drunk of the milk of human kindness, have no feeling for their fellow creatures but would as soon strike a man down the skull with a hanger as the unfeeling butcher does the ox who has more right to the benefit and advantages of life than his executioner.

Be you, my successor, grand president of this glorious band, and as there is no likelihood but rewards for apprehending of robbers will still exist you may come in snacks, as they call it, for part of the reward and have at the same time no occasion to go in quest of adventures; leave that to the brave fellows under you while you, like their monarch, dispatch them at your will upon various expeditions for the public good; and at the same time manage your affairs in such a manner that your own fortune may increase daily, so shall men say unto themselves: 'This young Jonathan has more wit than his ancestor, who, though he gained wealth, was at last an object of the public scorn and made a sacrifice to the gallows.' You may secure yourself from such a fate provided you follow my rules and keep in with the power that you have most reason to fear.

In a time when real thieves are scarce there are ways to bring honest men into scrapes whereby they may, if the *plumpers rapp* hard, come in for a *scragging bout*, as well as the worst rogues in the nation; and as the reward for taking an honest man is the same as for taking a real thief I don't see why any one of my profession should be against it, provided you or your emissaries can make them appear guilty, as undoubtedly it will lie in their power to outswear any honest witness that can be brought for the prisoner, because I have previously advised you to let no one into the herd but such as will swear to anything that you shall please, as their grand president to desire.

Let the party who goes out on such a *lay* be men of feared consciences lest they should *blow the widd* and bring your character into dispute: always have some claw upon them in order to secure your own safety and profit – when any of these brave fellows are determined and resolute upon any affair where innocence and honesty are to be made the prey of villainy and craft, provided it be upon the highway the first poor labourer or traveller may become an easy instrument in their hands – let two or three of these brave fellows be fixed in proper places within call. Let one be in the character of a farmer or a tradesman, then let one of the others come up to the first and rob him in the sight of the first passenger that comes by and immediately laying hold of him force the money on the poor object. Let the third then come up and with the two others secure him, carry him before a magistrate, and there swear the robbery before him. What can the other say in his defence when there are three others in opposition desiring him to make his confession – the only way to receive His Majesty's pardon – what can the wretch do in this situation?

He is brought to a gaol, tried, cast, condemned and hanged while you and your emissaries share the reward. This has been done several times by me and my associates, and whoever succeeds me, be he who he will, may find these arts absolutely necessary to the enriching of his own private coffers.

Whoever shall be adventurous enough to become my successor will think at first that this last scheme cannot be carried into execution, that the discernment of those who try the poor wretch will naturally lead them to enquire more closely into the character of those persons who swear so positively against him. One would indeed think so, but I know, and so does everyone that has often attended the courts of judicature, that there ever was a set of fellows, whose business it is to swear whatever is put to them, and will find in the evidences without the least variation from the beginning to the end, though at the same time their very faces would betray them. But notwithstanding the stamp of villainy is so strongly marked in their countenances yet no notice is taken, though every sessions brings them about for many years; their persons, though remarkably striking, make no impression on the memories of those about the court. What can this regardless principle proceed from? If I see a man once I always know him again; if his business or discourse was particular I remembered it: but here are the same persons upon the same business one sessions after another. One would think it almost impossible, but so it is; and I don't doubt but others have remarked it as well as myself who are not half so conversant with people of that stamp.

I have seen a known thief give in his evidence, who has been heard with as much attention, as ever was given the tongue of honesty; nay, when honesty has been brow-beaten and a person that has not been used to appear in such places and on such business have through simplicity and timidity boggled, by that means has been baffled out of them evidence by the fallacious C—, and the honest person has perhaps been threatened with punishment for false swearing, while the real perjurer has gained his point though life and death has depended on the truth. This is a plain proof how blind justice is, though it was not meant by the emblem that she should be blind to truth, but blind to partiality, and that the external appearance of a rogue in gold should not in the least bias justice from doing that which is right to the poor man in rags. How far this sort of blindness is observed nowadays anyone can easily discern. However, it is not always to be imagined that justice can take place, for wherever the reigning principle of avarice shall diffuse itself through all ranks of man the great will feel it in proportion with the Newgate solicitor, split pettifogger or any of the inferior members of that honourable fraternity.

As I have thus pointed out matters in the fairest light as they are in my times, and I believe there is no fear of any alteration for the better in the law, for whoever comes after me will find matters in *statu quo*, though an hundred years hence, and therefore villainy of all kinds may be as easily perpetrated then as it has in my time, provided you can artfully cover it over with a specious appearance that may dazzle the eyes of those in power and authority.

No very great abilities – I mean intellectual ones – are required in the person who shall hereafter make a figure upon my plan. Law, craft and cunning in this case is superior to sense and learning. You who may hereafter endeavour to copy my character may do it on a sure principle without the least expense, either of money or application, and provided it should now and then infringe upon the former the power under whose sanction you act will be very capable of making a retribution; but in the latter it will always pay itself, and your leisure, or rather lazy hours, may be made somewhat lighter in revolving in your mind the little arts and subtleties that may be of service in any future schemes, whether private or public.

The public good, which has ever been the mask of self-interest and private avarice, must be always on the tip of your tongue. This notable phrase is swallowed down by the multitude with great approbation, and they turn their eyes with reverence upon the man who only makes use of the mean external show of it. They cannot be made to think ill of the person whose favourite topic is the welfare of his country, notwithstanding his more secret intentions are upon the most selfish principles in nature; for who can imagine that he who constantly brawls forth his good sentiments, his esteem and affection for his fellow creatures, and is at every juncture wracking his brains for schemes and plans for their benefit should have any such principle as his own interest at heart?

True virtue is a starving principle. No man ever got a fortune by it, as I know, but who could speak of thousands who now loll in their chariots who have gained that situation by the contrary. But the mask of it is so very essential that no man can be a complete rogue without it, nor will he ever carry one scheme into execution unless he is externally as good a man as he is internally a bad one.

Take care, provided you should take upon you the office of —, to act with caution. Don't suffer a whore to be committed to Bridewell while she has any money or a *cull* of fortune to back her. If a blood of quality should be brought before you for breaking a watchman's head in the night, treat him with complacence, but make him come down sufficient. But if a poor fellow should by chance reel against a feeble old watchman, or the watchman push against him purposely, let him, when brought before you, be saluted with a volley of rascals and villains. This serves to intimidate and look important. It well becomes the chair of authority when its expletive lolls from side to side and with a haughty air menaces the trembling caitiff; and this sort of behaviour, if he has any friends, brings them to light. But as there is commonly a private connection between a — and a gaol keeper let the wretch be sent to gaol, and then you come in snacks for the prison fees, provided his friends can procure his enlargement.

As undoubtedly many a bawdy house may act with timidity on

your account such fears may be soon removed, provided they will be condescending enough to pay so much per week or month privately to you for your good nature, with a night's lodging now and then with one of the finest, freshest, youngest and tenderest lambkins of their flock. But if on the contrary they should obstinately persist in their lewd calling without making proper concessions let them be punished according to law and at the same time with the greatest show of hatred and antipathy to such vile occupations.

And if any officious person, from an unhappy turn of humanity, should put you in mind that your indulgence to any class of lewd woman made your severity to another more observable you might tell him that he is no sufferer by the removal of the lower sort of prostitute. But were you to banish those who figure it in high life it would make a sad notch in the rent roll of somebody's estate.

A man of a cunning turn of mind might, I think, get a handsome fortune by insuring bawdy houses, gaming tables, night-houses; for suppose a man, after he has got on the blind side of his betters, should by a private certificate become their protector, which certificate should be renewed weekly or monthly at the person's will who presides, or suppose a person in some little power should (by renting such houses of the parish, company or persons, whose real estates they are) upon leases for a certain number of years, at certain sums stipulated, which again let by the lessee, weekly or monthly, for sums much larger, paid either weekly or monthly, might not a man get handsomely by such a scheme as this, it being then in his power to raise their rents to what height he pleases? There is no fear of convenient houses standing empty upon that account, for those who are in possession will take care to make their *cullies* pay for the extraordinary charge.

Therefore a great man might be a bawd without the reflections of the world, for who shall say that a landlord could help the vices of his tenants or that he is in any way culpable for suffering such persons to live in his houses? When he has this grand maxim of his side, that no sober family can afford to pay him the rent of them, or provided they could would choose a more creditable neighbourhood.

But should murder or the appearance of it be committed in any of those houses, which may be hereafter under his protection he will naturally say, 'What must become of me then?' for should the enraged multitude grow outrageous, and by forcing the doors and breaking the windows revenge themselves on him in this manner, where must he fly to? Peace, my good successor, whoever you may be! Don't you know that the office I advise you to get will secure you from harm? Will it not be in your power to call for the assistance of a detachment of soldiers on such an occasion, and if that won't do send a few of your brave fellows with bludgeons etc.? I warrant the mob will soon quit their purpose. As for the persons who were in possession of the house they have got off, Lord knows how. Then put a bill upon the door of the said house signifying that it is the property of another person; and you have no connection with it, and it will soon blow over!

To drive away all the dregs of clamour and censure that may yet remain in the breasts of some sort of people, soon after come out with some grand scheme for the good of the public; let your puffers be dispersed in every company with panegyrics on your great goodness and philanthropy. Half a dozen lines now and then in some newspapers may be of service to you, but be sure let them be well *plaistered* with your extraordinary care, diligence and public spirit. If you can't make them yourself you may have a copy of verses made in your praise for half a crown by any of the Grub Street train, who would as leave sing 'Jack Catch's'[1] praise as His Lordship's, provided they are to eat and drink for it.

Thus far have I set everything in the fairest light, with this view only – that as I could not escape hanging myself, to endeavour to furnish any other who may succeed me with the arts how to thrive in a profession so profitable as mine, and likewise to show the world that I am not void of all goodness, but that I would willingly caution and instruct others who may hereafter pursue the same game which I have many years, and not only that, but to act in such a manner as

---

[1] Ketch; see p. 163 note 1.

may gain them the sanction of those in power and repel the little censures of the vulgar; and all this without the fear of the gallows. And I hope that whoever shall take my character upon them, or anyone whom the world shall think fit to bestow it upon, may be truly worthy of his occupation.

This is the sincere wish of

The unfortunate

JONATHAN WILD.

JOHN HOLMES AND PETER WILLIAMS
Convicted of grave-robbing, and publicly whipped in 1777
From Knapp and Baldwin's *Newgate Calendar*

Continuing the theme of religious conservatism, the Newgate Calendar *claims that grave-robbers should be known as 'Sacrilegious Robbers of our Holy Church'. The sanctity of a corpse was a firmly held belief, rooted both in church doctrine and superstition, which had not been supplanted by the recognition that in order for science to progress and medicine to improve doctors needed newly dead bodies on which to experiment and teach. It was not until 1752 that a law granted surgeons' colleges the corpses of all murderers, but this was still an inadequate supply. The surgeons were reliant on grave-robbers for corpses, and were willing to pay large sums for them; and they were never responsible for the crime, even though they were the reason it occurred. Undertakers, gravediggers and sextons might all be involved in the scam, perhaps burying a coffin at the correct depth but leaving the actual body in the loose earth near the surface to make it easier for the 'sack-'em-up' man (who put corpses into sacks to take away) to get to. (The complete entry is given.)*

JOHN HOLMES and PETER WILLIAMS,

PUBLICLY WHIPPED, BY THE SENTENCE OF THE MIDDLESEX COURT OF QUARTER SESSIONS, FOR DECEMBER 1777, FOR STEALING DEAD BODIES

The sum of all our long list of thieves, and their different deceptions and modes of plunder, surely are those detested monsters of depravity, who break into the sacred deposit of the dead, and rob the graves of the putrid bodies of our departed fellow-creatures, for the sole purpose of selling them to surgeons for dissection.

The impious robbers are vulgarly called, in London, resurrection-men, but rather should be called Sacrilegious Robbers of our Holy Church, not even confining the unnatural crime to men alone; the gentler sex are connected in this horrid traffic, whose business it is to strip off the shroud, or whatever garments in which the body might have been wrapped, and to sell them, while the men, through the darkness of night, drag the naked bodies to be anatomised.

Though it matters not where we would return to our original dust, yet there is something offensive to the living, to hear of grave-yards being broke open for this base purpose; and for any of us to know, that the remains of a parent, a wife or a child, have been basely removed, our nature is shocked at the sacrilege.

When Hunter[1] the famous anatomist, was in full practice, he had a surgical theatre behind his house, in Windmill-street, where he gave lectures to a very numerous class of pupils. To this place such numbers of dead bodies were brought, during the winter season, and which is yet practised there, and among the lecturing surgeons, that the mob rose several times, and were upon the point of pulling down his house. He had a well dug in the back part of his premises, wherein was thrown the putrid flesh and with it, alkalines, in order to hasten the consumption thereof.

---

[1] William Hunter, who with his brother John in the 1740s instituted medical courses with each student working on a corpse apiece.

Numberless are the instances of dead bodies being seized in carrying to the surgeons. Hackney-coachmen, for an extra fare, and porters with hampers, are often employed by these resurrection men for this purpose.

A monthly publication, in March 1776, says, 'The remains of more than twenty dead bodies were discovered in a shed in Tottenham-Court Road, supposed to have been deposited there by traders to the surgeons; of whom there is one, it is said, in the Borough, who makes an open profession of dealing in dead bodies, and is well known by the name of the resurrectionist.'

Still more shocking is it to be told, that men who are paid for protecting the sacred deposit of the mortal remains of their fellow-parishioners, are often confederates with these carcase-stealers, as the present case will demonstrate.

Holmes, the principal villain in this case, was gravedigger of St George's, Bloomsbury. William was his assistant, and a woman named Esther Donaldson, an accomplice. They were all indicted for stealing the dead body of Mrs Jane Sainsbury, who departed this life on the 9th of October, then last past, and the corpse was interred in the burying-ground of St George's, above-mentioned, on the Monday following. They were detected before they could secure their booty; and the widower, however unpleasant, determined to prosecute them. In order to their conviction, he had to undergo the mental pain of viewing and identifying the remains of his wife!

The gravedigger and his deputy were convicted on the fullest evidence; and it was regretted that it did not reach the woman, though no doubt remained of her equal guilt. She therefore was released, but Holmes and Williams were sentenced to six months' imprisonment, and to be whipped twice on their bare backs, from the end of Kingsgate street, Holborn, to Diot-street, St Giles's, being half a mile, and which was inflicted with the severity due to so detestable an offence, through crowds of exulting spectators.

> RENWICK WILLIAMS *Convicted of assault and sentenced to six years' imprisonment in 1790*
> From Knapp and Baldwin's *Newgate Calendar*

This curious case is notable not because it forms a part of any criminal development or form, but for the sensationalist, moralizing, romantic tone of the entry (given in full) in Knapp and Baldwin's Newgate Calendar, *and the behaviour of the protagonists – almost like a Victorian novel. Williams would now be called a 'stalker'.*

RENWICK WILLIAMS, COMMONLY CALLED 'THE MONSTER',

CONVICTED OF A BRUTAL AND WANTON ASSAULT ON MISS ANNE PORTER

Several months previous to the apprehension of this man, a report ran through all ranks of society that young females had been secretly wounded in different parts of their bodies, in the public streets, and often in the day-time, by a monster, who, upon committing the brutal crime, effected his escape.

Sometimes, as reported, the villain presented a nosegay to a young female, wherein was concealed a sharp instrument; and, as he offered them the flowers to smell, stabbed them in the face. Other tales were told, of some being stabbed in the thigh, and behind; in fine, there was universal terror in the female world in London.

At length a man named Renwick Williams was apprehended on the charge of one of the young ladies thus brutally wounded, and his trial came on at the Old Bailey, on the 18th of July 1790.

The indictment charged, that with force and arms, in the parish of St James on the king's highway, Renwick Williams did, unlawfully, wilfully, and maliciously, make an assault upon, maim, and wound, Anne Porter, against the peace, etc. A second count charged the said Renwick Williams, that, on the same day and year, he did unlawfully, wilfully, and maliciously, tear, spoil, cut and deface, the garments and clothes – to wit, the cloak, gown, petticoat and shift, of the said Anne Porter, contrary to the statute, and against the peace, etc.

Miss Anne Porter deposed that she had been at St James's, to see the ball, on the night of the 18th of January 1790, accompanied by her sister, Miss Sarah Porter, and another lady; that her father had appointed to meet them at twelve o'clock, the hour the ball generally breaks up; but that it ended at eleven, and she was therefore under the necessity either of staying where she was, until her father came, or to return home at that time. Her father, she said, lived in St James's Street, and that he kept a tavern and a cold bath. She agreed to go home with her party.

As they proceeded up St James's Street her sister appeared much agitated, and called to her to hasten home, which she and her company accordingly did. Her sister was the first to reach the hall door. As the witness turned the corner of the rails, she received a blow on the right hip; she turned round, and saw the prisoner stoop down: she had seen him before several times, on each of which he had followed close behind her, and used language so gross, that the Court did not press on her to relate the particulars.

He did not immediately run away when he struck her, but looked on her face, and she thus had a perfect opportunity of observing him. She had no doubt, she said, of the prisoner being the man that wounded her. She supposed that the wound was inflicted with a sharp instrument, because her clothes were cut, and she was wounded through them.

Miss Porter farther deposed that on the 13th of June last she was walking in St James's Park, with her mother and her two sisters, and a gentleman of the name of Coleman. The prisoner at the bar met and passed her; she was struck with his person, and knew him; she found he had turned to look after her. Upon appearing agitated, she was questioned, and pointed him out to Mr Coleman. She said she knew him when he was brought up to the public office at Bow Street.

Her gown, of pink silk, and her shift, which she wore the night she was wounded, were produced in court, and were cut on the right side, a considerable length.

Miss Sarah Porter was next called. She swore that she had seen the prisoner at the bar prior to the 18th of June last, but had no acquaintance with him. He had followed her, and talked to her in language the most shocking and obscene. She had seen him four or five different times. On that night, when her sister was cut, she saw him standing near the bottom of St James's Street, and, spying her, he exclaimed, 'O ho! are you there?' and immediately struck her a violent blow on the side of the head. She then, as well as she was able, being almost stunned, called to her sister to make haste, adding, 'Don't you see the wretch behind us?' Upon coming to their own door, the prisoner rushed between them, and about the time he struck her sister he also rent the witness's gown. There were lights in the street, and she knew him.

Two more sisters, Miss Rebecca Porter and Miss Martha Porter, also bore unequivocal testimony as to the identity of the prisoner, with respect to his having accosted them, in company with their sisters, with the most obscene and indecent language.*

Mr John Coleman was the next witness called. He swore that he was walking with Miss Anne Porter, and the rest of her family, in St James's Park, on the evening of Sunday, the 13th of June 1790. That, upon observing Miss Porter much agitated, and inquiring the cause, she pointed out the prisoner at the bar, and said 'the wretch had just passed her'. Having pointed him out, the witness followed him to the house of Mr Smith, in South Moulton Street, and, upon going into the parlour where he was, expressed his surprise on the prisoner's not resenting the insults he (the witness) had offered him; and demanded his address. Mr Smith and the prisoner both expressed their surprise at such a demand, without a reason given; he therefore said, that he, the prisoner, had insulted some ladies, who had pointed him out, and that he must have satisfaction. The prisoner denied

* This is a practice among a set of scoundrels of the present day, in the public streets, wherever they find a modest, well-dressed, unprotected female. They not only whisper the most abominable bawdry in her chaste ear, but often pinch her on the side or behind, so as to put her in both bodily and mental pain. Such rascals ought to be whipped at the cart's tail through every street in London.

having offered any insult; but, upon his persisting, they exchanged addresses.

The prisoner's address was produced by the witness, No. 52, Jermyn Street. The witness and the prisoner then mutually recognised each other, as having been in company with each other before, and the witness then departed. On his departure he repented having quitted him, and, turning back, he met with him at the top of St James's Street: he then accosted him again, saying 'I don't think you are the person I took you for; you had better come with me now, and let the ladies see you.' The prisoner objected, as it was late at night; but, upon his saying it was close by, he went with him.

On his being introduced into the parlour, where the Miss Porters were sitting, two of them, Anne and Sarah, fainted away, exclaiming, 'Oh! my God! that's the wretch!' The prisoner then said, 'The ladies' behaviour is odd; they don't take me for the monster that is advertised?' The witness said they did.

The prisoner was there an hour before he was taken away, and in that time said nothing particular.

Mr Tomkins, surgeon, was next called. By his description the wound must have been made by a very sharp instrument. He had also examined the clothes, and they must have been cut at the same time. The wound itself was, at the beginning, for two or three inches, but skin-deep; about the middle of it, three or four inches deep, and gradually decreasing in depth towards the end. The length of the wound, from the hip downwards, was nine or ten inches.

The prisoner, being called upon for his defence, begged the indulgence of the Court, in supplying the deficiency of his memory, upon what he wished to state, from a written paper. He accordingly read as follows: –

'He stood,' he said, 'an object equally demanding the attention and compassion of the court. That, conscious of his innocence, he was ready to admit the justice of whatever sufferings he had hitherto undergone, arising from suspicion. He had the greatest confidence in the justice and liberality of an English jury, and hoped they would not suffer his fate to be decided by the popular prejudice raised against him. The hope of proving his innocence had hitherto sustained him.

'He professed himself the warm friend and admirer of that sex whose cause was now asserted, and concluded with solemnly declaring that the whole prosecution was founded on a dreadful mistake, which, he had no doubt, the evidence he was about to call would clear up to the satisfaction of the Court.'

His counsel then proceeded to call his witnesses.

Mr Mitchell, the first evidence, was an artificial flower-maker, living in Dover Street, Piccadilly. The prisoner had worked for him nine months in all; he had worked with him on the 18th of January, the queen's birth-day, the day on which Miss Porter had been wounded, from nine o'clock in the morning till one o'clock in the day, and from half past two till twelve at night: he had then supped with the family. He gave the prisoner good character, as behaving with good nature to the women in the house.

Miss Mitchell, the witness's sister, told the same story.

Two other witnesses, domestics in the same house, likewise appeared on behalf of the prisoner; but the whole of the evidence, on his part, proved rather contradictory.

Mr Justice Buller, with great accuracy and ability, went through the whole of this extraordinary business, stating, with great clearness and perspicuity, the parts of the evidence that were most material for the consideration of the jury, with many excellent observations.

He said it had been stated, in various ways, that great outrages had been committed by the prisoner at the bar, and therefore, in his defence, he had, very properly, not only applied to the compassion of the jury, to guard against the effects of prejudice, but also to their judgment. It was very proper to do so, and in this he only demanded justice: prejudice often injured, though it could never serve, the cause of justice.

In this the jury would have only to consider what were the facts of which they were to be satisfied, and on which it was their province to decide. This being done by them, and if they should find the prisoner guilty upon the present charge, he would reserve his case for the opinion of the twelve judges of England; and this he should do for several reasons: first, because this was completely and perfectly a new case in itself; and secondly, because this was the first indictment of the kind that was ever tried. Therefore, although he himself entertained but little doubt upon the first point, yet, as the case was new, it would be right to have a solemn decision upon it. So that hereafter the law, in that particular, may be declared from undoubted authority.

Upon the second point he owned that he entertained some doubts. This indictment was certainly the first of the kind that was ever drawn in this kingdom. It was founded upon the statute of the 6th George I. Upon this statute it must be proved that it was the intent of the party accused, not only to wound the body, but also cut, tear and spoil the garment; (here the learned judge read the clause of the act;) – one part of this charge was quite clear, namely, that Miss Porter was wounded, and her clothes torn. The first question, therefore, for the consideration of the jury would be, whether this was done wilfully, and with intent to spoil the garment, as well as to wound the body. That was a fact for the jury to decide; and, if they agreed upon this, then, whether the prisoner was the man who did it.

He observed that there might be cases in which the clothes were torn, and yet where this act would not apply; such, for instance, as a scuffle in a quarrel, where clothes might be torn wilfully, but not with that malice and previous intent which this act required.

It should be observed, that here there was a wound given, with an instrument that was not calculated solely for the purpose of affecting the body, such, for instance, as piercing or stabbing, by making a hole; but here was an actual cutting, and the wound was of a very considerable length, and so was the rent in the clothes. It was for the jury to decide whether, as both body and clothes were cut, he who intended the end did not also intend the means.

He left it to the jury to say, upon the whole of the case, whether the prisoner was guilty or innocent.

The jury immediately, without hesitation, found the prisoner guilty.

Mr Justice Buller then ordered the judgment in this case to be arrested, and the recognizances of the persons bound to prosecute to be respited until the December sessions.

The court was crowded with spectators by nine, when this trial began, which ended at five o'clock at night.

All the witnesses were examined separately.

At the commencement of the sessions at the Old Bailey, on the 10th of December 1790, Judge Ashurst addressed the prisoner nearly in the following terms: 'You have been capitally convicted under the statute 6 George I. of maliciously tearing, cutting, spoiling and defacing, the garments of Anne Porter, on the 18th of January last. Judgment has been arrested upon two points – one, that the indictment is informal; the other that the act of parliament does not reach the crime. Upon solemn consideration, the judges are of opinion that both the objections are well founded: but, although you are discharged from this indictment, yet you are within the purview of the common law. You are therefore to be remanded, to be tried for a misdemeanor.'

He was accordingly, on the 13th of the same month, tried at Hicks's Hall for the misdemeanor, in making an assault on Miss Anne Porter.

The trial lasted sixteen hours: there were three counts in the indictment; viz. for assaulting with intent to kill, for assaulting and wounding and for a common assault.

The charge was that he, on the 18th of January 1790, made an assault on Anne Porter, and, with a certain knife, inflicted on her person a wound nine inches long, and, in the middle part of it, four inches deep.

The same witnesses were then called in support of the charge as appeared on the trial at the Old Bailey: they gave a very clear, correct, and circumstantial evidence, positively swearing to the person of the prisoner.

The facts proved were nearly the same, with very little variation indeed, with those which were given in evidence on his trial for the felony at the Old Bailey; for which reason we forbear to enter more fully on his trial.

The prisoner produced two witnesses, Miss Amet and Mr Mitchell, who attempted to prove an *alibi*, and the credit of their testimony was not impeached by any contradiction. The question therefore was, to which the jury would give credit; for the evidence on both sides was equally fair and unexceptionable.

The prisoner was again put to the bar at ten o'clock the next morning, and tried on the remaining indictments, on three of which he was found guilty; when the Court sentenced him [to] two years' imprisonment in Newgate for each, and at the expiration of the time to find security for his good behaviour, himself in two hundred pounds, and two sureties in one hundred pounds each.

Thus ended the case of this man, which had greatly interested every rank of people; but all were by no means satisfied of his guilt, believing that the female witnesses, a circumstance which we have shown too frequently to have happened, mistook the man who wounded and ill-treated the prosecutrix. The particulars we have given of the uncommon and brutal attack on the defenceless, by a monster of the stronger sex, with out full report of the trial, will sufficiently prepare our readers to judge for themselves on the case of Renwick Williams, divested of the popular prejudice then strong against him.

10

Cant Glossary

academy	brothel
Adam-tiler	pick-pocket's comrade; look-out
altitudes	drunk, as in 'In his altitudes'
anglers	thieves sitting on roofs or the top of coaches who used fishing poles to hook up valuables from people passing below them in the street
baggage	slut
bagnio	famous Covent Garden steam bath-house with private rooms for hire; entrance 5 s.
banditti	highwaymen
bingo	brandy
bingo-boy	great drinker or lover of brandy
bit	purse
bite	rogue or cheat; also woman's genitals
bleed freely	part with money easily, either by spending or being robbed
blow the widd	to give the game away
blowes	mistress or whore
Boarding School	Bridewell House of Correction
bowman	safe, sure
bowse	drink, or to drink
bulls-eye	crown (five shillings)
bunter	prostitute
cackle	to inform on another criminal
case	house or shop
chapman	dealer
cloak	watch-case

click	to snatch
cole	cash
cove	man or fellow, or rogue
crap	money
cull, cully	as *cove*, above
dancers	stairs
darbies	irons or fetters
dim mort	pretty girl
dun	debt
equipped	rich, or well-dressed
fence	receiver and securer of stolen goods
flash	safe for thieves, a compliment in thieving terms, as in 'He's a flash cull'
foot-pad	highway-robber who worked on foot (and often in a gang) rather than on horseback; noted for their violence
fork	to pick the pocket of, as in 'Let's fork him'
George	half-a-crown (2½ shillings)
glaziers	eyes
glim	candle or lantern
heaver	chest, breast
Jacob	ladder
jade	hussy
Joseph	cloak
Kate	pick-lock
ken	house
kid	confidence trick
King's Head Inn	Newgate Prison

lappy	drunk
lay	good prospect
lift	to shoplift
link-boy	boy with a lantern hired to light the way down dark streets
make	to steal
member-mug	chamber pot
mill	to break into, rob or kill
moon-curser	link-boy that robs the men whose way he's lighting, or leads them into a gang of footpads
munge	the dark
nab	cap or hat
nim	to steal or whip off, as in 'To nim a nab'
ogles	eyes
'peach	to betray to the authorities (short for impeach)
plumper	man hired to swear the truth of a false story; padding put into the cheeks to make them appear full
prancer	horse
prig	thief
queer	base, roguish
rattler	coach
ready	cash
rhino	cash
rum	gallant, genuine, excellent, as in 'A rum cove'
scragged	hanged
snack	share or part of the spoils
squeak	to betray to the authorities

swag	a shop
tail	sword
thief-taker	one who recovered stolen property and brought criminals to justice through his connections with the underworld, and usually himself was involved in crime; Jonathan Wild ('A Miscellany') was the pinnacle of this profession
twang	prostitute's companion, or bully
velvet	tongue
wap	to have sex
wipe	handkerchief

Appendix

The Black Act

ANNO NONO GEORGII I. C.22.

An act for the more effectual punishing wicked and evil-disposed persons going armed in disguise, and doing injuries and violences to the persons and properties of his Majesty's subjects, and for the more speedy bringing the offenders to justice.

    I. Whereas *several ill-designing and disorderly persons have of late associated themselves under the name of* Blacks, *and entered into confederacies to support and assist one another in stealing and destroying of deer, robbing of warrens and fish-ponds, cutting down plantations of trees and other illegal practices, and have, in great numbers, armed with swords, fire-arms and other offensive weapons, several of them with their faces blacked, or in disguised habits, unlawfully hunted in forests belonging to his Majesty, and in the parks of divers of his Majesty's subjects, and destroyed, killed and carried away the deer, robbed warrens, rivers and fish-ponds, and cut down plantations of trees; and have likewise solicited several of his Majesty's subjects, with promises of money, or other rewards, to join with them, and have sent letters in fictitious names, to several persons, demanding venison and money, and threatning some great violence, if such their unlawful demands should be refused, or if they should be interupted in, or prosecuted for such their wicked practises, and have actually done great damage to several persons, who have either refused to comply with such demands, or have endeavoured to bring them to justice, to the great terror of his Majesty's peaceable subjects:* for the preventing which wicked and unlawful practices, be it enacted by the King's most excellent Majesty, by and with the advice and consent of the lords spiritual and temporal and commons, in parliament assembled, and by the authority of the same. That if any person or persons, from and after the first day of *June* in the year of our Lord one thousand seven hundred and twenty-three, being armed with swords, fire-arms or other offensive weapons, and having his or their faces blacked or being otherwise disguised, shall appear in any forest, chase, park, paddock or grounds inclosed with any wall, pale or other fence, wherein any deer have been or shall be usually kept, or in any warren or place where hares or conies have been or shall be usually kept, or in any high road, open heath, common or down, or shall unlawfully and wilfully hunt, wound, kill, destroy or steal any red or fallow deer, or unlawfully rob any warren or place where conies or hares are usually kept, or shall unlawfully steal or take away any fish out of any river or pond; or if any person or persons, from and after the said first day of *June* shall unlawfully and wilfully hunt, wound, kill, destroy or steal any red or fallow deer, fed or kept in any places in any of his Majesty's forests or chases, which are or shall be inclosed with pales, rails or other fences, or in any park, paddock or grounds inclosed, where deer have been or shall be usually kept; or shall unlawfully and maliciously break down the head or mound of any fish-pond, whereby the fish shall be lost or destroyed; or shall unlawfully and maliciously kill, maim or wound any cattle, or cut down or otherwise destroy any trees planted in any avenue, or growing in any garden, orchard or plantation, for ornament, shelter or profit; or shall set fire to any house, barn or out-house, or to any hovel, cock, mow or stack of corn, straw, hay or wood; or shall wilfully and maliciously shoot at any person in any dwelling-house, or other place; or shall knowingly send any letter, without any name, subscribed thereto, or signed with a fictitious name, demanding money, venison or other valuable thing; or shall forcibly rescue any person being lawfully in custody of any officer or other person, for any of the offences before mentioned; or if any person or persons shall, by gift or promise of money, or other reward, procure any of his Majesty's subjects to join him or them in any such unlawful act; every person so offending, being thereof lawfully convicted, shall be adjudged guilty of felony, and shall suffer death as in cases of felony, without benefit of clergy.

II. *And whereas notwithstanding the laws now in force against the illegal practices above mentioned, and his Majesty's royal proclamation of the second day of* February *which was in the year of our Lord one thousand seven hundred and twenty-two, notifying the same, many wicked and evil-disposed persons have, in open defiance thereof, been guilty of several of the offences before mentioned, to the great disturbance of the publick peace, and damage of divers of his Majestys' good subjects;* It is hereby enacted by the authority aforesaid, That all and every person and persons, who since the second day of *February* in the year of our Lord one thousand seven hundred and twenty-two, have committed or been guilty of any of the offences aforesaid, who shall not surrender him, her or themselves, before the twenty-fourth day of *July* in the year of our Lord one thousand seven hundred and twenty-three, to any of the justices of his Majesty's court of kings bench, or to any one of his Majesty's justices of the peace, in and for the county where he, she or they did commit such offence or offences, and voluntarily make a full confession thereof to such justice, and a true discovery upon his, her or their oath or oaths, of the persons who were his, her or their accomplices in any of the said offences, by giving a true account of their names, occupations and places of abode, and to the best of his, her or their knowledge or belief, discover where they may be found, in order to be brought to justice, being thereof lawfully convicted, shall be adjudged guilty of felony, and shall suffer death as in cases of felony, without benefit of clergy.

III. Provided nevertheless, That all and every person and persons, who have been guilty of any the offences aforesaid, and shall not be in lawful custody for such offence on the said first day of *June* and shall surrender him, her or themselves, on or before the said twenty-fourth day of *July* as aforesaid, and shall make such confession and discovery as aforesaid, shall by virtue of this act be pardoned, acquitted and discharged of and from the offences so by him, her or them, confessed as aforesaid; any thing herein contained to the contrary in any wise notwithstanding.

IV. And for the more easy and speedy bringing the offenders against this act to justice, be it further enacted by the authority aforesaid, That if any person or persons shall be charged with being guilty of any of the offences aforesaid, before any two or more of his Majesty's justices of the peace of the county where such offence or offences were or shall be committed, by information of one or more credible person or persons upon oath by him or them to be subscribed, such justices before whom such information shall be made as aforesaid, shall forthwith certify under their hands and seals, and return such information to one of the principal secretaries of state of his Majesty, his heirs or successors, who is hereby required to lay the same, as soon as conveniently may be, before his Majesty, his heirs or successors, in his or their privy council; whereupon it shall and may be lawful for his Majesty, his heirs or successors, to make his or their order in his or their said privy council, thereby requiring and commanding such offender or offenders to surrender him or themselves, within the space of forty days, to any of his Majesty's justices of the court of king's bench, or to any one of his Majesty's justices of the peace, to the end that he or they may be forth coming, to answer the offence or offences wherewith he or they shall so stand charged, according to the due course of law; which order shall be printed and published in the next *London Gazette*, and shall be forthwith transmitted to the sheriff of the county where the offence shall be committed, and shall, within six days after the receipt thereof be proclaimed by him, or his officers, between the hours of ten in the morning, and two in the afternoon, in the market-places upon the respective market-days, of two market-towns in the same county, near the place where such offence shall have been committed; and a true copy of such order shall be affixed upon some publick place in such market-towns; and in case such offender or offenders shall not surrender him or themselves, pursuant to such order of his Majesty, his heirs or successors, to be made in council as aforesaid, he or they so neglecting or refusing to surrender him or themselves as aforesaid, shall from the day appointed for his or their surrender as aforesaid, be adjudged, deemed and taken to be convicted and attainted of felony, and shall suffer the pains of death as in [the] case of a person convicted and attainted by verdict and judgment of felony, without benefit of clergy; and that it shall be lawful to and for the court of king's bench, or the justices of *oyer* and *terminer*,[1] or general gaol-delivery for the county, where the offence is sworn in such information to have been committed, upon producing to them such order in council, under the seal of the said council, to award execution against such offender and offenders, in such manner, as if he or they had been convicted and attainted in the said court of king's bench, or before such justices of *oyer* and *terminer*, or general gaol-delivery respectively.

V. And be it enacted by the authority aforesaid, That all and every person and persons, who shall, after the time appointed as aforesaid, for the surrender of any person or persons, so charged upon oath with any the offences aforesaid, be expired, conceal, aid, abet or succour, such person or persons, knowing him or them to have been so charged as aforesaid, and to have been required to surrender him or themselves, by such order or orders as aforesaid, being lawfully convicted thereof, shall be guilty of felony, and shall suffer death as in cases of felony, without benefit of clergy.

VI. Provided nevertheless, and it is hereby declared and enacted, That nothing herein contained shall be construed to prevent or hinder any judge, justice of the peace, magistrate, officer or minister of justice whatsoever, from taking, apprehending and securing, such offender or offenders, against whom such information shall be given, and for requiring whose surrender such order in council shall be made as aforesaid, by the ordinary course of law; and in case such offender or offenders, against whom such information, and for requiring whose surrender such order in council shall be made as aforesaid, shall be taken and secured in order to be brought to justice, before the time shall be expired, within which he or they shall be required

---

[1] a commission of the peace; literally, 'to hear and determine'.

to surrender him or themselves, by such order in council as aforesaid, that then in such case no further proceeding shall be had upon such order made in council against him or them so taken and secured as aforesaid, but he or they shall be brought to trial by due course of law; any thing herein before contained to the contrary in any wise notwithstanding.

VII. And be it enacted by the authority aforesaid, That from and after the first day of *June* one thousand seven hundred and twenty-three, the inhabitants of every hundred, within that part of the kingdom of *Great Britain* called *England*, shall make full satisfaction and amends to all and every the person and persons, their executors and administrators, for the damages they shall have sustained or suffered by the killing or maiming of any cattle, cutting down or destroying any trees, or setting fire to any house, barn or out-house, hovel, cock, mow or stack of corn, straw, hay or wood, which shall be committed or done by any offender or offenders against this act; and that every person and persons, who shall sustain damages by any of the offences last mentioned, shall be and are hereby enabled to sue for and recover such his or their damages, the sum to be recovered not exceeding the sum of two hundred pounds, against the inhabitants of the said hundred, who by this act shall be made liable to answer all or any part thereof; and that if such person or persons shall recover in such action, and sue execution against any of such inhabitants, all other the inhabitants of the hundred, who by this act shall be made liable to all or any part of the said damage, shall be rateably and proportionably taxed, for and towards an equal contribution for the relief of such inhabitant, against whom such execution shall be had and levied; which tax shall be made, levied and raised, by such ways and means, and in such manner and form, as is prescribed and mentioned for the levying and raising damages recovered against inhabitants of hundreds in cases of robberies, in and by an act, intituled. *An act for the following hue and cry*, made in the twenty-seventh year in the reign of Queen *Elizabeth*.

VIII. Provided nevertheless, That no person or persons shall be enabled to recover any damages by virtue of this act, unless he or they by themselves, or by their servants, within two days after such damage or injury done him or them by any such offender or offenders as aforesaid, shall give notice of such offence done and committed unto some of the inhabitants of some town, village, or hamlet, near unto the place where any such fact shall be committed, and shall within four days after such notice, give in his, her or their examination upon oath, or the examination upon oath of his, her or their servant or servants, that had the care of his or their houses, out-houses, corn, hay, straw or wood, before any justice of the peace of the county, liberty or division, where such fact shall be committed, inhabiting within the said hundred where the said fact shall happen to be committed, or near unto the same, whether he or they do know the person or persons that committed such fact, or any of them; and if upon such examination it be confessed, that he or they do know the person or persons that committed the said fact, or any of them, that then he or they so confessing, shall be bound by recognizance to prosecute such offender or offenders by indictment, or otherwise, according to the laws of this realm.

IX. Provided also, and be it further enacted, by the authority aforesaid, That where any offence shall be committed against this act, and any one of the said offenders shall be apprehended, and lawfully convicted of such offence, within the space of six months after such offence committed, no hundred, or any inhabitants thereof, shall in any wise be subject or liable to make any satisfaction to the party injured, for the damages he shall have sustained; any thing in this act to the contrary notwithstanding.

X. Provided also, That no person, who shall sustain any damage by reason of any offence to be committed by any offender contrary to this act, shall be thereby enabled to sue, or bring any action against any inhabitants of any hundred, where such offence shall be committed, except the party or parties sustaining such damage, shall commence his or their action or suit within one year after such offence shall be committed.

XI. And for the better and more effectual discovery of the offenders above-mentioned, and bringing them to justice, be it enacted by the authority aforesaid, That it shall and may be lawful to and for any justice of the peace, to issue his warrant to any constable, headborough or other peace officer, thereby authorizing such constable, headborough or other peace-officer, to enter into any house, in order to search for venison stolen or unlawfully taken, contrary to the several statutes against deer-stealers, in such manner, as by the laws of this realm such justice of the peace may issue his warrant to search for stolen goods.

XII. And be it further enacted by the authority aforesaid, That if any person or persons shall apprehend, or cause to be convicted any of the offenders above-mentioned, and shall be killed, or wounded so as to lose an eye or the use of any limb, in apprehending or securing, or endeavouring to apprehend or secure any of the offenders above-mentioned, upon proof thereof made at the general quarter-sessions of the peace for the county, liberty, division or place, where the offence was or shall be committed, or the party killed, or receive such wound, by the person or persons so apprehending, and causing the said offender to be convicted, or the person or persons so wounded, or the executors or administrators of the party killed, the justices of the said sessions shall give a certificate thereof to such person or persons so wounded or to the executors or administrators of the person or persons so killed, by which he or they shall be entitled to receive of the sheriff of the said county the sum of fifty pounds, to be allowed the said sheriff in passing his accounts in the exchequer; which sum of fifty pounds the said sheriff is hereby required to pay within thirty days from the day on which the said certificate shall be produced and shewn to him, under the penalty of forfeiting the sum of ten pounds to the said person or persons to whom such certificate is given, for which said sum of ten pounds, as well as the said sum of fifty pounds, such person may and is hereby authorized to bring an action upon the case against such sheriff, as for money had and received to his or their use.

XIII. *And whereas the shortness of the time within which prosecutions for offences against the statute made in the third and fourth years of the reign of their late majesties King William and Queen Mary, intituled,* An act for the more effectual discovery and punishment of deer-stealers, *are limited to be commenced, has been a great encouragement to offenders*; be it therefore enacted by the authority aforesaid, That any prosecution for any offence against the said statute, shall or may be commenced within three years from the time of the offence committed, but not after.

XIV. And for the better and more impartial trial of any indictment or information, which shall be found commenced or prosecuted for any of the offences committed against this act, be it enacted by the authority aforesaid, That every offence that shall be done or committed contrary to this act, shall and may be enquired of, examined, tried and determined in any county within that part of the kingdom of *Great Britain* called *England*, in such manner and form, as if the fact had been therein committed; provided, That no attainder for any of the offences made felony by virtue of this act, shall make or work any corruption of blood, loss or dower, or forfeiture of lands or tenements, goods or chattels.

XV. And be it further enacted by the authority aforesaid, That this act shall be openly read at every quarter-sessions, and at every leet or law-day.

XVI. And be it further enacted by the authority aforesaid, That this act shall continue in force from the first day of *June* one thousand seven hundred and twenty-three, for the space of three years, and from thence to the end of the then next session of parliament, and no longer.

XVII. And be it further enacted by the authority aforesaid, That if any venison, or skin of any deer, shall be found in the custody of any person or persons, and it shall appear that such person or persons bought such venison or skin of any one, who might be justly suspected to have unlawfully come by the same, and does not produce the party of whom he bought it, or prove upon oath the name and place of abode of such party, that then the person or persons who bought the same, shall be convicted of such offence, by any one or more justice or justices of the peace, and shall be subject to the penalties inflicted for killing a deer, in and by the statute made in the third and fourth year of the reign of their late majesties King *William* and Queen *Mary*, intituled, *An act for the more effectual discovery and punishment of deer-stealers.*

Acknowledgements

My grateful thanks to the British Library, the London Library and the New York Public Library; Robert Mighall, whose idea this collection was; Lindeth Vasey; my agent, Georgina Capel; and Euan Rellie.

The half titles have details from William Hogarth's illustrations, and the frontispiece is 'Claude Duval stops a Knight and his lady', in Charles Johnson, *Lives and Actions of the Most Noted Highwaymen* (London: Willoughby & Co., 1853), facing p. 140, courtesy of General Research Division, The New York Public Library, Astor, Lenox and Tilden Foundations.